Butoh

Sondra Fraleigh

Butoh

Metamorphic Dance and Global Alchemy

UNIVERSITY OF ILLINOIS PRESS
Urbana, Chicago, and Springfield

Manufactured in the United States of America
1 2 3 4 5 C P 6 5 4 3 2
⊗ This book is printed on acid-free paper.

Library of Congress Cataloging-in-Publication Data
Fraleigh, Sondra Horton, 1939–
Butoh : metamorphic dance and global alchemy / Sondra Fraleigh.
p.   cm.
Includes bibliographical references and index.
ISBN 978-0-252-03553-1 (cloth : alk. paper)
ISBN 978-0-252-07741-8 (pbk. : alk. paper)
1. Buto. 2. Modern dance—Japan.
I. Title.
GV1783.2.B87F72   2010
792.80952—dc22   2010007687

Dedicated to *butoh-ka*
(ancient dancers) everywhere.

Contents

Acknowledgements ix

Introduction 1

Part One

ALCHEMY AND MORPHOLOGY

Chapter 1. Butoh Alchemy 11

Chapter 2. The Morphology of Butoh 37

Chapter 3. Is Butoh a Philosophy? 63

Part Two

ALCHEMISTS: ESSAYS AND POETRY ON TRANSFORMATION

1. One Thousand Days of Sunshine and Peace 81

2. Whole World Friend 91

3. History Lessons 102

4. Crocodile Time 112

5. Goya La Quinto del Sordo 116

6. The Sounding Bell 123

7. Ancient Dance and Headless 129

8. Salt 135

9. Da Vinci 139

10. The Cosmos in Every Corner 149

11. Risky Plastic 155

12. Fine Bone China   161

13. Moving MA   167

14. Weak with Spirit   172

15. Waking Woman   183

16. Torn   187

17. Butoh Ritual Mexicano   191

18. Mourning the Earth   196

19. Quick Silver   201

20. Daemon of the Riverbank   205

Part Three

URSPRUNG UNFINISHED

21. *Ursprung*   213

22. *Kuu* (Emptiness)   218

Biographies of Dancers   227

Notes   237

Bibliography   247

Index   253

Acknowledgments

I would like to thank the many butoh artists who have contributed immeasurably to this work and, as always, my family and students who inspire all of my endeavors.

Butoh

Introduction

Dance should be intoxicating.
—Ohno Kazuo

Alchemy is an early unscientific form of chemistry exploring the power of enchantment and transformation. Alchemists sought the conversion of base metals into gold and a universal cure for disease, just as *butoh-ka* (butoh dancers) attend to metamorphosis and healing through the body. In butoh, as in alchemy, the darkness of material needs to be undergone before transformation and integration can occur. Hijikata Tatsumi, the principle founder of butoh and an outspoken agnostic, created his dance under the sign of darkness, but it morphed throughout his lifetime. In his final workshop, he encouraged students to disperse into *nothingness*—quite a Buddhist turn—and at his death, he uttered: "In my last moment, God's light."[1]

Butoh, a metamorphic form of dance that had its origin in Japan, is fast becoming a borderless art for a borderless century. In this book, I trace its transformative alchemy and study the international movement inspired by its aesthetic mixtures, moving forward from the founding of butoh in 1959 to its international assimilation in the twenty-first century. I describe the work of a wide range of contemporary butoh artists, weaving an aesthetic tapestry with philosophical and political threads. Not least is my visit in June 2006 with Ohno Kazuo in his hundredth year, twenty years after my first class with him. In part 2, I write of this visit and my improvised dance with his son and dance partner, Ohno Yoshito, at their studio in Yokohama. (Last names come first in Japan, and I follow this convention throughout the book.) Through their association with

Hijikata, Ohno Kazuo and Yoshito also became important in the founding of butoh. Tamah Nakamura and I completed a book on butoh founders in 2006, *Hijikata Tatsumi and Ohno Kazuo,*[2] to document their work and words and the origination of butoh.

Part 1 of this work consists of three chapters that define the morphology of butoh, its metamorphic context, and its alchemy. Chapter 1 is historical and explains butoh elements and global fusions. Chapter 2 is analytical as pertains to conceptualization of the body and lived experience, and chapter 3 is philosophical. Part 1 sets the theoretical framework for the essays of part 2, which describe a wide variety of butoh and related performances spanning 1973 to 2008 and further develop themes introduced in part 1. These essays vary in length but are consistent in their descriptive thrust, and they take advantage of the creativity of the essay form in its interpretive function. The essays begin with Hijikata's 1973 rescue of Japanese identity in his antiwar dance *Summer Storm*. Part 3 returns to the *ursprung* (original leap) of butoh and signifies its unfinished nature, pointing toward emptiness in the description of *Kuu* (2007), Ohno Yoshito's dance of nonattachment. This work, discussed in the final essay of the book, furthers a fifty-eight-year history of butoh and spiritual metamorphosis through its inclusion of Yoshito's father, Ohno Kazuo, on film. At the root of butoh, Yoshito performed *Kinjiki* (Forbidden Colors, 1959) with Hijikata and figured prominently in the subsequent development of this original dance genre.

The text as a whole shifts between voices of exposition, analysis, poetry, and personal experience. I include my own experience in phenomenological descriptions and set apart longer ones. The essays show that butoh has retained a special identity related to its Japanese background, while creating at the same time a tolerant and inclusive morphology. Butoh had its source in the limited political surrealism of Hijikata and his identification with Japanese nativism, but its ability to adapt to new ethnicities and circumstances provides it wider appeal and staying power. Compassion, the patient mind of Buddhism, which is able to endure difficulty calmly, is the subtext of much butoh. Erasing outlines of the confining self, butoh revives this Eastern ethos in an unexpected alchemy: through a transformational form of theater dance bridging cultural differences.

I explain butoh's genesis and how the butoh aesthetic eventually extended beyond the borders of Japan, first through the extensive dance tours of Ohno Kazuo and Yoshito. I studied with Ohno and became fascinated with his life—as a dancer, soldier, and finally an unassuming spiritual guru. Ohno is a very sensitive Japanese man who converted early in his life to Christianity, even as he retained Buddhist teachings and beliefs. A pacifist, he was nevertheless conscripted for service before and during World War II, where he served as a soldier for nine years, the last two as a prisoner of war. His experiences in war shaped his outlook on life and dance. "When I dance," he says in his workshops, "I carry all the dead with me." Ohno teaches that we "cannot turn away from the messiness of life." As a nonviolent revolutionary, he teaches, like Mahatma Gandhi, the importance of making "the whole world" your friend. As of this writing, Ohno is past one hundred, and in advanced age continues to dance from his bed and chair. Still mixing it up in his late nineties, he liked to move his arms to the songs of Elvis Presley, shifting without blinking to "Ave Maria."

Artists, dancers, theater directors, and photographers—all have been struck by the originality of butoh, one of the most compelling arts of the second half of the twentieth century and still evolving. Its manifestations are many, including staged productions, environmental dance, community rituals, and healing dances. *Butoh* means "dance step" and "ancient dance." *Ankoku Butoh* through Hijikata means "darkness dance." From its origins in Hijikata Tatsumi (1928–86) and Ohno Kazuo (born 1906), butoh has developed a new genre of dance in jigsaw fusion of global aesthetic elements. In its reaction to modernism, it could be called postmodern, but this designation does not entirely suffice. Butoh, with its intense physicality and theatrical flair, is unlike other postmodern dance forms, whether these focus on the pedestrian body and worklike expression or on development of technique.

As a theater art, butoh draws upon the traditional Japanese dance forms of Kabuki and *Noh,* even as it seems to repudiate them, and it also travels back to the foundations of Expressionism in the Western modern dance of the early twentieth century. In so doing, butoh retrieves something essentially Japanese, as a glance at the relationship between Japonisme and Expressionism reveals, and we will take up. Japonisme refers to the influence of Japanese and Eastern arts on European and American taste extending at least as far back as the mid-nineteenth century. This history lies behind the international assimilation of butoh.

At the foundation of butoh, traditional Japan, the same Japan that inspires Japonisme in the West, is a primary source of inspiration for Hijikata Tatsumi, Ohno Kazuo, and Ohno Yoshito. Out of their Japanese traditions and through their contact with Western aesthetic and intellectual life, they develop an original form of dance that cultivates movements of transformation and healing, or as Hijikata often puts it ontologically, "the body that becomes." In a word, they are alchemists.

Dissolution and Butoh Alchemy

Darkness, the major trope of butoh, is not a corruption of the flesh to be purified as in biblical alchemy. Rather—as in Jungian explanations of alchemy—the darkness of material is something that must be experienced consciously before transformation and integration can take place.[3] Some forms of dance purify movement through geometry and bodily sublimation, as in classical ballet and its continuing influence in contemporary dance techniques. Butoh, however, does not purify and sublimate; it is muddy and often ugly, but it seems to understand that ugliness wakes up beauty. Meanwhile, it is not a progressive art; instead, it looks back and takes stock. Its direction is not upward and outward as in Western ballet, but more downward and dissolving. *Butoh* is one of several words for "dance" in Japan, but it has become more than this internationally, attaining an identity through the work of adherents who seek a more satisfying rapport of East with West than has been established in Japan—where the United States bases nuclear warheads. One can see exhibits of these and other continuing reminders of America's influential presence in Japan in Hiroshima's Peace Park.

We witness that the promise of Western-style freedom is disappointing as a formula for all. It has had limited success in Russia and is even hated in many Muslim societies. The promise of improved policies through democratic experience and the upward march of a global economy are unfulfilled in today's world. Hijikata was one of the first to seize the problem of importing Western values into his own culture without questioning them, and currently his skepticism seems warranted. John Nathan's book *Japan Unbound: A Volatile Nation's Quest for Pride and Purpose*[4] maps Japan's continuing shift toward Westernization. Not since World War II has it faced such an identity crisis—with the weakening of traditional communal values and children turning classrooms into battlefields. The proponents of butoh seek something more basic than promises of progress. They turn back time and investigate themselves in basic terms of the human body and, even more broadly, the human.

Not forgetting where he came from, Hijikata wanted to rescue the Japanese body from colonization after the war. He sought to rescue his Japanese identity from Western effacement. In this, he overcame his training in German Expressionist dance, even as he used the creative opening it provided and courted European surrealist tactics. Now in the new century, butoh dancers wage a battle against lethargy, tending to the human body and the ecological body, exhuming what Hijikata famously calls "the body that has not been robbed." The art, drama, and dance of butoh seek cultivation of bodily truth and inner life as an antidote to the numbness of American-style homogenization—the view from McDonald's and Starbucks everywhere in Japan, imports of Disneyland, corporate models, and violent pornography and entertainment.

Since the early 1990s, I remember conversations from my visits to Japan about what soda pop and fast food were doing to Japan's future generations. Now in the first decade of the twenty-first century, the Japanese, despite their legendary longevity, continue to watch their children fall into depression and obesity. Since 1995 and the Aum Shinrikyo cult's gas attack on the Tokyo subways, memories of mass destruction have been revived. The results of retreat from the hazards of modernity and varieties of bodily terror are acutely felt in the phenomenon of the *hikikomori,* the tens of thousands of young Japanese who early in the new century have withdrawn from active life, refusing to go to school or to work as they confine themselves to home. Another specter of withdrawal is seen in young women who refuse to get married, staying home until their late twenties and thirties and saving their money for travel, designer clothes, and good times.

The question of young men in this regard seems not to be discussed, and in any case the issue would not be parallel, because the gender problem in Japan is unique. I noticed on my recent visit to Tokyo in 2008 how my Japanese friends there complained about a loss of boundaries that leaves Japan without its traditional moorings, as schoolgirls proposition businessmen like common prostitutes in the street in order to buy Gucci bags and sunglasses. If Westerners have not always understood Japanese sexual mores, the Japanese themselves have held clear boundaries. As an outsider, I listen and observe. I don't judge or interpret, but I do notice how butoh, with its antimodern political stance and muddy countenance, continues to plague commercial tendencies. Addressing societal ills directly, it builds community and stands against empty progress, as we will explore in various contexts. Butoh looks metaphysically inward, leveling desire and dissolving materialism. In this respect, its psychological core and healing alchemy is Buddhist.

My Connections with Butoh and German Expressionism

As a *butoh-ka* myself, I am fortunate to have studied dance with two important founders of related Expressionist schools: German Expressionism with Mary Wigman and, later, Japanese butoh with Ohno Kazuo. As a dancer and historian, I was reminded of the Expressionist foundation of butoh from my very first dance experiences with Ohno in 1986. At the time, however, I didn't know of his connection to German Expressionism and Mary Wigman who was my teacher twenty years earlier. Through my research into the entry of modern dance into Japan, I discovered the connection between Ohno and Wigman.

Along with Rudolph von Laban, Mary Wigman is at the foundation of German Expressionism. I studied dance with her in Berlin as a young student in 1965–66 on a Fulbright scholarship. I studied briefly with Ohno in Japan in 1986 and later in 1990 when I was a teaching fellow at Ochanomizu University in Tokyo. Ohno's dance lineage traces directly back to Wigman, and we know that he also admired Wigman's student Harald Kreutzberg. Ohno's first influential modern dance teacher, Eguchi Takaya, studied with Wigman from 1931 to 1933 and carried her teaching of German *Neue Tanz* (also called German Expressionism) to Japan. Thus, *Neue Tanz* through Eguchi and others was the first form of modern dance to enter Japan and, because of its perceived potency, was dubbed "poison dance." In this book, we will see a rare photograph of 1930s *Neue Tanz* in Japan: Eguchi in his solo *Prometheus*. American modern dance came later to Japan in more lyrical and sometimes narrative forms. I have seen a great deal of this highly technical, expressive modern dance and some of its objective postmodern developments in my visits to Japan.

The primary founder of butoh, Hijikata Tatsumi, twenty years younger than Ohno, studied *Neue Tanz* with Eguchi's student, Ando Mitsuko. Hijikata and Ohno met through Ando between 1952 and 1954 and performed *Crow* (1954), their first work together, under Ando's direction and in his Expressionist style. *Neue Tanz* provides a background for butoh but is not its direct inspiration. Butoh finally developed its own identity as a unique form of dance through Hijikata's surrealist struggle for the Japanese soul and in continuity with Ohno's world-friendly East-West amalgamations.

Ma

In this book, I hope to capture a spark of the esoteric fire and ashen bodies of butoh. Artists in Africa, Australia, Brazil, Burma, Canada, France, Germany, India, Israel, Japan, Mexico, New Zealand, Scandinavia, Spain, the United Kingdom, the United States, and elsewhere are now affecting a global alchemy and spiritual passage through butoh as they morph through multicultural imagery and gather liberally from history. Theirs is a theater of sense impressions and the space *in-between* through which they move. In Japanese (and in Zen), this space is called *ma*. We have no equivalent for this experiential concept in the West.

Ma, the space between, is the global connective tissue of butoh, allowing the permeable passage of images in butoh alchemy. Moving through *ma, butoh-ka* awaken self-reflexive moments in themselves and their audiences. *Ma* is not merely a perceptual and spatial concept; it is also an expansive state of mind. The mind that has been freed from thought can dwell in-between, not looking back with regret or forward in anticipation. A calm mind is free from the need to judge. Ugliness and beauty are let be, as perceptual and impermanent. Endo Tadashi, Japanese, born in China, living in Germany, and teaching internationally, says in his classes that he "holds a surprise inside" when he performs. He is not afraid of silence and waiting and likes to include people with disabilities in his dance classes. In part 2, I include a description and photographs of Endo's work *MA*.

Many today dance through their contact with butoh and their study of its methods but would not necessarily call themselves butoh dancers. Some like Maureen Fleming, who lives in New York but grew up in Japan, still identify closely with butoh, having performed with several of butoh's originators. When I see her dance, I am aware not only of butoh in her background but also how completely she has moved into her own original quest. Like artists everywhere, she finds her own voice and style, moving past her background, past butoh in fact. Many who have studied butoh with teachers in Japan and elsewhere would not necessarily call themselves butoh dancers. They want to move beyond this designation, as they must in order to allow themselves to progress and their dance to morph where it needs to. Nevertheless, butoh provides the basis for their opening into the future. *Ma* rings the globe in metamorphic dances, calling up the primordial shape-shifter in everyone. Metamorphic dances, as such, would not be what they are without the advent of butoh; my dance would not. It is the purpose of this book to trace the global alchemy of butoh and, with the poverty of words in relation to dance, to document it.

Part One

Alchemy and Morphology

FIGURE 1. Butoh founders Ohno Kazuo and Hijikata Tatsumi rehearse *The Dead Sea* for the 1985 Butoh Festival in Tokyo, the first of its kind. As choreographer, Hijikata whispers instructions to Ohno, who is costumed ambiguously, bridging genders, the human word, and other life forms. Miniature flags of several nations adorn Ohno's hair. Nourit Masson Sekine, a witness to the beginnings of butoh as a photographer and author, calls the work "a fusion of polarities" through the opposing yet complementary talents of Hijikata and Ohno. Photograph by Nourit Masson Sekine, © 1985. Used by permission of Nourit Masson Sekine.

Chapter One

Butoh Alchemy

There is an orientalism in the most restless pioneer, and the farthest west is but the farthest east.
—Henry David Thoreau,
  A Week on the Concord and Merrimack Rivers

Butoh is a form of dance theater born in Japan out of the turmoil of the post–World War II era, partly as a refraction of America's bombing of Hiroshima and Nagasaki and more generally in protest of Western materialism: "I don't want a bad check called democracy," is how butoh founder Hijikata Tatsumi sometimes put it. I first saw butoh at the Festival of New Dance in Montreal in 1985 with Nakajima Natsu's dance *Niwa* (The Garden). I wrote about *Niwa* and sent Nakajima the article. She invited me to Japan and took me to a butoh class with her teacher, Ohno Kazuo, who cofounded butoh with Hijikata. Ohno was eighty when I met him in his studio in 1986 and as of this writing is a centenarian. I have been a butoh addict ever since.

I understood this form of dance immediately, because it is not filtered through classical or folk forms, but its basic material is the body itself in its changing conditions. It is furthermore a hybrid form of dance, linking physical and spiritual cultures from around the world, also accounting for aging bodies as well as the buoyant qualities of youth. I have studied many dance forms, including ballet and modern dance with its postmodern offshoots. Butoh fascinates me most because of its shape-shifting potentials and its somatic shamanistic basis, not marking race so much as metamorphic change. The manner in which metamorphosis is achieved becomes part of the aesthetic of the dance and is individual, as the essays in part 2 explore. Metamorphosis and alchemy are linked as the very words suggest; they both point toward transformative change and connectivity, even when the change seems to come magically from nowhere.

Butoh has several translations as well as differing meanings in Japanese. Most basically, it means "dance step," but Hijikata evoked an older meaning, that of "ancient dance." It also refers to Western social dances imported to Japan, and some say it refers to Western dance in general, but this would not be its central meaning.[1] Butoh now identifies a genre of dance, and as a term in use internationally, it accrues meaning.

This chapter introduces butoh as alchemy, how its various Eastern and Western elements come together, fuse, and transform into something new. The values and means of metamorphosis arise in this context, and we see how butoh morphology rests on globalizing elements in dance throughout the twentieth century.

Shape-shifting

The therapeutic potentials of butoh are founded in shamanic alchemy, and by this I'm not suggesting the paranormal or supernatural but rather the very real ability of the body to manifest healing through dance and movement. Dance as therapy (also called "dance movement therapy" and "dance therapy" in America) is widely practiced by professionals in America, Japan, Europe, and elsewhere. Dance therapists wouldn't call themselves "shamans," because they don't consider themselves mediums between this world and another; rather they employ dance and movement toward healing as shamans often do. Shamans—also known as shape-shifters—are healers first and foremost; dance and repetitive movement (such as shaking, stamping, leaping, and whirling) are part of their seemingly miraculous means toward healing. As shamanist, butoh uses movement to pass between conscious and unconscious life, finally distilling this in various forms of dance and theater. This might be said of other kinds of dance as well, but butoh methods cultivate this passage in-between in unique ways, one of which is called *ma* in Japanese, as we mentioned in the introduction and explore throughout the text.

At the New York Butoh Festival in 2007, Tatsuro Ishii spoke about the shamanistic basis of butoh as a dance form.[2] He further outlined how butoh moves out internationally because of this. Shamanism is deeply embedded in Asian sensibilities, as he showed on film. I also recognize shamanism in butoh, a kind not based in religious or ritual practices. Butoh is based in creative arts and draws upon the shamanic aspect of metamorphosis; it involves several core shamanic practices that transcend cultural boundaries, as we will see.

If butoh has a shamanist basis, that doesn't mean that butoh dancers are taught how to be shamans or that they have this as a goal. They will, however, encounter core values of shamanism, whether explicitly stated as such, or not. Shamans exist in all cultures and many religions, from Judeo-Christian to Hindu, and many are independent of any specific faith. Shamans aim to heal at the soul level. They work with their own awareness in relation to nature, dancing with plants, rocks, and trees, paying attention to the weather and the land, the seas and the mountains. Consciousness through movement and sound is their primary tool in healing, and thus they are often dancers and musicians.

Shamans respect death and the ancestors: This is also a key element of butoh. Like Hijikata and Ohno, *butoh-ka* (butoh dancers) are often aware of the spirits of their ancestors. Hijikata said that his dead sister danced inside him, and Ohno said that the dead spoke to him, as we will see further in part 2. In one of my early butoh experiences, I saw my mother's face. Subsequently, I wrote about what this experience meant to me and how seeing my deceased mother connected me to feminine divinity and ancestry.[3] Ohno teaches that there is a thin separation between the living and the dead, and he encourages states of consciousness that dance into the gap. He himself danced about embryonic life as also the life/death/life cycle.

For the shaman, everything is alive: As for Ohno, stones speak. He likes to dance with stones, and a popular exploration in his workshops is "be a stone." Everything carries information for the shaman. In butoh we might call this spirit, energy, movement, or consciousness. Shamans shift through states of awareness in order to connect with the spirit or energy of the thing with which they seek resonance. This can be done through meditative movement, wild and uncontrolled movement, concentrated movement in natural environments, and embodiment of surreal imagery that stirs the unconscious, as was Hijikata's primary means. The performative issue is how one embodies the image: pictorial, poetic, natural, metaphysical, or surreal—transforming through consciousness— morphing (changing) from image to image. Metamorphosis is the metaphysical method of butoh, its alchemical aspect, and its shamanist basis.

Soul Retrieval

The shamanist basis of butoh is seldom pointed out in workshops, and it may be implicit rather than explicit in performance. It takes some acquaintance with the practices of shamanism to gain a perspective on alchemy in butoh. The shaman's work is soul work. And, as we will explore further in the text, soul work also motivates butoh. We notice, however, that shamanist healing principles appear in many movement forms and are not exclusive to butoh. Soul retrieval is practiced in meditative forms of yoga and in some forms of Qi gong. In my practice of Taoist Light Qi gong, I invite the return of my soul, one of the explicit practices in the form. This presupposes that my soul is lost, and sometimes it is—through a sense of dissociation, lack of wholeness, or "sorrow" for something missing. The shifting state of awareness that allows the return of the soul is essential in shamanism, as it is in some meditative movement forms and butoh.

In addition to healing people, shamans have traditionally performed rituals to heal the earth, using the power of consciousness to that end. One of the most interesting tangents of butoh has been precisely this. From Ohno Kazuo who traveled to heal rivers, seas, and prison camps with his dance, to Takenouchi Atsushi who dances in deep caves and on the killing grounds of war around the globe, butoh has developed the special mission of healing the earth.

We know that shamans are responsible for discovering the healing properties of plants, especially in South America where their explorations later form the basis for specific medicines, and that they also communicate with the spirits of animals, shifting their states of awareness to include nonhuman life. It is significant in this regard that Hijikata slept with a chicken to remind himself of his hunger, he said, and that chickens (also the ritual sacrifice of chickens) entered into his dance. His student and chronicler of his *butoh-fu* (dance notation collages), Waguri Yukio, is especially gifted in dancing animal essence. I took a workshop with Waguri in Tokyo that revolved around the instruction: "Be a chicken." As absurd as it may sound, I found it fascinating and far more difficult and nuanced than one might suppose. In keeping with Hijikata's concern for dancing into the margins and paying attention to the dispossessed, his identification with chickens and their commodification is apt. SU-EN's butoh also takes chickens seriously. Her *Chicken Project* in Sweden is covered in the seventh essay of part 2.

In most cultures, even in current times, a particular shaman will be gifted in working with one or another shamanic activity. *Butoh-ka* practice the shamanist art of transformation, which, we have said, requires the ability to cross over from image to image, shifting shapes and bodily forms, while relating to others and the outer world. The purpose of this shape-shifting, as I study it, is to release and heal the subconscious mind. The practice of butoh is inspired through hidden messages from the subconscious; not relying on the linear mind, butoh works with nonlinear processes, giving less attention to controlling the body than to cultivating a listening-body. Questions that suppose surprise flow though such processes: "What is waiting to emerge," the dancer asks her body without forcing an answer. "How might it speak? Does it have a color or a sound, a shape or a smell? Can I let my dance find its own way out?"

The trust that is asked of the dancer is how she can stay with the emergent image, let it be, let it move and morph, and not fix it. Then she can be surprised by her dance. And if she is performing, perhaps she can also surprise her audience by awakening something in them of their own hidden truth. In these affective connections, butoh holds healing potentials, as many dancers have experienced, not only committed *butoh-ka,* but also those who take butoh classes and workshops for personal growth. Healing and celebration are basic purposes in all forms of creative arts—though seldom stated as such. In butoh they appear oddly and unexpectedly, often as interactive aspects of world community, through personal intuitive insight, and in theater performances.

Sand and Footprints in Water

Now that we can see images of our planet from space, we understand how all life is connected. We are related—sharing a small home spinning in the vastness of space. As a hybrid art that expands this sense of kinship, butoh as it developed through the second half of the twentieth century continues to move across cultural boundaries. If its shamanist basis promotes a healing ethos, its aesthetic tendencies further a Buddhist psychology of nonviolence and compassionate interdependence. The individual, as such, is not as important as the whole in butoh, even as individuality is represented and respected. The particular features of the dancers are often indistinguishable in the butoh company Sanki Juki, for instance, as white faces and powdered bodies blend and sand drops from the ceiling in sprays across them.

The use of sand that occurs a lot in butoh is profoundly mesmerizing. It prompts the mind to spread out and dissolve and the ego to give up its attachments to limited individuality. The shifting qualities of sand point directly toward shape-shifting and the transcendence of individual ego. On the cover of this book, we see Yoshioka Yumiko drenching her head with sand in *Before the Dawn,* her work premiered at the Daiwa International Butoh Festival in London in 2005. In an earlier work, *It's All Moonshine* (1997), she is buried completely in a large pile of sand. We see only the mound in the beginning, as we wait through a long period of emptiness and silence. Then she comes plowing out, dancing. Finally she spits sand, ritualistically, propelling us into its grit. Yoshioka loses herself to the dancing and the sand, shaking, shedding her skin like a snake, and morphing through several states of being.

Likewise, I have seen Ohno Kazuo bite into paper in dance class, using illogical behavior to prompt laughter and release ego, then through poetry motivate dancing with a barrage of images: a moth's wing, the fetus in its mother, the ocean, orchids, racing sperm, the dead, and more. He projects students past the solidity of ego and imbues empathy in a global sense. His more linear lectures assert care and gratitude for those whose lives we share, the living and the dead.

Butoh comes rolling through the wind with its bones on fire, in the shape-shifting imagery of Hijikata Tatsumi. The first performance of butoh, *Kinjiki* (Forbidden Color), was in Tokyo in 1959. Seeded by Hijikata, Ohno Kazuo, Ohno Yoshito (Kazuo's son), and Kasai Akira, butoh redefines beauty in dance.

In its beginnings, several women were also important, including Ashikawa Yoko, Nakajima Natsu, and Motofuji Akiko (Hijikata's wife). Its heart-searching images pose new imperatives for contemporary life. Butoh can also be irritating, as any alchemical form would. It rubs through in bravura performances, even as it covers its tracks, erasing pride.

Whether amateur or professional, butoh performers challenge inner enemies, mourn the living and the dead, carry ancestors, resonate with fear and faith, and, in the unlikely manner of alchemy, leave evanescent impressions like footprints in water. Unlike ornamental European ballet, the democratic designs of American modern dance, or the improvisational games of the postmodern, butoh masquerades human weakness. It exposes the watery subtle body ready to dissolve and go under. Not moving outward in decorative lines or aspiring upward, *butoh-ka* around the globe effect a metamorphic signature through inward dances of spiritual transformation. They show how our global survival depends on empathy with others—not control. This is, moreover, not a conceptual empathy, but one that is lived through the vulnerable body we all share.

Sheer strength is not the quality that leads to feelings of gratitude and love. Rather, compassion for others and ourselves deepens through the experience of vulnerability, especially as we contemplate the impermanence of everything on the globe—*mono no aware* (evanescence)—and transform the earth we share. As in meditation, butoh offers a slow contemplative space within consciousness, somatically transforming: one pace, one synapse, and one cell at a time. This space of passage is known as *ma*. We have no Western term for *ma*. It is a middle, a hyphen in-between in any case. Sometimes I visualize this metaphysically as the space between the top of white and the bottom of black or more physically as a wide yawn where I lose myself in the middle, not the top of the wide inhalation or the bottom of the release moving down. *Ma* comes to me similarly as I form my own Zen question: What is the middle of gray? The essays in part 2 explore the Japanese concept of *ma* in several different butoh contexts.

Broken Path, Global Scattering

In several ways butoh is an arresting mixture of East and West, beginning with Japan. First, Japonisme strongly influenced the development of Western Impressionism in art as well as the Symbolist and Expressionist aesthetic movements that followed, as we consider next. As part of its global alchemy, butoh adapts elements of Expressionist dance, German *Neue Tanz* (known in Japan as "Poison Dance"), borrowing back what the West had already borrowed from Japan. We take this up more fully in several contexts. Not resting there, butoh continues to scatter internationally—but not in a smooth unbroken path—more like a faltering figure eight or a spotted infinity line askew, its center passing through

Japan. Breaks represent emptiness and *ma,* the mysterious spaces in between. In both a local and global sense, *ma* (as empty space) proffers the unexpected, allows the ego to soften, and permits the dance to transform.

Concerning global scattering, pure identities are difficult to find in butoh. Hardly utopian, the muddy, ashen bodies of butoh disclose a shadow side of the global economy and negative consequences of technology turned toward material accumulation, thus ensuring that as an East-West synthesis it can never be recuperated in the interests of political globalization. I question how this dance resists control of dominant cultures and modern notions of progress? What provides its staying power? And how does it create world friendliness? Dancing beyond ethnicity and the borders of Japan, butoh has developed a world-friendly, healing alchemy largely through Ohno Kazuo and Ohno Yoshito and owes its surreal alchemical morphology, "the body that becomes" (the body in states of change), to Hijikata Tatsumi—as we explore further from several vantage points.

The lineage of Ohno and Hijikata constitutes a global genealogy. To consider just one instance among many: Min Tanaka declared himself a son of Hijikata and took his butoh cues from there. In turn, Stuart Lynch of Copenhagen is certified to teach the *Body Weather* work of Tanaka, carrying this perspective from Tanaka's dance farm in Japan to Denmark and New York. Lynch performs his work internationally, ranging in appearance from powder-caked androgynous nudity harking back to Hijikata to gender ambiguity characteristic of Ohno and butoh in general. Lynch's solos morph through all of this and fast forward as well. In an old overcoat, he carries farm buckets across trails of stones with a feeling for the rustic appreciated as *wabi* in Japan. He splays his ribs like Hijikata, and, like Min Tanaka, he shows up the inner sides of boredom and bedlam. We see this in *The Touch of a Vanished Hand* made for his ensemble of dancers, the Perfume School. This work is a conceptual butoh collage and soft machine dedicated to Lynch's mother with further remembrance of the American choreographer Ralph Grant (1947–2007). In his reviews, critic Janus Kodal calls it "a fragile rite . . . of sorrow and loneliness."

Background: How the West Assimilates Japan

Behind the global scattering of butoh lies Japonisme, a continuing fascination with Japanese art and fashion that began in the West in the late-nineteenth century after the Meiji restoration of 1868 and the opening of Japan to trade and travel.[4] Japan opened its borders for trade under threat of military intervention from the United States when Commodore Matthew Perry of the United States Navy sailed his tar-covered ships into Tokyo Bay and leveled his cannons on the city. Thus, butoh's alchemy has origins in art history and military history, including concerns for commerce. When Japanese dancers began to travel to Germany and the United States in the 1920s and 1930s to study the innovative modern dance of the West, the expressively stylized and much admired Japanese ukiyo-e woodblock color prints were popular in America and Europe. Japanese art, clothing, textiles, and ceramics exerted a strong influence on the growth of Western art in the nineteenth and twentieth centuries. Assimilation of Japanese stylization and technical acumen in the West became known as Japonisme.[5]

One of the best practitioners of Japonisme is Vincent van Gogh, who evolved a technique of drawing with dots and lines, using a reed pen, with Japanese artist Hokusai Katsushika as his preferred aesthetic model. The adoption of Japanese modes can also be seen in Henri Toulouse-Lautrec and the *mie grimace* of the Kabuki theater and Paul Gauguin and the *ishizuri* technique.[6] The everyday quality of gesture in matter-of-fact bathing and squatting, sprawling, and sleeping in Hokusai's studies of ordinary movement served as a model for Gauguin and other artists of his time when European art still felt the "indecency" of a basic pose. The fact that Hokusai had often depicted people in postures that offended the norms of nineteenth-century European prudery made him the founding father of new Impressionistic conventions, with which Edgar Degas, Toulouse-Lautrec, and a host of second-generation Impressionists shocked their society.[7]

Many artists of the Impressionist movement, including van Gogh and Degas, were strongly influenced by the abstract, suave, and flowing style of the Japanese ukiyo-e artists. Impressionism came to identify this style of painting in Europe and entered into music, especially of late-nineteenth- and early-twentieth-century France, characterized by the use of rich harmonies and tones to express scenes or emotions. Claude Debussy (1862–1918) and Maurice Ravel (1875–1937) were widely known for their Impressionistic style.

Ohno Kazuo based his dance *Suiren* (Water Lilies, 1987) on the water lily canvases of Claude Monet (1840–1926), a French painter and leading exponent of Impressionism in the late-nineteenth-century art movement. Monet's paintings captured scenes of everyday life and the qualities of light in nature. His use of bright colors in short strokes became an identifying mark of Impressionism. As with several French Impressionist painters, Monet was also influenced by the style of Japanese ukiyo-e. His idea for painting varied images of his pond garden at Giverny in several time frames came through Hokusai's *Hundred Views of Mount Fuji* and Hiroshige Ando's *Hundred Views of Edo*. In basing his dance on Monet, Ohno was vicariously participating in his own cultural roots, completing a circle of aesthetic exchange. I have previously described Ohno's *Suiren* extensively, including its relationship to the Impressionist nature paintings of Monet with their watery feminine essence.[8] Behind *Suiren*, one senses the spiritual luminosity of Monet's work, the surface of the still or rippling water emerging through the flat leaves of the water lilies, floating in repose like the lotus lilies of Buddhist tranquility. But Ohno textures *Suiren* with startling elements in juxtaposition. His son Yoshito's jerky dance against his father's quiet gliding entrance is performed in a seething staccato style to the music of Pink Floyd—and this devious ploy makes all the difference between Monet and Ohno, Impressionism and butoh.

Concerned with illustrating the exceptional phenomena that welled from their own inner beings, artists such as Edvard Munch and Aristide Maillol experimented with black backgrounds in their woodcuts based on Japanese *shiro-nuki,* a black-and-white technique. They abandoned the clear outlines of Art Nouveau and plunged into dark, associative depths of the psyche in work that became known as Symbolism. Through groupings of light spots, they imbued their work with abstraction and mobility sustained by an underlying rhythmic pulse. With the post-Impressionist work of Gauguin, *shiro-nuki* exerted an important influence on graphic art in Europe at the turn of the century. Its traces can be recognized in the members of the German group Die Bruke (The Bridge), a group of painters living in Dresden in 1905 who explored emotional styles. "It supplanted the ornamental arabesques of Art Nouveau and prepared the ground for Expressionism."[9] Butoh can be traced to Expressionism, in part, as we will see, cycling materially back—through Symbolism and Impressionism—into the very elements that Europe found so fascinating in Japanese art before the Westernization of Japan. Butoh's pre-Western Japanese origins inspire this history in a novel way, as we consider next.

Pre-Western Japanese Roots of Butoh

The international exhibitions of the nineteenth century fostered a positive understanding of the art of Japan and China.[10] Interest shifted to Japan when through the military pressure of Commodore Matthew Perry of the United States Navy, Japan opened its ports to the world on March 31, 1854. A year later, Japan concluded trade agreements with Russia, Great Britain, the United States, and France, and after more than two centuries of isolation, Japan opened its doors and its arts to foreigners in 1868 at the beginning of the Meiji era.[11] Inevitably, as art exited Japan, Western influences also entered. Thus, effects of the West were felt in Japan long before the end of World War II in 1945. In several ways, butoh is the inheritor of the confluence of East and West in Japan, as we will see throughout this book, but its alchemy began in Hijikata's frustration, his love-hate encounter with the West, and his deep identification with his native Japan.

The indigenous, pre-Western Japanese roots of butoh will become increasingly clear throughout the text. For now, we take a brief look into these and link back to our examination of Japonisme in art history. Ukiyo-e wood-block prints depict pre-Western Japan, the actors and passions of the original Kabuki theater, and capture everyday scenes of sleeping, eating, washing clothes, and traveling. These prints, now dimmed with age, show nature in highly stylized forms, especially the ocean and the mountains of Japan. The favorite preoccupations of the ukiyo-e artists were Edo (the original name for Tokyo), bold theatrical costumes, sex, and *onnagata* (gender transformation from male to female in Kabuki). Hijikata was inspired by ukiyo-e, especially as he turned toward the original Kabuki, stating that he wanted to create a "Tohoku Kabuki" in his dance.

While dancing in the avant-garde movement in 1960s Tokyo, he looked back to these sources, creating a contemporary form with indigenous roots. However, it would be difficult to say that his butoh assimilates native Japanese elements in a literal way. Rather does it bring these forth in a new context? Butoh is a cauldron for these. Through Hijikata, the pre-Western roots of Japanese culture inspire butoh and take on a new complexion.

Butoh also thrives on European aesthetic movements of the late-nineteenth and early-twentieth centuries, as we consider more fully in the next section, but we might notice a curious cycle in this; creatively, Hijikata and Ohno and those influenced by them reclaimed from Europe what Europe had already borrowed from Japan, namely indigenous Japanese aesthetic elements. Inevitably these elements change in translation, acquiring new characteristics.

One of these borrowings concerns the virtue of detail embedded in the art and sensibility of Japan. There one learns to look for details, whether in the silken kimonos of endless color combinations and pictorial elements, the traditional woven cottons in subtle stripes, or the lacquerware with tiny inlaid jewels. Even the little purses in the open marketplaces for tourists are decorated in great detail, with flowers, kittens, owls, smiles, and endless more ornaments. Japanese food is also creatively detailed, as Westerners who love sushi discover. Each shop and restaurant has its own varieties, and sushi is just the beginning of original dishes, served as singular artworks, each plate different. Portions are small, and every tiny detail is important. Sometimes I don't know whether to eat the food or just look at it.

Attention to detail has a long history in Japan and its influence on the West, especially through art. As we just saw, pre-Western Japan had an enduring effect in the work of the Impressionists, the Symbolists, and even the Expressionists after them. Japanese exemplars gave the West "the wave and its ornamental form, new types of posture and movement, the abstraction of nature, the rock in the sea."[12] The exhibition Weltkulturen und Moderne Kunst (World Culture and Modern Art), mounted to mark the Olympic Games in Munich in 1972, brought forward the global influence of Japanese art and cataloged elements of Japonisme. It shows that Western artists learned a variety of highly detailed methods from Japan—compositional ones—"such as silhouette, the diagonal principle, the imposition of a grille pattern or of cut-off objects placed in the foreground."[13]

Furukawa Anzu, represented in two essays of part 2, is one of many dancers, butoh and contemporary, who use silhouette, striking diagonal designs, angular and grille patterns, and cut-off objects or fragments of movement in collage. Furukawa makes obvious use of these techniques, moving simultaneously westward toward a French-born American artist, Marcel Duchamp (1887–1968), and back to the Japanese artists who preceded him. Duchamp is significant to discussions of butoh because he provides the avant-garde a bridge between Dada and surrealism, and as we will explore further in our study, butoh carries surrealism into dance, morphing it into a global art, still growing in the twenty-first century. Duchamp became famous for his highly detailed and fragmented collage images and for his "found art" conceptual work, playing a major role in the development of twentieth-century art, also influencing late modern and postmodern dance. We discuss him further in the first essay on Furukawa. Concerning collage and detail in choreography, we might bear in mind how Hijikata and butohists who followed him introduced collage pictorial records (*butoh-fu*) to dance and theater, following a long line of Japanese innovation in art.

How Butoh Assimilates the West

Now to look westward: Historically and methodologically, butoh draws on several Western sources, especially Expressionism and surrealism as we have just mentioned. Expressionism is an imprecise term, referring to art and literature that attempts to convey a subjective, psychological, or spiritual essence. It developed roughly over the first half of the twentieth century, first in Europe. This artistic movement originated in Germany between 1905 and 1925; its advocates sought to represent feelings and moods rather than objective reality, using bold colors and forms in highly stylized and subjective manners of representation. In dance, Expressionism arose primarily in Germany through the work of theorist Rudolph von Laban and dancers Mary Wigman, Kurt Jooss, Harald Kreutzberg, and others. Their work represented German Expressionism in dance and was also called modern dance or New Dance (*Neue Tanz* in German). The modern dance movement also grew in America through such figures as Ruth St. Denis, Doris Humphrey, and Martha Graham—who would later be associated with early modern dance, alongside the Expressionists.

Dalcroze Technique and German *Neue Tanz* were imported to Japan through Kosaku Yamada and sustained in the influential teaching of Ishii Baku. Eguchi Takaya, who studied with Mary Wigman, imported Expressionist dance to Japan, its creative experimental nature, and its developmental physical techniques. Eguchi's teaching influenced the growth of lyric and dramatic modern dance. Much later in the twentieth century and into the twenty-first, Japanese modern dancers developed experimental work using deconstructive postmodern methods similar to those in America, but with a significant difference, as seen in the unique dance of Teshigawara Saburo existing in the cracks between postmodern deconstructive dance and butoh. (I introduce his work in *Dancing into Darkness*.)[14]

Eguchi's teaching of German Expressionist dance in Japan is also in the background of the more gestural and raw dance of butoh performed by Ohno and Hijikata. Ohno studied Expressionist styles with Eguchi in 1936 (and before that with Ishii Baku in 1933). Hijikata studied German-style modern dance under Masumura Katsuko, a student of Eguchi, and with Ando Mitsuko, Eguchi's student. Ohno and Hijikata met through Ando between 1952 and 1954. In Ohno's six-page vita and biography, he notes his experience of seeing Expressionist Harald Kreutzberg, a student of Mary Wigman, dance in 1934. This inspired him to study with Eguchi and his wife Miya Misako. Thus, both Hijikata and Ohno had significant training in German Expressionist dance, or *Neue Tanz*.

Hijikata's choreographic inspirations through Jean Genet (1910–96) look even deeper into European sources. Genet was a French novelist and dramatist whose writings reveal societal margins and sometimes grotesque aspects of human existence, which are undercurrents of surrealism and Expressionism. Genet is the literary inspiration behind Hijikata's performative surrealism. His early subversive themes are drawn from the writings of Genet that he read in the mid-1950s—*The Thief's Journal* (1949) and *Our Lady of Flowers* (1944)—just translated into Japanese. He even performed for a while under the stage name of Hijikata Genet. In his program note for his first butoh, *Kinjiki,* in 1959, Hijikata wrote: "I studied under Ando Mitsuko, consider Ohno Kazuo a brother, and adore Saint Genet."[15]

One year after *Kinjiki,* Hijikata choreographed *Diviinu sho* (also called Divinariane) in 1960 for Ohno Kazuo, a solo based on Divine the hero/heroine of Genet's novel *Our Lady of the Flowers.* Like his hero Genet, Hijikata attempted to give voice to those on the margins of society, giving songs to those who don't have voices.[16] This spirit that he adopted from Genet transfers politically to his *Ankoku-Butoh*. In "To Prison," Hijikata quotes from Genet's *The Thief's Journal:* "Talent is courtesy with respect to matter; it consists of giving song to what was dumb. My talent will be the love I feel for that which constitutes the world of prisons and penal colonies."[17] As a performative rather than product-oriented movement, Hijikata's radical experimentation carries through a political purpose of questioning social mores in a vanishing medium.

Surrealism, a complex early-twentieth-century movement in art and literature, permeates Hijikata's aesthetic. In a long line of surrealists, he draws imagery from the unconscious. Like the European surrealists, he creates fantastic, erotic imagery juxtaposing dream states and reality in contradiction, further projecting this into an avant-garde movement. Antonin Artaud's call for a theater of the senses and his theatrical innovations inspired Hijikata's surrealism directly.

Artaud's *The Theater and Its Double* was translated into Japanese in 1965 and had a profound influence on a new generation of Japanese directors and performers, including Hijikata. This is evident in the anarchy of his dance *Hijikata Tatsumi to Nihonjin: Nikutai no hanran* (Hijikata Tatsumi and the Japanese: Rebellion of the Body), also known as *Rebellion of the Body* and sometimes *Revolt of the Flesh.* This shamanist dance choreographed in 1968 demonstrates Hijikata's maturity as a surrealist and his explicit use of the unconscious. His dance is cast amid the turmoil of the late 1960s in Japan (as throughout the world).

In this work, Hijikata enters the stage through the audience, borne on a palanquin, a long kimono covering his naked body, and holding a golden phallus—as in Artaud's *From Heliogabalus, or The Anarchic Crowned.* He transforms from one episode to the next as though possessed, wearing a large strapped-on golden penis, dancing in a heavy gown, and binding himself with ropes, his sleek and artificially tanned body wrapped in swaths of white cloth. He contrasts costumes with his personal characteristics as he dances, at one point jumping in a girl's short dress and kneesocks with his wild beard and hair flying. Kimonos and Western dresses exist in clashing collage with Hijikata's masculine body as it transforms, his ribs lifting high as he casts his gaze downward, flaunting his extended fake penis like a satyr. Through *Rebellion of the Body,* performed nearly a decade after his first radical experiment *Kinjiki* (1959), Hijikata's butoh is gradually understood as a new form of dance.[18]

Global Borrowing in the Modern Period

It is worth considering the wide global borrowing of dance during the modern period in general, because this foregrounds butoh's somatic elasticity. Butoh arose in the creative ferment of the 1960s on the heels of the modern dance movement, developing roughly over the same time period as American postmodern dance. Modern dance (also called New Dance and sometimes creative dance) grew in Germany, the United States, Canada, Mexico, South America, and elsewhere in the first half of the twentieth century. In Japan it took firm root through such figures as Eguchi Takaya, as we have seen. Ito Michio was arguably the most globalizing of the early modern dance pioneers in Japan. He gained wide recognition early in the twentieth century with much of his work being performed in Europe and the United States, including Hollywood. His work was greatly admired by Claude Debussy, Auguste Rodin, William Butler Yeats, and George Bernard Shaw and gained recognition in the United States. In those times, the Oriental was imagined in the West as a spiritual being; paradoxically, this refinement coexisted with the devious, lazy, and sensual stereotype.[19] Ito walked this perilous line through his representations of Oriental themes in Hollywood. He also taught at the Denishawn School in the 1920s but returned to Japan after World War II to focus his clearly defined modern dance work on universal themes and emotions, not simply Oriental content. Ito's dream of merging East and West utilized both his Japanese background and Dalcroze training. Émile Jaques Dalcroze (1865–1950) was a Swiss musician who developed his educational techniques through movement. Dalcroze techniques exalted bodily, psychic, and cosmological integration, as symbolized in the yin-yang interlocking teardrop symbol over the door of its school.[20]

Dance in the United States during the first decade of the twentieth century appropriated the East—borrowing from it openly and often quite literally through trite Oriental imitations in ballet, interpretive dance, and Delsarte Orientalism. François Delsarte (1811–71) was a French singer, philosopher, and teacher, whose philosophy of gesture and expression was highly influential in the development of modern dance in the United States. The dance world was permeated with the exotic and Oriental, including the Ballets Russes. Michel Fokine created the exotic ballets *Scheherazade, Cleopatra,* and *L'Oiseau de Feu* in 1910. Modern dance pioneer Ruth St. Denis created *Radha,* based on a Hindu legend, in 1906, and in 1913 she premiered *O-Mika,* a Japanese dance drama. Charles Weidman created *Japanese Actor* and *Singhalese Drum Dance* in 1928, inspired by his work with artists Mei-lan Fan and Koshiro Matsumoto on Denishawn's Oriental Tour of 1925–26.[21] Ted Shawn choreographed *The Cosmic Dance of Shiva* in 1926.

As it grew, Western modern dance incorporated the Far East as exotic and "Oriental." Although its sources were often clearly stated in such titles as those listed previously, they were not always so transparent. Martha Graham used elements of yoga in developing her very popular dance technique, and Noguchi Isamu designed many of her sets in suave and flowing Japanese styles, as can be seen in the Noguchi Museum in New York City. Graham's themes, however, drew heavily upon Greek mythology, and they included Americana. Modern dance also borrowed from the South Sea islands and Africa, assimilating undulating rhythms, bold shapes, and abstract masks that it deemed "primitive." As late as 1963, Louis Horst taught modern dance composition in America as a sophisticated form of primitivism. I experienced this approach as a student in his "modern forms" class that year. He writes about this approach in his book, *Modern Forms,* written in 1961.

The use of the term *primitive* has long since been expunged from the language of dance scholarship, except as an artifact in the thinking and art of the early modern dance period. The rituals of Native America also inspired the emerging modern dance of Martha Graham, Eric Hawkins, and Ted Shawn. African American music inspired a great deal of modern dance in the United States. Eventually, black artists themselves accomplished a global diaspora, fusing modern dance and African American culture. The Alvin Ailey American Dance Theater represents a prominent example of this fusion, and Garth Fagan

Dance another. African American dancers studied and acknowledged African sources, beginning with modern dance pioneer Katherine Dunham and her first company of dancers in 1940. The voluminous scholarship of Brenda Dixon Gottschild has detailed the influence of African American culture on American dance and American culture at large.

The emerging modern dance looked back into Western sources as well, incorporating classical aesthetics and ancient Greek archetypes. These were in vogue with early dance Expressionists in Europe and the United States; certainly they motivated Graham and Wigman.[22] Even the technically systematic Austrian modern dancer Rosalia Chladek choreographed classical dramas. Thus we see that during the first four decades of the twentieth century, a global cycling of aesthetic substance began to unfold in the original stew of modern dance, and it also involved Japan. In figure 2, we see a photograph of Eguchi Takaya, who studied *Neue Tanz* with Wigman and eventually became the modern dance teacher of Ohno Kazuo in Japan. Here Eguchi dances *Prometheus,* bearing fire from the gods in representing the Greek legend of Prometheus; thus, did he carry the passion of the West to Japan.

Butoh Fusions and Interspaces

Prior sections have explored butoh's Eastern and Western assimilations as well as its revival of elements native to Japan. I have said that butoh represents a point of fusion. How does fusion happen in butoh? And what is the difference between assimilation, appropriation, and fusion? Can we rightly speak of fusions in dance? Fusion implies that parts are being fused together, physically or even mechanically, as in welding. In the arts, with pitfalls of abstraction and interpretation, an understanding of fusion is harder to come by, referring as it does to the merging or blending of ideas, aesthetic styles, or entire genres (as when we speak of blends or fusions of modern dance and ballet).

Fusions of aesthetic styles and cultural elements from more than one tradition are not uncommon, for instance the fusion of African polyrhythm with Euro-American architectural harmony and Western musical instruments in jazz. A good example of this can be found in the jazz piano style of Erroll Garner, whose rhythmic lag in syncopation and stride on the keyboard is still without peer. My early research into jazz dance via jazz music, more than anything else, taught me about fusion. It also taught me to look for vital fusions, weak links, and breaks.[23]

Concerning assimilations of Eastern and Western sources in butoh, this is what we can say about butoh fusions thus far. Reading from East to West: Butoh revives Japanese nativism, including its shamanist aspects, and it employs the myriad stylizations belonging originally to Japanese culture that we have explored as Japonisme in the West's fascination with Japan. As Japonisme crops up

FIGURE 2. Eguchi Takaya in a photograph from the early modern
dance period. Eguchi is seen here in his dance *Prometheus,*
bearing fire from the gods to earth. From the collection of Kanai
Fumie, Eguchi's assistant for many years. Photographer unknown.
Used by permission of Kanai Fumie.

in butoh, however, it is recycled, having gone from Japan to the West and back
to Japan, which poses the intriguing question of whether a country through its
art can be fascinated with itself? I believe it can, especially through the eyes of
the other, just as we can admire in ourselves what others admire in us. Reading
from West to East: Butoh cultivates the raw, gestural, and sometimes grotesque
nature of Expressionism without its narrative and symbolic tendencies. Drawing

upon sense experience, butoh juxtaposes dream states in an avant-garde form, thus borrowing from European surrealism; it employs the creatively unfinished nature of modern dance, leaving aside its lyrical connectivity and narrative; it provides a unique example of postmodern eclecticism in blending historical periods and different cultural styles of music and costumes.

The reach into subconscious life, the unconscious body, and metamorphic methods are also important in butoh fusions. These matters are beyond ethnicity; yet the model for them is Hijikata. We are beginning to see that he carries a nativist/shamanist Japanese sensibility toward the unconscious in his dance and that his stylistic manner and inspiration come from surrealism, especially Genet and Artaud. His leap into what he called "the unconscious body" may well be the *ursprung* (original leap) that allows his assimilation of the other in several guises, opening a hole for his passage, and ours, between East and West. In his love-hate relationship with the West, he distanced himself from American materialism while embracing European theater and intellectual life. Eventually, Hijikata's work nudged physical theater in the West toward the power of a fully performed nonrestrictive gesture and further away from literal acting. Hijikata's influence on theater has been profound.[24] The first essay of part 2 will describe his unique dance theater.

If we look more closely at postmodern aspects of butoh, it is easy enough to seize matters of eclectic borrowing and conscious appropriation. Suddenly in the postmodern era it became popular to mix styles, periods, and cultures. I have written more extensively about this in *Dancing Identity,* especially using the example of Karole Armitage's postmodern ballet works.[25] The Judson dance movement in America provides a contrasting example of the postmodern as based on pedestrian movement and tasks. Butoh, more than postmodern dance in America, thrives on an overabundance of images and at the same time harks back to some of the first examples of appropriation in 1917–18 when the Berlin Dada artists began to make their surreal montages. Collage is not a marker of the American postmodern dance, but it does identify butoh—as from the beginning Hijikata based his choreography on his creative *butoh-fu* collages, selecting fragments and fusing them together, then sending them through the alchemical fire of his performances.

In summary, something new arose in butoh through the fusion of Japanese aesthetics and spirituality with Western intellectual movements in the arts. Of course there are many ways into butoh fusions, and these court an array of results, depending on individual artistry, as we see through the essays in part 2.

I tend to think of assimilation as the process behind fusion, the absorption if you will of the motivating idea or the stylistic element. When I lower my center of gravity, for instance, and begin the slow meditative pace of the butoh walk, *hokotai* (or *hoko*), I am in a process that bears a relationship to traditional Japan.

I am aware, if I bring it to mind, of the pace of *Noh* theater and the tea ceremony and the Eastern ethos of inwardness developed in meditation. The last time I experienced an extended butoh walk was in an improvisation that I devised for students at a retreat in Wales in the summer of 2008. We moved outside in the dewy farmland, slowly spreading out in an early morning walking meditation, and then we returned still walking the same way, each person carrying something that could, or might, become apparent to them through the process, a surprise or realization from the unconscious.

How can you carry something that is not material? Don't we do this everyday? We carry burdens, hopes, and illusions, the lies we tell ourselves, and the things we can't let go of. These are just a few of the "things" we carry. Their particular features can become apparent to us in meditative dance experiences. They resonate as questions that come to mind through the dance; as for me, for instance, What is this tender happiness I carry in my hands, what treasure, what shame?[26] In butoh walking, I find answers, as I often see myself in various life stages and relationships. Walking on, I always find a way to transform:

> I favor Japanese stylization in lowering my body's center of gravity and using small gliding steps, softening my chest and the proud bearing I learned in ballet. Moving in assimilation of an Eastern ethos, I embody and improvise movement meditations in smooth ways of walking—with the long strength of my back, my head sitting easily on my neck, and the steady power of my legs beneath.

Is this art? Butoh walking can be beautiful, and it can be beautifully odd as well. Is this therapy? Yes. Somewhere between East and West, it is.

It is obvious that butoh and work influenced by it would not be what it is without Hijikata's plunge into his own Japanese background, inspiring others toward personal ethnologies. It is also clear that he incorporated Western elements in his choreography and costuming. Tebby W. T. Ramasike and his TeBogO (TBO) Dance Ensemble provide an interesting example of how cultural synthesis works today. His recent work, "A Passage through Time-Space and the Traditional Body," is undertaken with other African artists in their respective fields, exploring how the body can encompass norms of African ritualistic ceremonies in new contexts. He collaborates with butoh artists such as Takenouchi Atsushi in Afrocentric and butoh environments designed to enhance responsive globalism. In Ramasike's statement about his work, he speaks of "artistic interspaces" that locate artists in the global art and media world. He and his associates look at "cross-pollination of art forms" with particular attention to dance, art, and music.[27]

Fusion is at the end of assimilation; it represents a synthesis or result and sometimes even an aesthetic or psychological transformation. It speaks of something that has been accomplished. Of course, fusion could also refer to process, and it does when used in its transitional sense. I speak of butoh fusions in terms of cultural and aesthetic elements that have come together to make something unique and new. These can bring psychological changes in their wake, because the material of dance is human in essence. Throughout the text, I describe such fusions. I don't always point them out as such, but I hope this discussion will open the reader's mind to them, to the several ways that butoh fusions are constituted and the myriad sources for them.

Spirit, Protest, and Obsession

Hijikata Tatsumi and Ohno Kazuo, the two major players in the founding of butoh, set the tone for much that was to come, affecting the wide span of this unique dance form. They had contrasting approaches to dance, as will become increasingly clear throughout the text. These two butoh founders represent opposite but complementary talents and life experiences. Ohno was twenty years older than Hijikata and had experienced war as a soldier and prisoner. I repeat this fact in different contexts, because Ohno's life and dance were strongly affected by the war. He never forgot his debt to those who died or lost his appreciation for life. Hijikata experienced World War II from another perspective altogether. He was too young to be a soldier, but his life spanned the problems of war, the rise of militarism in Japan, and the coming of American occupation.

Hijikata and Ohno also took different attitudes toward the West. Hijikata was more directly critical of modernism as it derived from mainstream Western ideas of material progress. And he wasn't alone in this view in Japan. His original butoh grew as part of the underground art scene in Tokyo, taking on aspects of Obsessional Art, an aesthetic expression in the 1960s that rebelled against the modernist movement sweeping Japan after the war. Ohno was friendly to the West but sometimes critical of Western dance and its objective orientation. He told me in an interview that he didn't like Merce Cunningham and Western choreographers like him who are "too abstract." This is less a criticism of the West than a declaration of aesthetic taste, I believe. Ohno's life has spanned the entire history of modern dance from its early-twentieth-century beginnings and into the twenty-first century. I feel fortunate to have heard him say, "Dance should be intoxicating," so it is not surprising that he appreciates the new Expressionism of Pina Bausch.

Hijikata's dance could be delicate, like Ohno's, and it progressed toward empathic tenderness toward the end of his performing career, as we will see in part 2, but it held a wide range of expression, including the grotesque. Violence against the body and identity was carried out through images of physical deformity in Obsessional Art and used as a tool of rebellion. Such "Happenings" and "Actions," as they are called, can be found in the work of Hijikata and Mishima Yukio, the author of the book *Kinjiki* (1953), which provided the impetus for Hijikata's first butoh. Photographer Hosoe Eikoh, who collaborated with Hijikata on the prize-winning book of butoh photographs, *Kamaitachi* (1969), was also linked to this protest art. His book of photographs captured butoh in compelling outdoor portraits of Hijikata in the rustic fields of Tohoku, showing the rugged beauty of rural identities in a time when these were being effaced by the escalating economic expansion of Japan under the United States-Japan security agreement, including the building of gigantic metropolitan centers.

Obsessional Art defined the work of many other avant-garde artists of that day. The relationship between artist and action as a central concept posited a critique of modern art and body-mind dualism. This widespread aesthetic movement in Japan and its protest of the West arose roughly at the same time as postmodernism in America. Because of its time in history, butoh became Japan's first postmodern expression in dance, especially with its eclectic mining of global sources for themes, costumes, and music, as eclecticism is a postmodern marker in architecture, art, and dance. Butoh is not simply eclectic, however; in its manner of metamorphosis, it is unlike any other art arising during the postmodern era of the 1960s and 1970s, as we will explore in the next chapter. The differences between Ohno and Hijikata at the root of butoh contribute to its breadth and metamorphic uniqueness.

The Cauldron

In its historical and cultural elasticity, butoh develops a globally sensitive dance theater still evolving in the twenty-first century. Like Japan itself, butoh bridges East and West, but with a conscience that is often skeptical of Western progress. We have said that surrealist literature and Expressionist dance from the West fueled the beginnings of butoh. Hijikata drew upon Western aesthetics, even as he sought to rescue the Japanese body from colonization, moving increasingly toward his own Japanese roots in his dances and speaking about them in "Kaze Daruma," his speech at the Tokyo Butoh Festival one year before his death in 1986. His final workshops encouraged experiences of disappearance and awakening, which are Buddhist and shamanist themes, and he also taught through his own surrealist poetry, speaking automatically, directly from the psyche, as surrealists seek to do.

His solo in *Summer Storm* (1973), which we consider in the first essay of part 2, is a transparent identification with leprosy and moves past ethnic boundaries in both costume and dance technique. Antiwar themes pervade *Summer Storm* in the material collage Hijikata favored, ever difficult to decode but clearly syncretic. Hijikata's genius lay in his ability to blend world sources in metamorphosis; this still marks the global way of butoh today. It also marks a great deal of butoh-influenced work, not necessarily claiming the term *butoh,* like that of Eiko and Koma out of New York, Djalma Primordial Science based in Lyon, France, and Kei Takei, who danced in New York City for many years and is now based in Tokyo. She danced her work *Woman Washing Rice* at the America Dance Festival in Durham, North Carolina, in 2008, and she performed her *Demon of the River* in a Tokyo premier in 2008. Her shamanist, butoh-influenced dance was one of six in various styles to honor Okuni, the female founder of the original Kabuki. I write about this dance in the last essay of part 2.

Taanteatro Companhia in São Paulo, Brazil, furthers Hijikata's shamanist, surrealist methods in *Máquina Zaratustra* (Zarathustra Machine, 2006), a work inspired by Friedrich Nietzsche. This work carries Germany to Brazil through Japan, significantly beginning on Brazilian soil. Hijikata's glance back and desire to rescue native or ethnic aspects of Japan as he saw the increasing encroachment of Western values also provided a glance back for others, who are now creating their own personal ethnologies in butoh and butoh-influenced metamorphic dance.

This includes a Samoan-born artist living in New Zealand, Lemi Ponifasio, whose Pacific butoh style is the most prominent butoh in New Zealand. His company, MAU, has toured globally but makes its home at the Corbans Estate Art Centre in Waitakere, a West Auckland maze of artists' studios and warehouses occupying an abandoned winery. Ponifasio's major work, *The Tempest,* has toured extensively to arts festivals around the world. Wilhemeena Isabella Monroe, another New Zealand choreographer contributing to the globalization of butoh, is heavily influenced by the philosophy and morphology of this art. She also works with Ponifasio and has danced with butoh notables Min Tanaka, Diego Piñón, Takenouchi Atsushi, and Yoshioka Yumiko. In her *Illusion Palace* (2008), Monroe integrates butoh and contemporary dance with a somatically inward eye, assuming the role of "the invisible container" for the whole, a way of "disappearing" in butoh. (Disappearing is an image we explore further in the next chapter.) I met Monroe through her somatics center in Auckland, which she established to play with the bridge between dance-making and somatic processes—including butoh. It is now the leading somatics research center in New Zealand and a hub for global somatics practice.

What Moves People

Now with butoh's international proliferation and other renewals of Expressionism in North and South America as well as Asia, the original stew of modern dance continues to brew. Is it "watered-down stew," as teacher Mathilde Thiele, who guided studies at the Wigman School when I was there in 1965, says, or like sourdough added to over a period of time, still getting richer? Expressionism, we may begin to see, has many faces; its dance media are as varied as the compelling *Tanztheater* of Pina Bausch. Dance that emphasizes expressive content over formal structure and abstract movement provides an avenue to the affective life that humans share, our varieties of desire, our suffering and self-interrogation. Bausch says she is not interested in "how people move"; rather she is interested in "what moves people," while contemporary dance in America continues to develop and diversify partnering and "release" techniques, emphasizing how people move and upping the ante in terms of technically difficult movement.

There is a degree of abstraction in any form of dance, but those that connect expressly to feeling and imagery cultivate the gestural body associated with an object outside of its own movement. This would be the objective material that Hijikata sought in creating his *butoh-fu,* the material collages and images that guided his choreography and with which he struggled. Hijikata's dance material did not come easily, as he wrote in "Inner Material/Material" in 1960. He struggled to embody it as "the most remote thing in the universe." Butoh is not movement for the sake of movement; it relates to an objective world, to the world of others, to dreams, and to life and death. Its somatic means are many, and its present-day seekers don't imitate past butoh. They take seriously the advice of Hijikata and Ohno that butoh is a discovery of the heart, as Yael Gaathon, an Israeli dancer, teaches in her butoh workshops. Ohno Yoshito continues to practice what his father teaches: that butoh comes from within and can be transferred from one person to another in the universal language of the heart. "Butoh doesn't have to be Japanese," Ohno would say in his teaching. We feel pain, we can love; these are fundamental and universal. "Butoh is just a word," Ohno said to me in my first class with him, "for dancing from the heart."

I am discovering, as Ohno taught, that there are many ways to express butoh and that the word itself is transitory. As we bridge cultures and histories in overtly expressive forms such as butoh and *Tanztheater,* we encounter a field of aesthetic differences and unique solutions. For me this is an occasion to turn toward the difference and try to understand it. Butoh presents a special case in this regard. It universalizes, as does Ohno's *The Dead Sea* (1985), inspired by an on-site visit and conceived on themes of mortality and nature. A museum of melting faces and dusty figures emerge as though from the flames of Hiroshima in Amagatzu Ushio's theater works for his world-renowned company Sankai Juku. His sublimely neutral dancers hang there in the air, crumble and fall, and then ascend without weight. Even as they grimace and their faces morph, they attain emotional distance. They distill existence and move behind the exterior face. Laughing and crying look alike, they seem to say; there is something eternal that connects the emotions in all their dizzy faints, however remote or light. Sankai Juku balances between a quintessentially Japanese feeling for restraint and minimalism and a universal quest for the human.

Ashikawa Yoko, one of the early virtuoso dancers of butoh who was close to Hijikata, also universalizes, but in a more personal way. She dances without representing anything, but she is nevertheless relating to discrete imagery that keeps her morphing from state to state. I read her morphology as osmotic. She invites the audience to pass through her dance, not to stop at her body. Ridding herself of "herself," she is a vehicle for spiritual passage, ever more absent as she empties herself. Hers is not the opaque body for itself; rather her dance is a transparency and her body a mystery. Ashikawa no longer performs, but many perform through the same mystique that she embodied. Her student SU-EN, a dancer from Sweden, was given her butoh name by Ashikawa. In part 2, I describe SU-EN's dance *Headless,* as well as the work of American Joan Laage, who studied and performed with Ashikawa.

Butoh is the result of the unique vision of Hijikata Tatsumi and the spiritual dancing of Ohno Kazuo, but its morphology also rests on globalizing elements in dance throughout the twentieth century. Born in Japan by way of Japan, Europe, and America, butoh now manifests still newer amalgamations through wider world influences. So one might wonder what tethers this dance form to some recognizable essence? This book attempts to describe some points of identification. Of these, metamorphosis and a feeling for the ground are key, as is paradox.

The global mixtures of butoh can baffle the eye and stir the soul, and its theatrical realizations can also temper, as in Frances Barbe's work. An Australian dancer living in London, she enters the space of her dance *Fine Bone China* (2003) carrying a fragile white cup clattering in its saucer as she walks. As her butoh continues from there, we soon understand that its source is not Japanese. It is also apparent to those who have studied butoh that she could not choreograph or perform as she does without a butoh background, but her study of the Suzuki acting techniques are also in play, as is her wide acquaintance with contemporary dance. She has performed *Fine Bone China* on stages in Australia, London, the United States, and Singapore. In Singapore, they gave her a green floor of spreading tropical leaves to substitute for the red dirt that was the original ground for the dance. I have seen the original, representing colonial Australia, and intriguing photographs of the Singapore version with Barbe hiding behind the giant leaves, spreading like fanning hands around her slight figure. She seems as vulnerable as the cup she carries and as strong as the tea it waits for. Her dance morphs and migrates globally; what migrates more globally than tea?

Deep in the Mix

In her consideration of "high Orientalism" (assimilating and learning from Eastern sources openly and with appreciation), dance scholar Katherine Mezur says that in butoh, "we inhabit a 21st century moment of 'trans-corporeal' nation/identity performance that is at once messy and visionary." She speaks of the San Francisco Bay area, where for thirty years butoh transformed from early enclave performances to a "global butoh" conference in 2003. Her conclusion, that California butoh transfigures Japanese butoh into a "transcorporeal" form, might be drawn in terms of London, France, Brazil, and New York as well. Tokyo, London, New York, and Chicago have all hosted butoh festivals. And butoh has migrated to Africa as well. Mezur's video clips in the presentation show how African choreographers have incorporated butoh in contemporary work.[28] Megan Nicely, a student of butoh and a dance scholar, also sees that butoh is a migratory practice, and not nation-specific.[29] Are we ready to say that butoh has become a transcultural form of dance? And that it evolves new cultural bodies? Butoh purists who remember Hijikata's highly specific dance form might not agree. Waguri Yukio, the foremost interpreter of Hijikata's dance, says he barely recognizes butoh in much work that professes this label today.[30] Certainly there are questions of identity in present-day butoh, and the past provides reference points, but we might realize that in order for any art to continue, it has to evolve or become a fossil of itself. Ohno's emphasis on improvisation encourages the global evolution of butoh; and while Hijikata's dances are highly stylized and choreographed, in their collage and syncretic constitution, they are also evolutionary. Metamorphosis, deep in the mix of the original butoh, spurs its global evolution.

As a synergic global art, butoh continues to change in terms of reference points. This is what I am learning. The metamorphic marker of butoh has permitted wide transformative travel. This does raise questions of authenticity, or maybe questions concerning the globalization of butoh tend more toward quality. What will pass as authentic experience for the performer, participant, and audience, since butoh from its beginning has been based in experience? Then what about the question of ownership? We might take a cue from Ohno Kazuo and Ohno Yoshito on this point. They and others associated with them have shared their art liberally. Ohno Kazuo was happy for Western students to learn butoh and encouraged their creativity, and he was just as happy dancing in mental hospitals as on stage. Butoh was never a "pure" form, needing to guard itself. Through Hijikata, Ohno, Kasai and others, it assimilated cultural aesthetics from around the world and gave dancers a way to build bridges. Suddenly it was fine to speak of universals in dance. In dance research circles, I had learned that nothing is universal if you search deeply enough. Butoh has taught me the opposite—that the more deeply I search, the more universals I will find.

Butoh-ka: The Last Samurai

The butoh of Hijikata and Ohno continues to evolve in new contexts, but it is the originality of their work that gives the term *butohist* its restive force, moving past modern and postmodern categories. As with Hijikata and Ohno, contemporary *butoh-ka* (dancers) pursue *experience* as the synonym of dance, appreciating the ongoing nature of life and the emptiness that plays an invisible role in form. Meaning in butoh comes through the immediate experience of the dance, not through a message. Hijikata and Ohno's theater of experience offers the audience a direct connection with the performer. Their butoh does not filter through centuries of dance stylization as in ballet, contemporary Kabuki, and *Noh;* nor does it move through the symbolisms of modern dance either. What you see in butoh, what you feel, is what matters. "The body must be caked with the essence of dance," Ohno says in his teaching. And because butoh rides the moment of experience in transition, its morphology has transformational potential, pointing in the direction of change and how you change—that is, in your never quite solid world.

Butoh, we will see throughout this book, thrives on transformative cycles. We could say that butoh dancers, *butoh-ka,* are the last samurai (with apologies to Ken Watanabe and Tom Cruise).[31] *Butoh-ka* hold onto something that is preciously fragile: emptiness and dimming light, the invisible inside of ourselves in our human multiplicities. When the world bears a single utopian stamp, it will dissolve. And the last warriors—like those "dreaming murder weapons" of Hijikata's dance against ennui—will literally embody butoh, as "corpses standing desperately upright," Hijikata's definition of his butoh.

Untamed in his signature work of 1968, *Hijikata Tatsumi to nihonjin: Nikutai no hanran* (Hijikata Tatsumi and the Japanese: Rebellion of the Body), compassionate and transparent in his ghostly *Leprosy* of 1973, Hijikata as fearless warrior and spiritual mendicant danced the painful metamorphosis of Japan. "All my seeds have been cut off," he declared, "the penis should be a radiant dagger." Hijikata danced through defeat, inspired by drastic changes in political and social values—growing to extremes in the 1960s. No area of Japanese life was immune to the political shifts taking place around the world at that time.

From a young age, Ohno was becoming acquainted with the West, growing up in the culturally rich port city of Hakodate. His mother created an international ambiance in their home through Western music and read Lafcadio Hearn's ghost stories to the young Kazuo. Hearn (1850–1904), a Western chronicler of things Japanese in the late-nineteenth century, saw well the changes coming to Japan. Writing his "Letter from Japan" in 1904, he captured the common everyday life during Japan's war with Russia and witnessed its first mighty struggle against the West. As Japan developed modern warfare, the old samurai culture began to crumble, but under the trappings of enchantment. When Hearn arrived in Japan in 1890 on a writing assignment from *Harper's Magazine,* Japan had its first constitutional government, but it was the land of boundless sea and sky that captivated him. There hearts are tender, people smile, cups are never empty, and there is no pollution or shame. Looking through this vision near the end of his life, Hearn describes an old painting of a Taoist paradise in his article "Horai," invoking a prophecy of modern Japan:

Evil winds from the West are blowing over Horai;—the magical atmosphere, alas! is shrinking away before them. . . . Remember that Horai is also called Shinkiro, which signifies Mirage,—the Vision of the Intangible. And the vision is fading,— never again to appear save in pictures and poems and dreams.[32]

Hijikata and Ohno never experienced Horai, and probably no one else did either. They did, however, go forth to wander in its ruins and to dance. "Dance into the dream," Ohno encouraged his students, "Walk on the bottom of the ocean." There is honor in sacrifice: "You are not the be-all and end-all of life."

The dance of Hijikata and Ohno continues to change in global circulation with *butoh-ka* framing their work in context of their own cultural matrix. Next we consider why butoh is uniquely positioned to carry across cultural boundaries through the way the butoh body is aesthetically constructed: *Butoh-ka* learn how to morph through bodily states and cultural facades, shedding, squatting, and waiting, seeking to uncover the dance already happening in the body in what-ever manner it appears, even as the costumes range from near nudity to elaborate theatricality. In the heat of bodily alchemy, they pass through *ma,* brightening the darkness that enchants the universe.

Chapter Two

The Morphology of Butoh

There are basically three kinds of rocks in the world: sedimentary, igneous, and metamorphic. Igneous rocks come from volcanoes and consist of melted rock or magma belched out of the earth's mantle. . . . Sedimentary rock is derived from combining tiny particles into one large rock. . . . Metamorphic rocks form when a mineral is subjected to intense heat and is compressed so hard by gravity or tectonic pressures that it literally changes into a different mineral. For example, squashed or metamorphosed sandstone makes quartzite. The Beaver Dam Mountains, just east of St. George, Utah, are metamorphic. The mountain range has made fortunes for miners exploiting its mineral resources.[1]

Images of Transformation

We find in butoh that everyone has a different rock quality, and that it comes to each of us as a different task and transformational gift, as in my experience:

Sometimes when I dance rock, I become still, solid, and fearless. And other times I melt into the rock, embracing, leaning, and giving myself to the shale. In my early sixties, I walked across a large field of hardened lava rock on the big island of Hawaii, hiking back to see the active flowing red fingers bubble up from under the earth's surface at dusk. With our guide, we watched the oozing dance of the morphing volcano way into the night, climbing high up above the sight on a craggy hill. I found the walking and climbing difficult at first, until I knelt down and touched the crusted glassy surface of the black magic rock. All the rest became

FIGURE 3. Takenouchi Atsushi dances in the deserts of southwestern Utah for the film *Ridden by Nature* by Kathi von Koerber. This feature-length improvisational butoh dance film was shot in environmentally endangered parts of the planet. Photograph by Hiroko Komiya, © 2003. Used by permission of Globe JINEN.

butoh, including a hula offering to Kilauea and the volcano goddess Pele. This adventure represented a turning point in my life. I needed heat to heal the chill in my feet and hands, and to melt the pain of living; at the same time to become solid and stop second-guessing myself.

"Be a stone" is one of Ohno Kazuo's singular instructions for a butoh workshop. Ashikawa Yoko, a female butohist who inspired the later work of Hijikata Tatsumi, also used stone imagery in her workshops, as I experienced in Tokyo. I have danced rock and stone in various butoh contexts in studios, theaters, and in nature. I learn the most from butohists who are dancing in the environment to heal themselves and the earth. Here I distill three poems from my solo dances filmed in 2007 in southwestern Utah near my birthplace. The first comes from red rock, the second from dream, and the third from fragments and rubble.

Worry Clouds

slip my eyes
Dowsing rose-bluffs underneath
The very purple peaks.
Pierce my feet, my hands
Wiggle through the holes in me
Root chakra lava.

Cliff Flyer

I fly,
Skimming the sheer cliff of pink rock,
In vertical sweeps to the next
Toehold as the ominous one pursues me.
With my saffron robe flying and holding
A magnetic distance, with my friend
I fly.

We watch the incredible doer's leaps
And denouement, marking the moments
Of his survival,
Til chocked and blazing he goes too far,
And the spell is broken.

Butch Cassidy's Cabin

My body is a vagrant among ruins,
The churchyard's damp stones,
And the cabin in the meadow.
Rain and wind pelt the window
Where I wait, as yellow tones
Rise from the dust and rot.
I will stay as long as it takes,
Or night brushes my cheeks.

When Ohno, a Japanese veteran of World War II, visited Auschwitz, he wanted to dance there for healing, but couldn't—not until he saw the pain in the stones.[2] Ohno saw the hidden morphology: that stone carries human history as well as geologic. He provides the example that others like Takenouchi Atsushi follow, excavating pain in the environment and transforming it through butoh. Such dance is not meant for show, but it might be witnessed on site or in film. Takenouchi has danced for healing after natural disasters and on the fields of war in every corner of the globe, carrying through his *Jinen Butoh,* dance in nature, to heighten global awareness and encourage peace.

Similarly, participants in Takenouchi's outdoor processions for healing seek "to dance and be danced and keep dancing," he says. He led his *Yin Yang Bu-*

FIGURE 4. Sondra Fraleigh dances in *Butch Cassidy's Cabin,* an environmental butoh film made in Circleville, Utah, in the Parker family cabin where Butch Cassidy (Robert Leroy Parker) was born and grew up. Circleville is also Fraleigh's birthplace. Photography and film by Mark Howe, © 2008. Used by permission of Mark Howe.

toh procession and open-door group improvisation in Paris in 2008, building on those performed at the Avignon Festival in 2005 and at the Centre George Pompidou in 2006 and 2007. He conceived *Yin Yang Butoh* to focus on transformation, "embracing souls that have been excluded or pushed away by society, or suffered from mental and physical disturbances." *Yin* is darkness and *yang* is light, and each carries characteristics of the other. In his processions, dancers can encounter the suffering of the dispossessed and keep dancing until they change their darkness into light.[3]

Metamorphic and transformational, butoh is a bodily type of alchemy that is often healing, partly through compression of global elements, especially through border crossings, accessing what Kasai Akira calls "the community body." Dancers embody images and elements, compress, expand, and morph through changing states in relation to others and the earth within a global community. Kasai, who has been dancing throughout the evolution of butoh as one of the founders with Hijikata and Ohno, says that if we are not dancing with a consciousness of community, we are not dancing at all. And the community he envisions extends toward nature, as he told me in an interview:

> The fingernail does not grow apart from the body, and the body of a human being does not grow apart from the community. It grows with the community, and that community includes all things in nature, not just the human community. No matter how hard dancers train—even if they are in superb condition—if they are not concerned for the larger body of nature, the dancer's body they develop does not mean much. This is one of the new concepts in dance. Your body does not develop unless you develop the community as well. . . . So far we have taken power from the earth, now it is time to return it. . . . This is an important new Butoh concept.[4]

Most recently, Kasai choreographed his highly responsive *Butoh America* (2007) for dancers in the United States, as we take up later.

Alchemy in Motion

I read butoh as alchemy in motion, as seen in the brief examples above. *Morphology*, the explanation of bodily types and transformations, is the encompassing theoretical task of this chapter. Three broad questions that guide me relate to this and derive from major phenomenological standpoints in dance, or we could also call these conceptualizations of bodily experience: (1) How is the body contextualized in butoh? This brings up issues of butoh choreography, including metamorphic inspirations and concepts of the body. (2) How is butoh performed and presented? This question pertains to *butoh-ka* (dancers) and the embodiment of butoh through the metaphor of alchemy. (3) How does the audience perceive or read butoh? I address the latter through acknowledging my own position as a witness to butoh, particularly through the essays of part 2, my readings of butoh performances in their global migrations, alchemical morphology, and unique aesthetic values. Being involved in butoh as a researcher and dancer, I am not an objective observer practicing the "disinterested" position of aesthetic perception described by Immanuel Kant in the aesthetic discourse of the West.[5]

Like most audiences, I come to theater and to dance with my past experience intact, but even as I try to suspend and refresh my experience, I certainly can't erase it. What we commonly call body memory will be there for me as for other audience members. Audiences bring a diverse set of experiences and expectations, but I think we hope to have our body memory jogged, to change in some way, if even in a small measure. When I'm watching something entertaining, I may simply expect to be entertained, but I don't attend to butoh in this way. Rather I understand that I am emotionally and spiritually "on the line," so to speak, and in a somatic process of "becoming," as Hijikata originally stated the metaphysical essence of butoh. Moreover, I am a *being becoming* in the transitive horizon of being. Nothing is settled. Akin to Buddhist psychology, butoh alchemy prepares me for uneven footing.

But why would I want to put myself in such a groundless place? Maybe it is because I need to learn how to live every day ready to respond and not to judge. In her book *When Things Fall Apart*, Pema Chodron outlines this Buddhist perspective brilliantly.[6] Similarly, butoh with its mysterious *pathos* often asks us to move toward pain and suffering, not insisting on answers, but lingering with curiosity. The dance in its metamorphosis offers us the possibility of relaxing into groundlessness. Admitting gravity and letting go of expectations, we may find that grace is indestructible, that we can trust our attention to odd juxtapositions, for life will surely bring the unexpected.

If butoh has a transformative purpose, and at best a healing ethos, how do we access this? Does transformation lie in the dance, the perception of the audience, or the performer's training and experience? In butoh, I understand metamorphosis as an aspect of the dance and of the performer's consciousness, performance personae, and training. Metamorphosis is transitive, suggesting a slow process or continuing change, while transformation often suggests culmination, and sometimes a sudden change, even as we can also talk about the act or process of transforming. A transformation can be a dramatic change, may be the result of a slow metamorphosis, and often indicates an enhancement of affect (a felt state) or appearance. "I am striving, not toward art: but toward love," is how *butoh-ka* Nakajima Natsu puts it in her teaching.

Phenomenologically (in essence), metamorphosis is what the dancer undergoes in butoh, and transformation is often the result. Receptive audiences in theater or witnesses to an environmental event may sense and experience the result, even if they don't understand it, but of course this is not always the case. Audiences for butoh are sometimes baffled, especially if they expect narrative logic. I had an interesting question from a woman at a lecture I gave on butoh: "I don't like butoh—is there something wrong with me?" she asked. Her dislike of butoh didn't surprise me—it is not what most people expect in dance—but the candor of her question was surprising. Of course there is nothing wrong with not liking butoh, but I think the question itself belies an attempt and interest.

Sometimes we want to know more about our attractions and repulsions. Butoh continues to teach me about mine.

What I am stating about the transformative potential of butoh is not a rule; rather it seeks to identify a tendency that I have observed from years of witnessing butoh performances and from participating in butoh training and therapy. Art doesn't usually follow rules, but the forms it takes display some common aspects of identity. What makes butoh butoh, we might well ask? I hold that butoh is most basically a metamorphic form of dance, and it is so in several ways. A primary means of butoh training is through the streaming or morphing of images ever in the process of change. Hijikata, the founder of butoh, gave the dance world a profound lexicon of paradoxical imagery in his *butoh-fu,* images in states of becoming and only seldom in states of arrival. *Fu* means "chronicle"; thus, his imagery became a record and collage notation for his choreographic morphology. He filled sixteen scrapbooks with profuse *butoh-fu,* including cut-out pictures of art and architecture from around the world and his own poetic streaming of word images.

These have been codified and saved in electronic format by one of Hijikata's longtime students, Waguri Yukio. He was a disciple of Hijikata from 1972 until Hijikata's death in 1986. He currently tours in Japan and internationally, presenting butoh workshops, lectures, and performances with his group Butoh Kohzensha. He started the Hijikata Method Study Group in 1992, and in 1996 he performed *Butoh Kaden,* a journey of seven *butoh-fu* worlds. Waguri's exposition is the first and, to date, only published source through which the public can access the alchemical process of Hijikata's *butoh-fu.*[7] While Hijikata's *butoh-fu* are poetic, they nevertheless show clear notation for performance, not in the style of Western notation like the Laban system, but pictorially and imagistically and within a cosmological outline, moving through seven worlds from wet and heavy to light and airy.

Butoh performances continue to explore states of becoming in metamorphic dances with transformational cadences, especially reflected in changes of facial expression and costume. Of course not all butoh endings are transformational; they might loop back to a previous state. The morphology of butoh becomes part of the choreographer's challenge and the surprise of the dance. In tandem with the dancer's metamorphosis, costumes, music, and stage settings also transform—often morphing from one cultural palette to another, as we see through the dances in part 2.

The audience is a witness to the performance and may undergo the imagistic transformations as well, but as is always the case with audiences, some witnesses will identify more with the intent of the dance and some less. What the audience gets from the dance, what they feel, is unpredictable, as Hijikata Tatsumi's primary disciple Ashikawa Yoko taught in our classes: "The audience may not get the changing images of the dance, but they cannot mistake the image-making process of butoh." I would agree to a large extent. Audiences are diverse; those who attend butoh concerts may experience its imaginative source material and transformative intent. Many are prepared for it. Butoh presents audiences with this possibility. This is one of the main reasons I continue to learn and write about this dance form. The life of human imagination in its changing terrain fascinates me in a way that narrative plots do not. Butoh presents a very full spectrum of imagery linked in odd and surprising ways—morphing who knows where. Thus the audience has the potential of being carried out of their habits. I never know where my psyche will land and what nuances of feeling will be stirred in me when I watch butoh. Maybe I will just be bored, but then there is the chance that the performer will connect and carry me into her unfolding stream.

Great butoh performers like Ohno Kazuo have become containers whereby audiences can experience transformative possibilities in their connection with the dance. Ohno stands for life in transition, making his aging process central to his dance. Aging is the ongoing metamorphosis that we all undergo. Ohno on his one-hundredth birthday gives us an aesthetic distillation of this: "Inevitably, the older I get, the more my body slowly withers away. Nevertheless, my dance still brims with life despite my physical limitations. As I see it, my performance should convey the reality of my aging process."[8]

Perhaps we also need to slow down, take a few steps back, and appreciate the beauty of age. Ohno provides a ready example, and there are others. The metamorphic alchemy of aging has been explored in butoh from the time Hijikata included the stooped postures of poor farmers in his homeland of Tohoku.

The Morphing Body

Morph is from the Greek *morphos,* meaning "form," "shape," or "structure." To morph is to change—as in dancing—where the human body is constantly in flux, stopping here and there for breath and only momentary glances. "Morph" is a relatively recent abbreviation of "metamorphosis," the word for transformation. Morphology, then, is the study of forms and their transformations, including that of rocks, plants, and animals. Like any living organism, the human body is constantly undergoing change, a dance of beginnings and arrivals: fading, falling, emerging, sleeping, waking, and walking. The whole of human life is morphology: a study of birth, death, and hope. The morphing body suggests the future and clings to it, etching cellular traces of the past, strangely sometimes, but with a possible second history. The morphing body as it touches the future involves the growth of the soul—in pain or sorrow and in love. Cultivation of the soul is the necessary project of life and not an intellectual endeavor but rather a transformative one. "The future is another word for the soul," professor of philosophy Jacob Needleman reminds us, and the development of the soul is the deep purpose in the founding of America. He sees America as a country still holding a promising future but weakening from within.[9] The tending of the soul, however, is not given to one people; it is a global project and the great gift of the wisdom teachings everywhere in the world.

Butoh dancers seem to get this! They consciously morph: from culture to culture and from birth to old age—transfiguring from male to female, from human to plant life, disappearing into ash, animals, bugs, and gods. Surprisingly, they transform without closure. Such nonlinearity might be confusing, but it can also call forth the present moment of awareness. In not needing to follow narrative logic, the mind is released into "the now" of listening and seeing. In the beginning of butoh, metamorphosis of the fetus in the womb was a major theme for Ohno, and it continues still in the butoh of today. This ability to inhabit an image and to change is basic to butoh. The dancer may go back into his own life, project himself forward, or inhabit an image to become something or someone other.

Becoming other is not a new idea. Transmigration of souls, a belief in ancient Egyptian cosmology, holds that souls of animals and humans can migrate to other bodies. Butoh, however, does not migrate so literally; rather it transforms through imagery, and as a dance form it is both spiritual and political. Hijikata associates it with darkness, which is his way of rejecting the forces of modernity, especially the secular ideal of progress he saw sweeping from America into Japan after World War II. Hijikata's bodily transformations presented the amorphous materiality of the body, and his call for the end of genres[10] set the stage for permeable boundaries in the international absorption of butoh methods. From the beginning, butoh artists produced postmodern amalgamations of East and West, moving their art beyond ethnic boundaries toward international participation.

On an ideological level, proponents of butoh deconstruct history and the evolution of reason, eschewing Western promises of progress. They turn back time and investigate themselves in terms of local cultures—as did Hijikata in exhuming "the body that has not been robbed," seeking his childhood roots and premodern Japan in the poverty of his homeland Tohoku. Hijikata also embraced universals in his world-friendly *butoh-fu,* using visual imagery from all continents. Now his vision of a theater of the senses fed by his own experience as channeled through world material resonates in butoh companies around the globe, like the archeology of pain he excavated from the cries of children in Tohoku.[11]

The art, drama, and dance of butoh have sought bodily truth. By backing into the shadow side of the psyche, butoh touches something basic to all humans. It acknowledges awkwardness and pathos; not getting stuck, it can always transform. Hijikata urged dancers to transform their concepts of the body, dispersing endlessly toward nothingness. Mikami Kayo, a student of Hijikata's, reports his words in his last training: "Your inner feeling is getting thinner and thinner to the extremity. Your outer feeling is getting higher and higher to the extremity." The moment the body becomes nothing, Mikami says, it begins to revive itself as everything universal in Hijikata's dance. The spiritual message is unmistakable—Buddhist, Hindu, and Taoist in tone: The body reduced to nothingness, will be revived in the "inexhaustible world of abundance." We know that Hijikata did not associate his dance explicitly with religion, yet this inexhaustible world, Mikami says, "was Hijikata's ultimate state to achieve in *Ankoku Butoh*."[12] The inexhaustible world is also that of the shaman who can shift his consciousness. Contemporary butoh and work influenced by it move beyond Hijikata but, at the same time, learn from methods he originated.

Nondualistic Morphology

We have noted that butoh has antecedents in German Expressionism and early modern dance, but its cultural matrix does not derive from there, even if its creative mien does. Hijikata and Ohno's study of German *Neue Tanz* introduced them to radical elements of creativity. They came into contact with ideas of the grotesque, beautiful ugliness, hysterical release, melodrama, and metamorphosis through *Neue Tanz*. They in fact tapped into the very root of *Neue Tanz* through Mary Wigman. We have noted that she taught Eguchi Takaya, who was in turn the teacher of Ohno, and we have also seen that Hijikata's dance lineage goes back to Eguchi and German Expressionism. There was variety in the creativity of German Expressionist dance, some lyrical examples as well as angular, and it seems clear that Ohno and Hijikata were acquainted with a full range of these elements from their first dance together, *Crow* (1954), which was choreographed by their teacher Ando Mitsuko in the German style of modern dance that he taught.[13]

But as the work of Ohno and Hijikata grew, it distanced from German Expressionism in important ways. Butoh is less melodramatic and its mystery more subtle. In this matter, it is less outwardly hysterical, although it resists the vanities of Western rationality with the same verve as Expressionism. Wigman's *Hexentanz* (Witch Dance, 1926) is a good example of theatrical uses of melodrama and aesthetic hysteria, what Peter Brooks has defined as the high end of melodrama in its capacity to push away the rule of reason toward underlying emotions.[14] This is also an apt description of butoh's revolt against Western rationality and the West's privileging of mind over body.

The nondualistic morphology of butoh draws upon the void of Continental existentialism, an aspect of theater of the absurd, but we should notice that concepts of emptiness underlying Buddhist sensibilities in Japan predate existential concepts of emptiness, nothingness, or the void in Western existentialism.

Theater of the absurd was part of literary existentialism and a partner to philosophical existentialism in its refutation of body/mind dualism. These links to the nondualistic morphology of butoh are not merely accidental. Refutations of dualism permeated continental philosophy through such figures as Jean-Paul Sartre and Martin Heidegger and were also part of Japanese phenomenology, as we shall take up in chapter 3. More important, Japanese artists and dancers themselves were rejecting Western body/mind dualism, especially Hijikata. His butoh rejected the separation of the body from its spiritual home, specifically refuting body/soul dualism.

Here the emphasis is on soul. Hijikata developed a technique called "killing the body," his surrealist language for shedding the material body. My understanding of this is through butoh processes of "appearing and disappearing" in workshops with Nakajima Natsu, one of the female originators of butoh with Hijikata. As you "kill the body" in disappearing, you shed materiality in consciousness, letting go. And at will, you can return. I often feel such letting go in watching *butoh-ka*. Later we take up various means of shedding in butoh, and in the next chapter on philosophy, we glimpse the importance of the body beyond matter in Japanese phenomenology.

The morphology of butoh also derives directly from the nondualistic mien of surrealism, as we touched upon in chapter 1. Its eroticism is close to nature and contrasts that of Pina Bausch's *Tanztheater*. Butoh and Bausch are both reviving Expressionism but with very different results. The aesthetic of butoh is not built upon conflict between male and female as occurs in Bausch. Neither is the body in butoh sustained through dualistic tensions between nothing and something, emptiness and substance, subject and object, or man and nature. The bodily experience of butoh is fluid and cyclic. It is more about identity in the making than finished arrival.

Butoh morphology dances not through dualistic tension but rather in muddy forms and flowing exchanges throughout a whole gestalt. Hijikata writes in "Kaze Daruma" about his childhood experiences of chill and sinking into the muddy landscape of Tohoku that infused his limbic memory and the stricken contours of his dance.[15] Butoh has diversified since its beginnings with Hijikata. Now it morphs from mud to light in the metaphysical aesthetic of the popular dance company Sankai Juku, where we see form coming into being—timelessly, meditatively—as in Buddhist thought. Their morphology is about emergence and part of the power of their butoh. "There is nothing so beautiful as form on the verge. This would be the beauty of emergence," says architect Raymond Moriyama.[16] This would also define the beauty of Sankai Juku. But as we will see, there is no singular method in the morphology of butoh.

Its morphing bodies gather up nature and culture at once, and its means are both Eastern and Western, with a foot in both worlds. Some butoh sings like grand opera, vibrating the body, as in Furukawa Anzu's *Crocodile Time*. Some whispers into disappearance, like the ghosts that inhabit *Noh* theater and Nakajima's butoh *Noh* dance *Sumida River*. In her performance of this work, Japanese Canadian Denise Fujiwara draws golden movement from leaden dream and a mother's vigil, slogging up from the mud, vibrating in bamboo, as we explore further in part 2.

Hokotai

Ascendant progress in the West depends on dialectical structure in which elements rub against each other or oppose each other. Dualism constitutes the genius of the West, as we gather in Richard Tarnas's book *The Passion of the Western Mind*.[17] But in butoh, as in the core doctrines of the East, especially Tao (origin), human energies exchange shapes within an unlimited whole in which beginnings and endings loop together. This is why butoh dancers often seem to float—but not like ballet dancers who defy gravity or hover above it. *Butoh-ka* sink and float at once. The basic butoh walk, *hokotai,* gives in the knees and lets the weight of the torso drop down, as I have experienced in classes with Ashikawa Yoko, Nakajima Natsu, and Yoshioka Yumiko. The body grounds so the head can float or hang, and the entire body seems light—as the deep roots of a tree allow sway in the limbs. The small steps skirt the ground slowly and continuously without inflection. The feet don't lift from the floor but slide along, remaining flat and in light contact, skimming eternally along. Because of its smooth continuity and floating lightness, *hokotai* creates a sense of timelessness: "How can you find eternity in the present," this walk seems to ask?

The Relational Body

Concerning intention in butoh: The butoh body is relational and not representational. It doesn't exist to display the self or show technical feats, and it is not about narrative. Its experiential somaticity, defined in bodily sensibility and capacity, is widely cast to incorporate material objects, images, and poetic collages. I hold that metamorphosis is at the heart of butoh and, therefore, that its aesthetic potency comes from the dancer's ability to embody otherness and to transform. This requires an elastic body-mind willing to risk and learn. Butoh can be understood in terms of the dancer's capability for conscious change and empathic embodiment. Such empathy is relational and somatic—belonging to the life of human feeling and therefore to the body as experienced by the self in relation to others and the environment. This is not so much the personal body as Self writ large. The butoh dancer expands the self to include others and to find otherness in herself; she universalizes in this sense.

The relational body, logically speaking and in terms of dance, is one that "feels with" others, an empathetic body so to speak. What does Ohno Kazuo mean, for instance, when he says "I carry all the dead with me"? I believe he is telling us something about how he senses his relational body when he dances. Ohno's empathic connection to the dead is probably not the only aspect of his consciousness, nor is it omnipresent, but it is a clear statement of one of the ways he experiences his body in dance and finds the other in himself. We note that his way of dancing his signature work, *La Argentina,* is through a profound somatic resonance with her, as we take up in the second essay of part 2. We also witness something of Hijikata's empathic embodiment of leprosy in the first essay.

Concerning the dancer's relation to the audience, and vice versa: The whole history of Western aesthetics is bound up in explanations of empathy, particularly in aesthetic attention as empathetic. But I am speaking of something else. I hold that we recognize dancers as empathic when we feel that they recognize and embody our values or motivations in their movement. It is not so much that we as audiences understand them, but rather that their movement itself proffers the immediacy of our own experience, and we identify.

Empathy by definition is simply to identify or feel in tune with someone else, to feel what they feel, though maybe not in the very same way. I like to speak of empathy as "somatic resonance," using the language of the body as experienced. In butoh this phenomenon takes a turn toward the East and is not a matter for control. It is not attained through any act of will but is cultivated through loss of self, spurring communal connectivity. Ask many a dancer what they are doing when they dance, and the common reply will be "expressing myself." Most *butoh-ka* won't say this; their intentions point in other directions. Their project is not self-expression; self-erasure would come closer. They invite moments of transformation, a unique alchemical possibility that I have been explaining in various ways.

Next we explore some of the transformative means of butoh through shifting the pain body, shedding, squatting, whitening, costuming, spiritual passage, ash, and "the body that becomes." We have already described the relational body as a performative stance and *hokotai* in terms of its nondualist timeless nature. These are some of the morphological methods of butoh. They don't exhaust all of the possibilities, but they do provide a glimpse.

Shifting the Pain Body

In its somatic alchemy, butoh is no stranger to pain, but this doesn't mean that the dancer is asked to endure pain. Rather, the morphology of butoh allows the dancer to transform at any moment, even in the midst of given choreography. There is always a somatic solution toward which the dancer with a listening body can move. Not insisting on one way, options arrive in consciousness. Culturally fixed forms, as in many codified dance practices, are not always so fluid. Dancing about pain and being in pain are two different things. One of my students wrote about her experience of pain in dance this way:

> Many times I found myself dancing in pain, with neither the courage nor permission to ask my teacher to sit out. It seemed OK to nurse injuries, limp along—dance beautifully onstage, and then struggle to walk for the following days. The effect on the psyche in practicing these "deconstructive" habits is quite powerful, and I have observed many dancers in similar positions who begin to believe (wholly in mind and body) that pain is a part of dancing.[18]

Pain is mixed with the deadly ingredient of denial in much dance today; butoh takes another approach. In morphing through somatic states of feeling, butoh reflects pain and expresses its changing contours. Audiences for butoh can empathize with the body in pain and with its shifting registers. Resonating with the body in its changing states, audiences can be moved in the direction of healing where the suffering body is not denied. In butoh there is no pedestal or point shoe, even as there are difficult and sometimes painful moments. Some butoh courts excess—as that of Hijikata quite often did—but butoh today as well as butoh-influenced work have other options. From the time of its beginning in Hijikata, the butoh body is encouraged toward change through incorporation of human otherness as well as of natural and objective otherness. The self is not for itself alone; it morphs through otherness and experiences interspaces through *ma,* so it can renew. Pain is not a necessary ingredient, but when it appears it is not denied, and neither is disease, as we see through Hijikata's example in *The Story of Smallpox* and *Leprosy.*

Shedding

We have seen that butoh has gathered liberally from many world sources and continues to do so. Because of this, the imagination cultivated in butoh is somewhat nomadic, if not panhuman. It sheds social specificity along the way, plowing beneath blank expressionless veneers of social constructions and abstract elements of dance. In university dance classes—both East and West—improvisations are commonly based on expressing "basic elements of dance." I have personally experienced many such classes in my studies of modern dance over the years. Form, space, and goal-oriented improvisations explore lines, circles, or level change. Time is another matter. It will split into mathematical rhythmic units in these studies and be conceived in gradations of slow to fast. Time and timelessness, however, will be left out. Form and emptiness as well. These seemingly mystical matters are too slippery.

Rudolph Laban's theories with their genesis in German Expressionism provide an exception because they do delve into timelessness, emptiness, and silence. Butoh dancers also explore these metaphysical elements, but they find the psychological shapes of these in a way that Laban's work does not. The way toward metaphysics in butoh is imagistic, often meditative, and sometimes wild. What you let go of is more important than what you put on. We have briefly explained Hijikata's technique of "killing the body," letting go material bonds. We see, however, that materiality can also be called back. The dances of butoh often begin with objective/material nature—with Ohno the fetus in its mother, and with Hijikata the material collages of his *butoh-fu*. The material associations of butoh dancers are just a springboard; subjective life in its incompleteness is their performative metaphysic, as we see further in part 2. Ohno, always poetic on these points, says he discovered butoh in his mother's womb.

In *Mr. O's Book of the Dead,* a film he undertook during a ten-year reclusive period after his first work with Hijikata, Ohno creates a wild metaphysical happening in the countryside where scenes change without closure. This film was first screened in 1976 and inspired by *The Tibetan Book of the Dead* with its progressive gates of passage after death. It strikes me as an afterlife parade, treading, nevertheless, the hilly ground of this life. There are beautiful scenes in this dance as well as surreal ones, including episodes in pigpens with Ohno sucking a mother pig's teat, morphing fearlessly into the real. It is a messy parade to be sure. And perhaps it allowed Ohno to shed part of his war trauma. Ohno Yoshito says his father didn't like to talk about the war, he just wanted to dance, and that dancing itself was a way for him to come to terms with his nine years as a soldier.

It would be difficult to cull abstract lines of space and time from Ohno's *Book of the Dead,* and why would one want to? Encouraging imagistic processes, Ohno Kazuo and Ohno Yoshito, Hijikata Tatsumi, Kasai Akira, Waguri Yukio, Murobushi Ko, and female butoh artists at the root of butoh, Motofuji Akiko, Ashikawa Yoko, and Nakajima Natsu, provoke a transformative body consciousness, shedding the logic of lines, shapes, and directions in space. *Butoh-ka* are interested more in the honesty of the body that sheds its social skin and in the highly individual ways this can happen. As they reach toward origins, maybe they will not succeed, but at least they give themselves a chance to experience something outside of their social habits and the abstract movements of modern/postmodern dance and ballet. Floating in the oceanic mother, *butoh-ka* shed the social body (and its dance practices) as they regress to what Hijikata called "a frog's-eye view." Ohno stated the importance of this for butoh: "As long as the body maintains an existence marked by social experience, it cannot express the soul with purity."[19]

Shedding (the social skin) is accomplished in various ways. It is certainly an ingredient of floating. Kasai Akira teaches what he calls "floating power," the very real sensation of going up or down with light intent. And conversely, you can counter such antigravity intentions with heaviness, suddenly "cutting the floating power." You have a choice, in other words. A sense of emptiness can also engender floating, as I experienced with Kasai.[20] In floating, you shed the mundane social world, removing its gravitational pull and obligations, and you also shed your personal body in this respect. You can let go of a lot in floating, especially in butoh improvisations and meditations. Kasai teaches the importance of shedding the social body in order to create a larger body that he calls "the community body," as we noted in the beginning of this chapter. The social body connotes the body of cultural manners and customs—social habits, obligations, and expectations. Community indicates sharing and purposes that go beyond self-interest, as Kasai teaches.

Shaking is another way of shedding the social. Mikami Kayo, one of Hijikata's students, provides a good example of this in *Kenka* (Consecration of Flowers, 1992). Her way of shedding is through shamanistic shaking. She sheds (gets rid of) her social self and moves like a shaman through entire sections in which her body seems thrown, seemingly beyond her predictable control, shaking in quivers, large and small, and inner trembling. Toward the end, she builds a shell of reeds and peeks out from underneath, still shedding.

Squatting

Squatting is another way of shedding and a typical butoh posture, one seldom found in Western dance forms, except as a passage through low-to-the-floor movements and in some folk forms. Russian folk dances use squatting and have well-developed techniques for it, including leg thrusts from this position, as well as leaps and jumps. Ballet dancers use the floor, grounding the feet for movements into the air, and they practice deep pliés toward this goal. It would be difficult to call these squatting, however. Butoh uses the squat creatively, imagistically, and unpredictably, so it is often emphasized in workshops, improvisations, and performances. As in hatha yoga, the squat in butoh finally becomes an act of nondoing, action without acting, a paradoxical movement of effortless ease. In Japan, you will find people able to squat well into old age. I see such limberness often in public baths (*onsen*) with women, and I try to stay young in practicing the squat, in butoh and in bathing.

Yoshioka Yumiko sometimes teaches entire butoh workshops with people in squatting sequences, coming up for air only to descend again for long periods. Western students have a difficult time with this at first but get better with practice. At age seventy, I am still able to squat because of my long acquaintance with yoga and twenty years of butoh practice. The squat requires deep flexion in the hip joints. You find that when you can lengthen the back in squatting, rather than leaning forward and doubling up, you build strength and lightness throughout the body. Squatting and sprawling ease are not refined motions; thus they are more taboo in contained and sophisticated society. Social constructions of the body in the West outlaw squatting in public. Sitting on chairs replaces squatting (or sitting on the floor, as in Japan). Of course, you can do any movements you want in private, but those who expect dance to be upright and graceful are shocked by what they see in butoh's close rapport with the ground. To many, public displays of squatting, even in theater performances, are repulsive and ugly. Children and monkeys do squat with ease, however, but most people lose this ability as they grow up in societies that never crouch.

Proponents of butoh don't want to lose the natural, animal, and childlike squat. Whether Western or Eastern, the human body can squat close to the ground, the back of the thighs resting on the calves, and from this position can dynamically fall or rise. There is nothing wrong with squatting, as I experience it:

> When sitting on my heels, I shed all thought of anything else. I become unified within myself for the time I can remain there—like a crouching animal or child, or maybe even a stubborn adult. I can't squander my thoughts on meaningless worries in the squat. It requires my whole attention, relieves me of cultural confinement, and frees my tailbone. In squatting I shed my cultural body and participate with all humans who can bend their knees and hips, hunker down, and refuse to move (as stubborn "squatters" do). This is a serious position, I find, not merely innocent, but I can always morph its character and move out of it. To squat, I need to let go of so much, breathe easily in my core, and make friends with the ground.
>
> When I explore movement freely from this position, I find that there are many ways to move through it; that there is not just one squat but many: with the heels down or lifted, turning, looking up, down, or around, and using my spine in all of its morphic abilities. Supporting myself on my hands, and then on my feet, I teach my shoulder how to love my knee in a froglike way. I can also perform an elegant motion out of squatting, striding one foot forward while remaining low and rocking my back knee to touch the floor. In this position, I am sitting on my heel in the back leg with my toes connected to the earth and in a low stride on the forward leg with my back easily upright. Meanwhile (I discover) that if I bow my head, I am kneeling on one knee, and I have morphed from frogness to knighthood, waiting for a tap on the shoulder.
>
> Squatting is a possible movement, neither beautiful nor ugly except we make it so.

The White Opus

Butoh-ka cultivate movements like squatting and somatic affects (expressions, shapes, moods, or qualities of feeling)such as shaking and extremely slow motion that are atypical in dance and often seen as odd and nonconformist in society. Women have found butoh workshops edifying in this regard, throwing off the movement restrictions that are placed on "femininity." But in its full practice, the butoh genre is not simply about allowing movements that are marginalized or taboo according to gender or social customs. Movements and their affects always appear in context in butoh as they would in any dance form. Contextually, butoh tends to dissolve movements and morph them one into another, rather than tell stories. It blurs held postures. Its stillness moves. Becoming a rock carries one into such moving stillness.

The butoh body is an incomplete opus; its power is not equally distributed, solidified, or funneled through democratic designs but is more anarchic, only gradually working toward structure. It is not that the study of butoh teaches disrespect for law, but it does not promote an authoritarian and orderly understanding of the body. Butoh sees beauty in weakness and disorder, looking into neglected corners. "We cannot turn away from the messy refuse of life," Ohno says in his workshops, echoing the deeper meaning of democracy, the charge of taking care of everyone and respecting differences. He does not speak about majority rule or social equality. What would true social equality really mean? We have forgotten if we ever really knew. People are not socially equal, but they can within their differences build community with fairness. Butoh does this through cultivation of marginalized movement, through its identification with nature, and through paradox, allowing differences to exist and to morph. Butoh builds upon community and grieves war, as does Ohno, finally dancing in a chair well into his nineties surrounded by his international students. Many carry his communal message of peace and understanding, not through talk but in their bodies.

Butoh-ka are typically powdered white, erasing personal features. This has a tendency to mask or universalize the body, erasing the willful-self and releasing the East's potential of no-self. The white, ashen bodies of butoh can float, descend, and settle lightly, having survived purgatorial fires as in the albedo stage of alchemy, the white opus. Some have said that butoh arises from the ashes of Hiroshima and Nagasaki, but this singular explanation does not suffice. It represents the limping imperfection in all of us, when we are able to embrace the darkness and let go. This seemingly odd dance form has therapeutic potentials as those of us who use dance for healing purposes are finding out. There are no good guys and bad guys in butoh, just the pinprick of an almost extinguished thought lighting up, flickering in a grimace, a strange laugh, or a painful limp. Like the albedo stage of alchemy, its light is indirect. The albedo is incident light, especially the fraction of sunlight reflected by the earth.

Butoh is not simply dark. How could it be if it is metamorphic? The light in butoh can be astounding. The butoh company Sankai Juku has been criticized for its beauty and polish, but I notice that it develops the albedo, the white opus, and that its power and beauty come from this. If Sankai Juku is popular, it is not simply through tricks. Butoh has liberally employed trickster mentality through nativism, popular in 1970s Japan. There is no butoh so full of light as that of Sankai Juku, and no dance company has been able to span the worlds of popular appeal and esoteric art as they have. Some great butoh artists have also come from this line, such as Toru Iwashita and Itto Morita. Significantly, both of these performers have also turned their butoh toward therapeutic means. They have escaped the cult designations that often plague butoh by taking their workshops into general communities and working with the mentally and physically disabled.

The Body That Becomes

Butoh morphs through gray tones and sharp edges; it has widely varying aesthetics and pan-cultural implications. At the New York Butoh Festival of 2007, speaker Ishii Tatsuro witnessed how Hijikata retained the spirit of the Japanese people while going beyond the boundaries of ethnicity in a shamanistic way,[21] but no one could anticipate the wide-reaching international results of his leap into darkness. Hijikata's *Ankoku-Butoh,* the Dance of Utter Darkness, is existentially human in its feeling for mud and ash, for wind and the transformative powers of nature. His onomatopoeia, or word paintings, conjured a body that moves against its will, stands up in spite of its folded legs, and walks toward death. This he called in existential terms, "the body that becomes," suggesting that the body we live is not an objective body that we can control but is more anarchic, the ongoing experience of being that lies beneath the surface of the will, living and dying at once. Butoh, he says, is "the weakened body" living in your own body. Just what would it mean to dance from this place? I wonder sometimes about this homunculus. I know at least that dancing from my weak body is not about overcoming the flesh as a means toward mastery. The magic in butoh metamorphosis is in how it does go under, rising from surrender and reflected light.

The dance of Denise Fujiwara represents just one example of surrender in the morphic body. She has created several site-specific solo dances, reflecting the butoh aesthetic of "the body that becomes" and in the real time that environmental work explores: the time it takes to carry a heavy rock from one place to another, as in her outdoor work *Unearthed,* for instance. Or in *Wellspring,* the time it takes to float a body in tranquility and toward danger. *Wellspring* is performed at the National Gallery of Canada in an intimate room with a large pool of still water formed into channels. Fujiwara performs it in a slate blue-green gown the same color as the water, moving smoothly and without inflection against the classical sounds of violist Valerie Kuinka. In contrast to *Unearthed,* this dance is not presented in wildness.

The whole performance of *Wellspring* progresses with the relaxed mind of meditation and dissolution of the separate self. As water trickles and drips in the dewy hall of the dance, Fujiwara walks in shallows along the channels, finally descending to float in the depths with her gown billowing round. A sequel moves outdoors as she inches her way down large rocks at the edge of a Newfoundland pond and rolls into the water. Letting herself slowly down, she floats. The video presentation ends with scenes of a waterfall, as we see the dancer and the dance drift in tranquility toward the pounding. Does she go under? I don't know. I see her drift, and I sense the potential of her crossing over. Most of all, I appreciate her surrender to an unknown outcome—the body that becomes its own unknown future—and trust.

Costume and Metamorphosis

Fujiwara wears a tattered dress in *Unearthed* and a long, flowing gown in *Wellspring*. These aid her relationship to rock and water. Nudity in butoh is also an aspect of costume and another form of shedding the social body. Costumes are incredibly important in any form of theater, even when they are selected from understated street wear. Butoh choreographers seem to understand this. They take pleasure in serendipity, surreal juxtaposition, exaggeration, and concentrated design. When the body appears nude in butoh, it is usually partially covered, often smeared with mud or whitened. Nudity is stylized in butoh, and costumes are metamorphic. They change along with the dance; often they assume fantasy shapes and collage appearance.

On the other side of nudity is the love of fabric: wrapping, draping, and folding to extend the lines of the body, to complement or hide them. Postmodern dance in America beginning in the 1960s introduced street clothes to the stage. The soft-pant, T-shirt look dominated dance in the United States for decades and is still a ready solution for a costume, seemingly neutral but with a signature of its own. Butoh, which is also a postmodern form, took historical eclecticism seriously in its costuming, echoing postmodern architecture in its fusion of styles from diverse historical periods. Clearly fashioned for the eye and soul, costuming in butoh is not left to chance or casual wear. Butoh dancers understand that no clothing or costume is neutral, much less natural. This also goes for blue jeans, the national dress of Western youth, now internationally adopted for all ages. One of my somatics students who just finished a master of fine arts degree in art at the University of Chicago advised me on the art of my own dress. "Wear an expensive pair of jeans, great shoes, and anything on top." This is the hip way to dress now, she told me. I picked out my best jeans and shoes and the rattiest thing I could find in my closet for the top. She said it really worked!

Marie-Gabrielle Rotie's contemporary dance often draws attention to costume. Her costumes are strongly influenced by the serendipity of butoh and its reach into the imagination. Recently, she choreographed seven vignettes for the enormous grandeur of the Raphael room at the Victoria and Albert Museum in collaboration with the London College of Fashion. Her work featured exquisite and fantastic costumes brought to life by advanced designers at the college and a team of nine dancers, with sound by Nick Parkin and lighting by Mischa Twitchin. Costumes created and conceived around diverse narratives were the starting point for the meeting of choreography and fabric. "Costume," Rotie says, "is the performer's universe. Fabric becomes another skin through which the performer can incarnate and transform."[22] We take up Rotie's work in the ninth essay of part 2.

In figures 5 and 6, we see two examples of the imaginative costuming of butoh. Figure 5 shows Rotie caught in a fantasy costume that Alwin Nikolais might appreciate, and in Figure 6 we see Kawamoto Yuko of Tokyo in *Shinonome Butoh*, inscrutable in her dress of ribbon and wire. Poised on the cusp of uncertainty, she might morph anywhere.

Historical Residue, Spiritual Passage

Butoh carries historical residue and metamorphic potency. Thus do *butoh-ka* perform through spiritual passages and in the cultural gaps, as they become vessels of transformation. Of course, performances are often unfulfilled, but that doesn't change the substance of butoh or its intention. If butoh is a healing form of dance, it varies only in kind from the healing essence of all dances undertaken in light of the spirituality of the body. The way butoh varies is most unique. We have already said that it does not separate body and spirit. There is a particular touchstone in butoh that reinforces this understanding. The concept is Eastern, but it has an interesting Western correlate.

I speak of the third eye, originally an energy center in the practice of yoga and now a wide metaphor for concentrated awareness and intuitive knowledge. Before my study of butoh, I had experienced the third eye through my study of yoga. Later through my travels in India—where the third eye is marked with a bindi on the forehead—I found it held a variety of meanings. This center of spiritual energy and strength between the eyebrows is the sixth chakra (or energy vortex) of yoga and considered the seat of concealed wisdom. Western views of chakras locate the third eye in the pineal gland, deep in the center of the brain. René Descartes believed it the dwelling place of the soul and tried to prove it scientifically. We know that it is an auspicious center for the production of melatonin, a central regulator of neural immune functions and patterns of rest and activity in harmony with the cycles of the sun and moon. In India, it is sometimes called the "blue pearl of bliss." As a visionary point of concentration and awareness, this mysterious eye can be prepared but not controlled. Unbidden, its spontaneous gifts appear to consciousness. The pineal cone is sensitive to vibration and associated with balance and hearing. Developmental movement studies hold that the pineal supports the spinal push from the head and is "both the birthing gland and place of exit into death," and there is further evidence that it translates bodily phenomena into dream imagery and visions.[23] Not surprisingly, the pineal is active in preventing premature aging. As the third eye (the sixth charka), it can be cultivated through yoga and meditation as well as in butoh and other forms of meditative dance.

In butoh, I have experienced many explorations that cultivate the third eye by design, especially through the workshops of Nakajima Natsu (who quotes Hijikata's use of the third eye) and in those of Ohno. I don't remember Ohno's mention of third-eye awareness as such, but I was conscious of it nevertheless,

FIGURE 5. Marie-Gabrielle Rotie in costume and butoh-influenced choreography for the London College of Fashion Show. Photograph by Sarah Ainslie, © 2007. Used by permission of Sarah Ainslie.

FIGURE 6. Kawamoto Yuko in *Shinonome Butoh,*
photographed by Naritada Takahashi, © 2004. Used by
permission of Yuko Kawamoto and Naritada Takahashi.

especially when he prompted us to dance as embryos in his class, and I also vi-
sualized the embryo growing inside me.

In the workshops of Ohno's son, Yoshito, students experience focused concentration while letting go of the effort to control, which encourages third-eye awareness. In his October 2007 workshop in New York, Ohno Yoshito presented his
butoh method by first showing ukiyo-e woodblock prints of the sea and Mount
Fuji, then discussing how to see through the eye of a bird, the eye of a fish, and
the eye of an insect. He often introduces themes of nature through ukiyo-e and
elicits nonlinear perception, relaxing the mind. Sometimes he distributes flowers
and discusses different ways of seeing them, accompanied by music imagined
in different kinds of light: morning, noonday, and evening. He dances himself
by walking with flowers, his body bathed in melodic music. In New York, his

teaching incorporated a theme of single-pointed consciousness. He distributed pieces of paper to a number of people and had them draw a single point on the paper as they stepped, walking and drawing at the same time, promoting single-pointed awareness and loss of ego.

"You are the point," he says, "you become very small—the perfect point." Then focusing on a global issue, he speaks of the changing center of the cultural world being in Paris for so many years and at some point moving to New York. "One point," he says again, then shifts, morphing back to visual images by showing calligraphy of kanji words: "snow, moon, flower."[24]

The third eye relates to spirituality and the soul for butoh dancers and those influenced by this movement. But if you asked butoh dancers about these connections, their answers would differ, because the words are understood in various ways. If we look beyond words and into the dances of butoh, we might simply say that butoh thrives on visionary imagery and that the soul, indefinable and uncontainable, characterizes the whole genre. Butoh is sometimes called "dance of the dark soul," because of Hijikata's identification with "the unconscious body." Many forms of dance develop complex attributes that have been attributed to the soul. Butoh is certainly one of these. How does one cultivate the soul through butoh, or what makes the attempt unique? The answer is empirical to some degree, because *butoh-ka* cultivate experience at the heart of their work. Not relying on theory, they practice the immediacy of experience. Many *butoh-ka* also have a specific relationship to third-eye nonlinear awareness, depending on their training and disposition.

It is important to acknowledge this bodily resource in butoh, especially in its connection to the ego. We need a healthy ego, or sense of self, as I have learned in Zen, but need not become attached to it or exert it (as willful). The ego can be acknowledged and let go when it seems confining, as Kasai Akira told me in an interview. He regards its appearance and then sends it to "the middle of the universe." In dancing, "we carry our body away from ourselves," he says.[25] Kasai, one of the originators of butoh who still performs internationally, includes meditation in his practices and often teaches release of the ego in a nonlinear manner of "shedding" through the use of paradox and riddles.

We have said that butoh has antecedents in German Expressionism with its extreme expressions. Behind this lurks early Kabuki rough-stuff *aragoto* depicted in a style of ukiyo-e woodblock prints with knobby-kneed dancers, fierce warriors in wide stride, and other bold images. We saw that ukiyo-e became fashionable with European and American artists after Japan opened its doors to foreigners in 1868. We explored how Japonisme took hold in the West, continuing into the early twentieth century and the growth of Expressionism. Butoh combines disparate bodily substance and historical residue—ranging from the mystical impulse and aesthetic flair of the East to the theatrical innovation and intellectual passion of the West. If butoh morphology is dark, the butoh body seldom seems heavy. It can float, but not like ballet, rather more like wood sinking lightly in water. Butoh morphology inculcates patience, magnifying small things through slow walking shifts with toes inching along, collage faces in transit, the blossoming and fading of these, and pictorial transformations of entire figures through the movement of an elbow or finger, the tilt of a chin or twist of a mouth. Time edges along in the beautifully slow emergence of a gesture, and as soon as one has arrived, another is beginning; then suddenly, as in nature, changes roll like thunder, and we find deep connectivity beneath the detailed collage.

Ash

It is no accident that butoh bodies are often powdered white. In the transmutations of alchemy we learn that:

> Ash can no longer be set on fire, and is, psychologically speaking, free from the turmoil of the passions. It is a synonym for the white stage of the opus, the albedo, when the dead, blackened body of bodies of united sulfur and argent vive have been whitened and purified by the refining fire.[26]

Ash erupts surprisingly in butoh and in odd ways, as dancers eat the air and blink their eyes like strobe lights or flail and stab the air as Furukawa Anzu does in her work on Francisco Goya's dark baroque paintings *La Quinto Del Sordo.* Furukawa travels back to Goya's blotchy huddled figures and reaches into the future, shaking off war, climbing, hanging, and burning in the aftermath, as we take up in part 2. Audiences can capture a spark of such esoteric fire in the ashen bodies of butoh. Earlier we spoke of the development of the albedo through Sankai Juku, and we reconnect this here to remember that ash and whitening in butoh represent a metamorphic process, not commensurate with classical ballet's upward ascent in its attempt to purify the body of earth and flesh. If butoh has the potential to purify, it is nevertheless not a pure dance. It represents a messy beauty, and its outcome is uncertain. Exponents of butoh tread the ground of aesthetic histories—East and West—forging a global art that resists globalization as utopia.

Hijikata's *butoh-fu* (notation) for "Ash Pillar" captures an important aspect of the alchemy of butoh. When performing "Ash Pillar," the dancer struggles for uprightness but can barely walk, having become a pillar of ash with an uncertain future. When I asked Waguri Yukio, the foremost authority on Hijikata's *butoh-fu,* to perform "Ash Pillar," he said he couldn't, "it is too difficult." So I began to show him my interpretation to bring out the performer in him, but he said no and told me not to move, but remain frozen. That was his memory of the essence of "Ash Pillar." "It is something like Hiroshima," he said. Then he showed me how "a wind like a knife" could come and cut the porous frozen pillar, causing it to fall in a sudden flash. I could feel it in my body.

Dancers around the world are now affecting a global alchemy and spiritual passage through butoh as they mobilize basic human material and gather liberally from history. Beginning often with the dark psyche, they set on edge a drama of the senses, through images of electric shock and stinking fish, for instance, and from panhuman phenomena such as desperation, clutching, itching, hiding, falling, reaching, recoiling, and moaning. Silence and listening guide them.

It is, however, the ineffable state in-between such happenings that moves them to a new condition. The state in-between states in Japanese (and in Zen) is called *ma*. Morphing through *ma, butoh-ka* pay attention to reflexive moments of self-remembering and spiritual awakening. *Ma* is more than a spatial concept; it is also a contemplative, expansive state of mind. Light as ash, the mind that has been freed from thought can dwell in-between, not being drawn into the object and not getting tangled in its own subjectivity. In this dispassionate place of nonattachment, the mind is free to see things as they are in the moment, free from the need to judge the beautiful and the ugly—like the impermanent Zen mind of Chokei (died AD 932): "Long I hovered in the Middle Way. Today the very ice shoots flame."[27]

• • •

In this chapter, we have concentrated on the transformative morphology of butoh. In the next one, we will see what kind of philosophy of the body emerges from this. The link between these two chapters rests on an understanding and feeling for the weakened body that Hijikata placed at the foundation of butoh. To study the body in butoh is to study the shifting structures and transformative habits of matter through dance—where in confusion and moments of weakness, we encounter our foreign body and experience again our original, spiritual body. I speak of "our body" because the body we encounter as spirit may not be so original as uniquely mine or yours. Butoh is about what humans have in common at the root, not about individual expression per se; the illusive matter of existence that underlies all experience is its true aim. Metaphysical yet unfinished, dark as night, and light as ash, butoh is still in the sway of becoming.

Chapter Three

Is Butoh a Philosophy?

Quantum mechanics describes a reality in which things sometimes hover in a haze of being partly one way and partly another. Things become definite only when a suitable observation forces them to relinquish quantum possibility and settle on a specific outcome.

—Brian Greene, *The Fabric of the Cosmos*

Hijikata Tatsumi said butoh was not a philosophy but that "someday it might be."[1] The previous chapter has already pursued some philosophical questions concerning morphology, how the body is conceived and presented in butoh, especially its nondualistic basis. We also considered the bodily lived ambiguity of butoh, its unfinished and vulnerable aspects. Here we ask whether butoh is a philosophy or if one can be discovered in it? To answer this, we need to continue to develop themes from the previous chapter, but in a philosophical context.

Dance Philosophies and Butoh

I believe there are philosophies implicit in dance forms if we take the time to study and uncover them. Once we understand what principles underlie a dance form, we can further analyze and develop these, and we can also relate these to the historical time frame of their unique development. For instance, classical ballet represents the balance and proportion of the golden mean of classical architecture, originating in ancient Greece and Rome. Ballet began in the Renaissance revival of Greek and Roman themes amid grandiose celebrations meant to consolidate the wealth and power of the ruling elite.[2] It continued to develop within the aristocratic courts and theaters of Europe for several hundred years, eventually evolving a codified classical technique, its well-defined practices spreading out internationally. The balanced proportions of classical architecture characterize the geometric mathematics of ballet technique, even as ballet choreographers can and do suspend the classical technique for specific purposes. It would be difficult to say that ballet represents classical philosophy, but it is easy to see that it does exhibit a classical context. Ballet has a formal enduring basis as opposed to a relativist and changing essence.

In stark contrast, the historic modern dance in America and Europe (including German Expressionism) represents an existentialist philosophy and approach to life that has individualism at its core. In this view, there is no objective enduring guide, certainly not ideals of balance and proportion. Individual expression, a radical creativity as poured through aesthetic visions, guided the discoveries of modern dance and eventually modernized ballet as well. Butoh lies outside the modernist enterprise, however, developing first as a protest against modernity, as we have explored.

If classical ballet exhibits a classical context and modern dance an existential one, how does butoh diverge from these? I hold that butoh can be explained through metamorphosis, that it has a metamorphic context proffering a unique understanding of the dancing body and that it promotes community and healing over the importance of the individual. Butoh shares an existentialist link with modern dance, however, because both rest on an understanding of the body that questions linear rationality and absolute knowledge. Not knowing is the compassionate quantum space in consciousness of the existentialist vision and the weak body images of Hijikata. This ethos compels the community-centered workshops of Harada Nobuo: waiting, not knowing how to move at the beginning, as I experienced in teaching a workshop with him in Fukuoka, Japan, in 2005. Trust of intuition and whole-body consciousness in modern/postmodern dance also presupposes a specific kind of lack. This is indeed the starting place for experiment, exploration, and discovery in all art. Creativity through individual discovery rather than established codified techniques has been central to the context of modern/postmodern dance. Throughout the twentieth century, dance developed with increasing respect for postulates of Freudian subconscious life and, later, the collective unconscious explained by Carl Jung. Martha Graham explored these extensively, as did many other choreographers. The psychological relativity of "not knowing" allowed quantum leaps toward new dance forms. The quantum lack that butoh displays is unique. Hijikata put the perspective of butoh well in a letter written in 1984 to his student Nakajima Natsu two years before his death, presenting his picture of the "hidden subconscious" and its tie to "the collective unconscious body" that he calls "our body." This letter has a Buddhist ring toward the end:

> We shake hands with the dead, who send us encouragement from beyond our body, this is the unlimited power of Butoh. In our body history, something is hiding in our subconscious, collected in our unconscious body, which will appear in

each detail of our expression. Here we can rediscover time with an elasticity sent by the dead. We can find Butoh, in the same way we can touch our hidden reality, something can be born, and can appear, living and dying in the moment.[3]

Butoh does not present an idealized body, as is often the case in ballet, or the technically normative display that one sees in many dance styles, including contemporary postmodern dance in which contact-partnering techniques are well developed and the look of released, relaxed, but difficult movement is prevalent. The struggle to be original is constant in modern and postmodern forms, as the very terms suggest, but genuine originality is hard to come by. Butoh asks less of originality, thus more of community and transformative potentials.

The morphology of butoh reflects an alternative to the Western social constructivist view of the body as a rational social actor. Western sociologists offer their social constructivist theories as universal, but in actuality they advance just one ethnocentric view.[4] As in all forms of dance, there is a concept of the body in butoh, and it is often stated in a poetically surreal way. The butoh body is one that "has not been robbed," as we have noted. This means that one acknowledges a native body living beneath the skin of society; such a body sheds the clothes of convention and social construction, as we explained through "shedding" in the previous chapter. Such a body squats and displaces the ego-bearing expansive chest. In squatting, the chest and whole torso must soften and descend, or the squat won't happen. This represents one aspect of how the body is lived in butoh, as we explored in chapter 2. We have also seen that imagery and intuition enter, sometimes elements of meditation as well, and that butoh plays upon small details of facial expression and slow, subtle movement. All of these become part of the way in which the body is lived in butoh.

The Original Body in Japanese Phenomenology

> *Tsuchi kara umareta* (I come from the mud).
> —Hijikata Tatsumi

Ichikawa Hiroshi and Yuasa Yasuo are Japanese philosophers who deal directly with the phenomenological concept of "lived body" from a Japanese point of view. These philosophers are not explaining butoh, of course, but their work gives us a way to uncover concepts of the body in butoh. Yuasa's valuable book *The Body: Toward an Eastern Mind-Body Theory,* originally published in 1977, was translated into English in 1987. This book gives us a rare phenomenology of the body from an Eastern perspective. I also published *Dance and the Lived Body* in 1987. In this book on phenomenology and dance, I explain the classical context of ballet that I have only just mentioned here, and I also posit the existential context of modern dance.

Ichikawa's prominent works *Seishin toshite no Shintai* (The Body as Spirit, 1991) and *Mi no Kozo: Shintairon wo Koete* (Structure of the Body: Overcoming the Theory of the Body, 1993) have not yet been translated into English, but his theories have been introduced to English readers in Nagatomo Shigenori's *Attunement through the Body* (1992). Ichikawa's main thesis—the body as spirit—refutes Western dualism. He employs the philosophical phenomenology of European philosophers Edmund Husserl, Jean-Paul Sartre, and Maurice Merleau-Ponty but carries their work further on Eastern grounds. He sees that the body we live can be better explained by the word *spirit* than through biology. This is not the material body we are so attached to in the West.

We can explain and understand butoh through Ichikawa's work. Unlike Western dance, butoh has techniques that project the body away from materiality and toward nothingness. The soma of butoh (its experiential substance) projects one beyond the physical self into a wider identification with spirit and nature. To understand this, we turn again to Hijikata's surrealist language and decode it according to his dance. Hijikata starts with the somaticity of the body, as one can catch in his writing of "Inner Material/Material." He begins fanatically, "You have to pull your stomach up high in order to turn your solar plexus into a terrorist."[5] Dance is his way of disclosing his body, of creating somatic awareness that is difficult to grasp through rational means. He uses dance both to construct and to dissolve materiality. Body is spirit in butoh, but it is not heroic or idealized. Spirit, moreover, has a link to nature, to rivers, birds, mud, sand, and flowers. Even when cathartic and metamorphic, the butoh body draws up the mundane and ineffable: "In boyhood the dark earth of Japan was my teacher in various ways of fainting" Hijikata says, morphing to a weaker somatic register.[6] In his first declaration, he expresses anger as a gut feeling in the solar plexus, pulling his stomach up high. Then he shifts toward his theme of the "weak body, living in your own body." He tries to jolt his audience awake, not with words but with his body, morphing from violence to surrender, fainting, and weakness, looking somatically inward.

Science provides a distance from the body, and medicine objectifies the body for its own purposes. Dance in its highly disciplined abstract forms can also distance us from the body through idealizing it and submitting it to harsh training. Dancing can distance us from the intimate contours of bodily life or bring us intuitively close to the nature bodies we are. The charm of butoh is that it seeks our original body before culture gets to it, an impossible task but one worth trying, as in attempting to unravel the Zen riddle, "What was my original face?" This original body is the spiritual body that Ichikawa explains. His phenomenology gives us a way to understand the body beyond the skin. This would be the body as spirit and origin that Ichikawa and Yuasa explain as the "immaterial body." This is the body beyond rationalization and without boundaries not accounted for in Western philosophy and, indeed, very suspect in materialist cultures that divide body from spirit and nature. The major project of Western phenomenology, as I discovered in writing *Dance and the Lived Body* (1987) and *Dancing Identity* (2004), is to mend the perceived body-mind split in Western philosophical traditions and their influence in bifurcated understandings of the body. The unlimited, immaterial body was not the project of continental phenomenology as it grew primarily in France and Germany. It *is* the project of Japanese phenomenology.

The unlimited, immaterial body is a difficult, mystical idea for the Western mind. What is beyond material is beyond calculation and scientific inspection. Western materialism refers us in fact to the material body: It represents the theory that physical matter is the only reality and that everything, including emotion and reason, can be explained as physical. Spirituality is left to religion and relegated to faith, but not trust. Devotion to material wealth and possessions at the expense of spiritual and intellectual values derives from materialist mentality. Greed grows from there. Hijikata's objection to the West was on the basis of its materialist orientation, as is clear in his dances and his writings. He was not skeptical of democracy as such, but of American-style democracy as it brought capitalist production in its wake.[7]

Ichikawa observes that studying the body "as phenomena" (as it appears) enables one to perceive the individual body on a conscious level, but not the unconscious body that supports it.[8] His phenomenology went behind individual appearance. Jung also studied what he finally called "the collective unconscious" through the symbols of psychology and myth, but not in view of constructing a philosophy of the body per se. In the next section, we look more carefully into his theory. Hijikata staged experiences of the unconscious in his dance, but not as posited by Sigmund Freud and Jung. Hijikata's spoken and written expressions were not grounded in Western psychoanalysis. He was exploring a particular darkness in his *Ankoku Butoh* (Dance of Utter Darkness), gestural utterances in a fluid state of becoming that he sometimes called "ecstasy without obstacles."

Ichikawa's claims that our existence itself unifies spiritual and physical levels of reality; existence is the gift of connectivity through the body. His theory of the body-as-spirit is based on the notion of various levels of unity. *Spirit* and *mind* are simply words, names given to the same reality (as I have also explored).[9] Ichikawa holds that when distinctions between spirit, mind, and body disappear, we become truly human and free. When distinctions disappear in bodily integrations, a high degree of unity manifests. This expresses our freedom, he says in his unique theory, while mental disorders are characterized by a low degree of unity: "When the degree of unity is low and we are controlled by the environment and have less freedom, we feel the body. The ultimate situation is that of a corpse."[10]

Hijikata often explained his butoh in terms of a corpse: "Butoh is a corpse standing desperately upright."[11] This would mean in terms of Ichikawa's theory and Hijikata's focus on death that butoh expresses a low level of unity and accepts the constraints of freedom. It is not unconditionally free and therefore heightens somatic sensations of bodily being as the body recedes or weakens and dies. Absence is made poignant. Hijikata's view of butoh as the weakened body ready to dissolve and go under is consistent with Ichikawa and with Friedrich Nietzsche's existential poetry in *Thus Spoke Zarathustra*.

> What is great in man is that he is a bridge and not an end:
> What can be loved in man is that he is an *overture* and *a going under.*
> I love those who do not know how to live, except by going under,
> for they are those who cross over."[12]

Butoh is not an orderly, unified form of dance, as we have seen. It does not idealize the body as ballet does; rather it brings the dancer into a metamorphic world where uprightness is a struggle and not taken for grated. Legs and arms are to be discovered, and time is experienced not in a straight line but in lived terms. Time is poetized by life and in dance, just as space is part of bodily experience. We can feel cramped or free, for instance, and we can feel painful constrictions; these feelings have spatial qualities. Death is a companion and teacher, as Ohno Kazuo reminds his students: "You owe your life to others," he says in workshops. "You are not the be-all and end-all of life." Clearly the butoh dancer cultivates neither the upward airiness of ballet nor the ballet dancer's control over gravity. In butoh there is no attempt to control, only the body that becomes the image, the strange metamorphic ally. The body can disappear in butoh imagery, but it can also reappear. How do you erase your body and then draw it newly all over again? The attempt is affective, and dancers experience this in various ways. As for me: I let go of my physicality and pain, clearing my mind of its rusty parts. Sometimes I cry.

Djalma Primordial Science, a butoh-influenced company founded in 1998 by Ephia and Jeff Gburek, provides a good example of how the body lives transformations in dance. Djalma is a Javanese word for metamorphosis. The Gbureks say that it signifies transformation toward the human on a metaphysical level, and when applied to chemical processes, it signals fermentation. In their work, they accent receptivity rather than production, receiving energies from ambient and inert environments throughout the United States and Europe—in theaters, galleries, music venues, derelict buildings, and gaping holes in the earth. Ephia as dancer and Jeff as musician describe the improvisatory process of Djalma:

> Through the practice of live improvisation we seek a restoration of the primordial physical body and exploration of its limits, the transmutation of the elements through unstable sound and volatile movement, a precarious position, an awkwardly silent situation. We reject the notion of "performance" in favor of "encounter." Our process involves the materiality of sound as onomatopoeia: wherein sounds evoke states of physical transformation (decay, agitation, coagulation, immersion). The dancer's bones reluctantly wring themselves out leaving a trail of

moisture on the brow, her limbs become delicate tissue paper catching fire, her form evaporates and condenses again. Like the origin of all sound in movement: the dance is not only seen but felt, transmitted directly from the body of the mover into the body of the viewer in this last and first frontier of connective tissue.[13]

Hijikata's weakened body is the starting point for Ephia Gburek's pursuit of the "unsound body," a body she sees as "fragile, unbalanced, imperfect, decrepit, cracked, lunatic, dangerous, risky." Her teachers include butoh originators Ohno Kazuo and Ohno Yoshito as well as Tanaka Min and Kasai Akira. She also pursued the study of ritual dance in Ghana, Java, and Bali. The vulnerable body she conceives penetrates the physicality of emotion, moving past it and into metamorphosis. Her material cousins, she says, are "saw dust, smoke, rusting metal, and sweating stone."

A metamorphic view of dance posits the body as evolutionary and relative. Likewise, Ichikawa develops a concept of bodily potential and relativity in his philosophy. The body he posits is unfinished. He explains it through the Japanese word *mi,* the body as a potential whole. *Mi* is an equivalent of body except that it has several more layers than the word *body. Mi* expresses what phenomenology developed as "lived body dynamic" rather than the material object we generally think of as body in the West. Through *mi,* the personal body connects to the body of others and to the earth's body. *Mi* expands finally to the whole of existence and moves by way of *ki. Ki* is a Japanese (and Chinese) concept that is often translated as "spiritual energy," an organizing field force and dynamic unity that pervades nature and therefore connects the body to nature; whereas in the West, the social constructivist convention conceives the body as a social/cultural actor distinct from nature and in control. Nature, however, keeps reminding us who is in control, sometimes disastrously, and that all of our actions have consequences.

Butoh as it originated through Hijikata and Ohno conceives a body resonating with nature and not above it. The dances of Ohno present a good example. He prepares his performances with spiritual poetry, conjuring rivers, birds, sea, and landscape. His vision of dance is one of flowering growth, recognizing birth and death. Hijikata moves with nature in another sense, excavating the sadness of his childhood. He explains that his invention of butoh comes from his early childhood memories of wind and mud:

In early spring the wind is something special, blowing over the sloppy, wet mud. Sometimes in early spring I would fall down in the mud and my child's body, pitiful to its core, would gently float there. I try to speak but it's like something has already been spoken. I have the feeling there is a knot of wood, somewhere in my lower abdomen stuck there in the mud, that is screaming something. . . . I am distinctly aware that I was born of mud and that my movements now have all been built on that."[14]

Shadow Dancing and Transformation

A philosophy of butoh would need to include psychology. Questions arise about butoh's relationship to a collective unconscious because of Hijikata's affinity to what he called "the unconscious body" and because of the unconscious as represented in Expressionism and surrealism. Western views of the unconscious are highly developed in the analytical psychology of Carl Jung (1875–1961), a Swiss psychiatrist and one of the founding fathers of modern depth psychology. Dance therapies such as Authentic Movement, as first developed in the work of Mary Whitehouse, grow from Jung's work. (Whitehouse originally called her work "Movement in Depth," as Joan Englander, a close associate of Whitehouse, told me.) The collective unconscious, Jung's most quoted concept, profoundly affects psychology, philosophy, and the arts.

In his development of this concept, Jung had great respect for the philosophies and religions of the East, bridging East and West. He broke with Sigmund Freud in the early history of psychoanalytic thought, inspiring the West's interest in Eastern religions, the *I Ching* (Chinese Book of Changes), and the power of mythologies across cultures. In his work, he integrates classical, Eastern, and Western literary sources.[15] Jung teaches that the artist is a vehicle for the psychic life of mankind.[16] Butoh with its globalizing tendencies might be interpreted as tapping into this collective, but with an Eastern ethos and philosophy of the body more in tune with that of Japan.

Like Jung in his work on alchemy, darkness, and symbols of transformation,[17] Hijikata embraced the darkness, naming his dance "darkness dance" and conceiving it in light of transformative potency. In his study of incipient schizophrenia, Jung believed that darkness through the opacity of myth manifests in the life of the body as fate when it is not acknowledged and allowed to transform.[18] In fact, the purposes of dance therapy might also be explained in this way. Undertaken in therapeutic contexts, dance can excavate the darkness or make clear what has been hidden in experience, allowing the body to clear away pain and trauma through movement. Likewise, butoh has therapeutic potential, particularly as it recognizes the shadow self.

I have experienced this directly in workshops with Nakajima Natsu and Ashikawa Yoko, expanding my darkness—not with a sense of gloom, but more as in a dream, moving shadows imagistically out to my sides, behind me, and in front. Or stated more experientially: Multiplying my shades of darkness, I expand into disappearance. Renewing my sense of self and connection to others, our subtly different shadows merge. Shadow dancing is a spiritual process, connected not to religion but to what Jung explained as "active imagination" and the emergence of the dream body. As a *butoh-ka,* I think in words, imagine in poetry, sound, picture, shape, and color, but finally dance beyond these and into "the dream," Ohno's image for unmediated bodily expression.

Despite butoh's similarity to Jungian active imagination, it would be a mistake to say that it derives from this Western basis. We cannot explain the imagistic process of butoh through Jung's psychology, even though we know his theory of the collective unconscious is cast inclusively across cultures and histories. The path to the unconscious for Hijikata is not archetypal in Western terms but is immediately available through the body in its spirituality. While Jung experiments with active imagination in silence and stillness and advocates dance to cull images from the unconscious and enrich mythic archetypes, Hijikata dances shamanistically into darkness, ancestry, and spirit: "Inside this one body there are various mythic things that are still sleeping intact," he says. "The work is how to excavate them at the actual site. . . . I would like to see something where such things float up like departed spirits."[19] As a poetic surrealist, Hijikata spoke often of his dead sister and how she danced inside him, "scratching away the darkness." Ohno Kazuo danced directly into the dream body through his spiritual poetry and love of flowers: "There is enough grotesqueness in the world," he says, "we should practice delicateness."[20]

Metamorphic Context of Butoh

Hijikata's reach into nature in tandem with surrealist imagery took him beyond the boundaries of the body as ordinarily perceived. His encouragement of latent powers of expression and the irrational content of the body lent impetus to new forms of dance therapy as well as theater and visual arts. Butoh wedges many faces of Eros and Thanatos (life and death) as it grows internationally in the manner of art and dance therapy. Its physiognomy twists and shakes through basic movements that most humans can do—but butoh shaking is profound, and its shuddering is stunning. The standards for such dance can be vague, which doesn't mean that butoh performers don't train assiduously. Kasai Akira, who is a contemporary of Hijikata and cofounder of butoh, has created his own unique style. He relates good butoh to good dancing in general, speaking of the butoh of Isadora Duncan and Vaslav Nijinsky. For Kasai, butoh is fully committed dancing (even that of Duncan and Nijinsky),[21] but it is more than this, as his butoh asks further: "Are we carrying our bodies into the world of the dead?"[22]

It seems that butoh is developing a range of applications and that the original cultic dedication of Hijikata's followers has given way to larger purposes and broader participation. We have seen that the butoh aesthetic is built upon imagery that activates the imagination. Here we see that in its philosophy, butoh suggests bodily potential, not unity. Neither does it drive toward conclusions;

as a genre it remains an unfinished opus. *Butoh-ka* move from positions of not knowing and waiting, as they excavate the body's cellular memory and allow it to morph from image to image. Concerning the future, there is increasingly an aura of discovery and renewal in butoh, and many more women are involved now than in the beginning.

Butoh and its metamorphic offshoots are local and global, and it has the stated purpose of community building for Kasai and others. His dance at the New York Butoh Festival, Butoh America (2007), explores present-day America. It is choreographed for himself and five well-trained dancers in American contemporary dance and ballet. This work is electric. It shows Kasai moving like a rock star, spurring technically proficient dancers toward new vistas as he blends his futuristic work with their sharp movements, globalizing butoh and expanding community at once. Kasai expands upon the great potential of America, still the dream, striking a chord of intercultural connection. Here is a Japanese choreographer dancing in America about America, a turnabout situation anthropologically, because it has been the habit of the West to colonize the East in its anthropology. Yes, America needs help to keep its promise alive, to rediscover its original purpose of developing the soul.

The Butoh group Seiryukai in Fukuoka provides another example of community building through the work of Harada Nobuo, who danced with Kasai. Harada's community process is more locally focused. For him, butoh begins from daily life experiences, observing self, and doubting every stereotype in order to grasp new relationships between the individual and the community. Harada designs experiences for the individual development of dancers in their personal quests—where the personal also strengthens community bounds. Tamah Nakamura, a member of his group, describes his dance practice:

> We begin by standing up and holding the lost feeling of not knowing how to move. Harada's improvisational exercises in dance class typically begin with painstakingly slow, careful steps as if petrified in a tight corner. We imagine carrying a delicate, precious object across the room to give to an imaginary person. We slowly cross the stage, a mountain, a river, the sea, calmly, alone, and together. We then discover a way to move alone and together. Momentary discoveries of reality occur through a connection of the inner force with bodily form.[23]

If ballet can be explained through its classical context as relates to balance and proportion, and modern dance through its existential context with its emphasis on freedom and individuality, as I have held,[24] we can add to this analysis that butoh cultivates a metamorphic context. Butoh dancers do not emphasize balance, nor do they express the self or represent anything outside the self, rather they are beings in transition; the self is not for itself alone. The self in butoh is a transitional self and a communal one. Butoh dancers perform in a process of transformation, guided by imagery, connectivity, and surrender. Thus they probe what Hijikata described as mythic images "sleeping" in the body.[25]

Anti-utopian Visceral Politics

> In our present state of degeneration it is through the skin
> that metaphysics must be made to re-enter our minds.
> —Antonin Artaud

We have seen that butoh holds a philosophy of the body that presents the human being as unfinished and metamorphic. As a philosophy, butoh also has political dimensions. Having diversified since its beginnings in Hijikata, butoh remains an anti-utopian form of dance, even as it extends the boundaries of ethnic identity. The butoh politic stems from communal memory and from a desire to salvage the significance of the body in the technocratic contemporary world. It questions the morality of global networks of information and shopping-mall aesthetics, seizing the violence against the body in society's acquiescence to technology and militarism. The Japanese theater director Shimizu Shinjin uses butoh's visceral physical techniques in spare dramas for his company Gekidan Kaitaisha (Theater of Deconstruction). Shimizu's *Bye-Bye: The New Primitive,* performed internationally, weaves names of places like Hungary, Assyria, and Crimea with those of Japanese emperors and a surreal simulation of a woman being beaten that nearly caused a riot in Zagreb, Croatia, in 1996.

Echoes of Japanese Obsessional Art and Artaud's vision of a theater of cruelty resound in Shimizu's work. By cruelty, Artaud did not advocate causing physical pain. He wrote rather of the cruelty it takes for the actor/dancer to express a truth that the audience may not want to see. Artaud says, "Without an element of cruelty at the root of every spectacle, the theater is not possible. In our present state of degeneration it is through the skin that metaphysics must be made to re-enter our minds."[26] Significantly, Artaud influenced Hijikata, and while not aiming toward an Eastern perspective, he saw the spiritual in the physical. For him all expression has physicality. His was a crusade to revolutionize theater so that it might connect people with the primal truth of the body.

The question of whether Artaud was attempting to purge himself through expression might also be asked of Hijikata, who finally chiseled Artaud's poetic vision into concrete relief. Butoh is the legacy of Hijikata, and some of its works can be interpreted as political in the sense of Artaud, but its expressions are not literally bound to cruelty, even though we know that Hijikata experimented with pain. I have been asked during my lectures on butoh whether it is a prime example of the theater of cruelty. I don't think so. Whatever its links to Artaud, I think it is not an example of the theater of cruelty any more than it represents Jung's view of a collective unconscious. Butoh holds an Eastern ethos, and its expressive means vary widely, even as it links to surrealism in literature, art, theater, and poetry. Its evolutionary path is metamorphic, and its challenge is the remembrance of the soul. It is specifically called to this mission through the darkness and shape-shifting of Hijikata and the world-friendly example of Ohno Kazuo. Soul work is inner work, and it can be emotionally painful; ultimately, it is the universal work of love and forgiveness.

If butoh is now global, it is nevertheless not utopian. Butoh artists challenge a utopian vision of the modern world to focus instead on human fear and senseless suffering—even redemptive suffering that Buddhism acknowledges at the core of human reality. Butoh actors and dancers counter global modernization with its quick-fix commodities. Dancers like Anzu Furukawa expose fascist tendencies of global homogeneity in historical flashbacks. I explore her work *Goya La Quinto del Sordo* in relation to Heidegger's flirtations with fascism in part 2. The political marks of butoh, like those of its relative *Tanztheater,* are unmistakable. Like the German *Tanztheater* of Pina Bausch, butoh develops repetitive righting rituals of falling down and getting up, of kissing without kissing, hurting without hurting, but with a difference that might well lay claim to a more mystical philosophy than that of the sexually conflicted visions of Bausch. Butoh lacks the sassiness of Bausch, and its transformations do not occur through ritual repetition of socially drenched actions, as so often in Bausch.

We have seen that *butoh-ka* are inclusive in their aesthetics, both in movement and culturally. The politics of butoh are equally clear. Dying and remembering, butoh dancers own nuclear fallout and its invalids—or the "invalid" position of war—as I describe in several butoh works in the following essays, beginning with Hijikata's *Summer Storm,* a work he choreographed in 1973 and that Arai Misao made into a film in 2003. Unlike ascendant forms of dance whose politics rest on overcoming gravity, butoh does not seek to escape the body. Its recognition of the immaterial body is about expansive connectivity of the human and universal and not about escape.

Emotion in Metaphysics

Emotion in Metaphysics is a dance by Hijikata in 1967. In his title we glimpse his postmodern view of metaphysics. We learn that his dances are drawn from feeling states and that they are also philosophically mitigated. They are not wholly abstract, yet his elaborate morphology as moving through dissimilar things (objects, images, and materials) goes behind material reality. If the body of butoh that he cultivated is flesh and blood in one sense, it is also much larger in another. In the view of Mikami Kayo, a student of Hijikata, the return of body to flesh is one of the techniques of butoh.[27] Flesh in the instance of butoh would be the physical earth body along with its needs and limitations, paradoxically unlimited in its morphological potentials.

The way of the flesh in butoh is the way of spirit, and flesh is also ambiguous, physical and metaphysical at once, in Hijikata's surrealist language. Butoh transformations are by way spirit, flesh, and material. In his first essay, "Inner Material/Material" (1960), Hijikata was already speaking about how he wrestled with "material" in dance and transformed from a dog into a human being. In "From Being Jealous of a Dog's Vein" (1969), he describes how emotions go astray in his body. The title of his work *Keijijogaku* (Emotion in Metaphysics, 1967) defies the logic of essentialist philosophies in which the mind is in control and emotions are what we are not supposed to have, or even bodies for that matter. The body of butoh from the time of Hijikata until now is material and immaterial, illusive, strange, and transformative. As such, it can't be pinned down with logic.

In various states of beauty and decay, the body of butoh, like the body of nature, always moves slightly beyond comprehension. It is certainly not the perfected body of ballet, the expressive body of modern dance, or the cool body of postmodern dance. Quite the opposite: Hijikata wanted to present a vulnerable body in decline. He sometimes said he sought "the emaciated body." At other times, he constructed his butoh ambiguously, presenting a tough exterior with a vulnerable core. In any case, the butoh body from Hijikata's time until now is not polished and presentational, nor is it cool and collected. It morphs through many faces and is not afraid to decompose. Modern dancers study composition; butoh dancers study decomposition.

Metaphysically speaking, change is constant in butoh, and it is less to be looked at than experienced. Through change, emotion can be magically, metaphysically diffused. And as through change, stillness is more visible. In the morphing of butoh, stillness seems to extend time, making it visible and expansive. We witness such stillness especially in surreal juxtapositions with nature, as in the environmental dances of Diego Piñón, Takenouchi Atsushi, Stuart Lynch, and Tanaka Min before them. Piñón's work *Ito* provides a good example of this, as I take up in a later essay.

Metaphysics of Awkwardness

We have said that surrealism influenced Hijikata at the root of butoh. This, coupled with his search for Japanese identity in a time of effacement, resulted in surreal (disorienting) butoh techniques known as "the hanging body." The edgy power and awkwardness of hanging techniques still motivates much butoh today. Ohno draws a portrait of hanging awkwardness in his dance "The Marriage of Heaven and Earth" at the end of *La Argentina Sho* (1977), holding a tenuous stillness, panting and hanging as though from a bent coat hanger with his knees knocking for several minutes, as I describe further in the essay, "Whole World Friend" in part 2. Most dancers would eschew awkwardness, and Ohno can certainly choose grace, but butoh manages to subvert intentional grace, making it more interesting, perhaps more real, and certainly more existential.

Butoh embodies the awkward, the painful, and the messy. Its metaphysical structure does not require the dancer to seek perfection. What a revelation, because most dance training is about mastery in this sense. Metaphysically speaking and contextually, *butoh-ka* are neither graceful nor awkward; rather, their movement is simply what it is. They seek to become the action at hand while moving on. Moreover, they create a structure where risky on-the-spot discovery and falling down might find a place. We know that the historic modern dance also used improvisation in its choreographic processes and that Doris Humphrey and other modern dancers cultivated falling motions. Perhaps this permission to fall down spans now to butoh? But modern dance was mannered and controlled in its approach to awkwardness and falling down, and Western postmodern dance takes a casual attitude to these matters. Like butterflies, *butoh-ka* settle into the images they inhabit with light control. With the whole of their being ready to disappear, they can land in seemingly awkward places, and are equally ready for grace.

Is Butoh a Philosophy?

Yes, it is an unfinished metaphysical philosophy of the dancing body that accounts for weakness and death, identifying with nature, decay, regeneration, and transformation. Its context is metamorphic and its politics anti-utopian. Its darkness is spiritual and beyond material. Born of mud and morphing to silk, its aesthetic is both beautiful and ugly, and it spirals emotion into metaphysics. Its alchemy moves through the ineffable spaces "in between" (*ma*, in Japanese). Its awkward "going under," or "frog's-eye view," seeks an end to heroic escalating power struggles and war. Its direction is descent, and its material tendency is toward dissolution. The cultivation of creative interspaces in butoh has promoted a global morphology that continues to evolve.

The Silk Inside of You

It is the express purpose of this book to show that the founding philosophy of butoh in its original approaches and morphology continues to motivate dancers today, even as they find their own distinctiveness at stake. American Maureen Fleming, who lives in New York City, provides a good example. We look briefly into her stated philosophy here and see its illustration in her dance. Her unflagging work has evolved continuously since her early study and performance in Japan. She has developed a unique practice of performance and teaching that reflects the use of butoh's transformative methods. In her lecture demonstrations, she depicts the history of butoh in films and slides and shows her original work alongside this history. It is clear that her roots in butoh are deep, but that she also grows beyond these through her own special talents, especially her desire to reach an organic state in movement and to draw upon several cultural bodies, from the animal dances of Africa to the undulating breath of Brazil.

Fleming was one of the first and most consistent Western students of Ohno Kazuo and Ohno Yoshito, and she is also no stranger to Hijikata's style. Her study with Tanaka Min took her toward Hijikata's surrealism and his concept of dance as experience. She has sought her own way in dance, uncovering the nature in human nature and our spiritual resonance with all creatures in organic flowing forms. She doesn't copy any of her butoh mentors, but her philosophy of dance reflects them all.

Butoh is dance work of course, and we have said that it is also soul work. The dances of Hijikata, Ohno, and more recently those of Fleming and many others ask the same perennial philosophical questions: Who am I, where do I come from, and where am I going? Fleming is clearly a butoh metaphysician, as can be seen in *Decay of the Angel* (2004) as she descends slowly to earth from high above the stage, lighting above a reflecting pool of water, her pliant body morphing into creature shapes. Broadly speaking, Fleming dances "archetypes," she says.[28]

She identifies herself as a choreographer and performance artist. Like Eiko and Koma, Takei Kei, Frances Barbe, Marie-Gabrielle Rotie, and several others represented in the following essays, she doesn't necessarily call her dance butoh, but she does credit butoh in her training methods and philosophical outlook. She was born in Japan, the daughter of an American Navy lieutenant. At the age of two, she was in a serious car accident with her mother. The effects of the experience, both physical and emotional, formed a thread through her life and influenced her devotion to the study of physical movement. In her multimedia performances, she invents what she calls "surreal movement poetry" and explores "the journey of the soul."

In performance, Fleming descends as from the air like a skein of silk, unwinding new shapes without pause or inflection. I saw this in Fleming's video dance in Geneva, New York (November 2, 2005), where I also saw her demonstrate her techniques and spoke with her about her work. Her body slips bonelessly down, undulating over ancient church steps, coiling and unrolling like a snake. As a dancer, she is like no other *butoh-ka,* yet I see butoh in her shading, in the murky background of her dance and in her stillness.

A diaphanous spirituality appears in her image of descent, or is it inside me? As Fleming states in her lecture and performance, she wants to become "the inside of the audience," to move inside body of the witness. For me, her dance in its

FIGURE 7. Maureen Fleming's *Decay of the Angel*
(2000), commissioned by the Japan-U.S. Creative Artist
Commission and premiered in Tokyo at the Saison
Foundation in 2000. Photograph by Lois Greenfield,
© 2004. Used by permission of Maureen Fleming.

nakedness is an inside. Or is it an outside that has been peeled and rendered liq-
uid essence? I sense my own watery soma in her constantly smooth flow—gently
moving on, insubstantial and oozing with no interruption. I tune my breath to
her continuum and resonate with her quiet descent.

Fleming embodies Eros in her metamorphic style, a silken pleasure that slips
toward disappearance. Speaking like a *butoh-ka,* she says the goal of her work
is to reveal the transcendent through images that focus on the human body as
a vehicle of transformation. She is interested in finding "a universal art which
touches the evolutionary traces imbedded in human experience and transcends
the limits of nationality and gender." Her dance morphs globally and holds healing at its core, providing an inspiring example of the philosophy of butoh, as do
others represented in the following essays, each in their own way.

Part Two

Alchemists

Essays and Poetry on Transformation

FIGURE 8. Hijikata Tatsumi in *A Story of Smallpox* (1972). This dance about disease came one year before *Leprosy* (1973), Hijikata's last solo performance. After that, he choreographed for others until his death in 1986. Photograph by Onozuka Makoto, © 1972. Courtesy of the Hijikata Tatsumi Archives at Keio University in Tokyo, Japan.

One Thousand Days
of Sunshine and Peace

Hijikata Tatsumi in Kyoto (1973)

> Be reborn always and everywhere. Again and again.
> —Hijikata Tatsumi

Hijikata is the dark soul and architectural genius of butoh. One of his final performances was his solo "Leprosy" in his dance *Summer Storm,* performed by his
company in the Westside Auditorium at Kyoto University in 1973. A year earlier,
his dance *A Story of Smallpox* (1972) also connected with thematics of disease.
He never performed publicly himself after 1973, but he continued to work with
his dance company until his death in 1986. Ohno Yoshito, who had known Hijikata throughout his revolutionary career, says that near his death Hijikata rose
on his deathbed in the hospital and performed his very last dance for all those
attending him. Arai Misao filmed the Kyoto performance of *Summer Storm,* and
his footage of this historic dance sat in a can for thirty years before he decided
to make it available in DVD format in 2003.

Arai's film documents one of Hijikata's last performances and his extraordi-
nary embodiment of leprosy in two sections. It is also important as a record of
one of Hijikata's most mature works as a performer and choreographer, showing
clearly delineated movement and compositional structures. As a concert-length
work, *Summer Storm* develops episodically and is choreographed by Hijikata
for his company members, all of whom have carried his butoh legacy forward
as choreographers and performers: Ashikawa Yoko, Kobayashi Saga, Tamano
Koichi, Waguri Yukio, and Hanagami Naoto.

When I spoke with Arai in London in 2005 and saw a screening of his film, he
told me that he finally understood the historic importance of this performance.
He was aware that very little had been recorded on film of Hijikata's unique

Ankoku Butoh (Darkness Dance) and that while parts of his own film were grainy, he knew the footage he had was a full presentation of Hijikata's work. In making his film, he decided not to edit the dance but give it a preface and epilogue with before-and-after images and have music made for the film. He asked YAS-KAS to create an understated score for his film to support Hijikata's dance without interrupting or distorting it. Arai's purpose was to let the dance and unpolished film with its sometimes-grainy texture stand as close to the original as possible.

I first saw butoh in 1985, a year before Hijikata's death, and subsequently studied it for twenty years by the time I saw him perform in this film. His solo, "Leprosy," had a surprisingly strong effect on me. I have seen many striking photographs of Hijikata, but photographs do not do justice to his subtle ability to transform and to touch audiences. So many of the performance photographs of Hijikata capture dramatically shocking moments, and he can be truly shocking, but he also has a very tender side. I felt close to Hijikata in this film of *Summer Storm,* connecting with a quiet center of affliction in his dance.

Hijikata's invention of original movement techniques is apparent throughout *Summer Storm.* His seemingly strange and nonconformist dance introduced an upside-down approach to dance technique. It does shine, but on its own terms. Unlike most dance, Hijikata's does not up the ante toward physical strength; rather, it excels in the use of yielding qualities, including weak and wobbly movement. His manner of letting go requires physical strength and also holds a psychic component, as he uses visual and verbal images to construct his choreography. These are not formal or literal images, and his morphing gestures are not mimetic. They are abstract as concretely distilled in essence. The weak body that Hijikata developed in his technique takes both physical and psychic strength, a technical paradox embodied in his butoh.

He was aware that the intuitive, tangible embodiment of imagery could condition the nervous system, producing dance experiences rather than emotional expressions. This is apparent in his imagistic teaching involving the life and death of the body. In the last chapter of *Hijikata Tatsumi and Ohno Kazuo,* Tamah Nakamura and I explore how Hijikata's deliberate approach to dance as experience, which he called DANCE EXPERIENCE (written in English with all capital letters), influenced subsequent generations of butoh dancers. We include techniques of nine dancers directly influenced by Hijikata in our book. Through his teaching and that of his students, we see that the dance experiences he sought varied widely. They could be ethereal, very subtle and ghostlike, heavy and dark, or violent and extreme. There are many dance performers and companies influenced by Hijikata, ranging from the highly minimalist and meditative Sankai Juku to the carnivalesque Dai Rakudakan. Companies and performers on every continent have been stirred by his work.

Hijikata continued to subvert conventional notions of dance and theater throughout his performing career. The dance that resulted from his *Ankoku Butoh* (Darkness Dance) is now called "butoh" and performed throughout the world, though not in the original style of Hijikata. Now there are many different styles and a great deal of metamorphic work that has benefited from the approach of butoh without claiming the name. Butoh and butoh-influenced work everywhere retain Hijikata's metamorphic signature. Because his dance is both yielding and penetrating, both yin and yang, female and male, it can morph through many states. In *Summer Storm,* we see the gentle reflective side of Hijikata, not the wild exterior and phallic metal thrust of *Rebellion of the Body* (1968), which established him as a noted surrealist choreographer. In *Summer Storm,* we can experience Hijikata's interacting yin and yang style, and his metamorphic choreographic method, which he calls "the body that becomes." This is not the dancer pretending to be something other. Rather the performance is metamorphic, living and dying at once, allowing an imagistic process to work its alchemy.

Summer Storm is in six parts: (1) "A Girl," (2) "Girls Picking Herbs," (3) "The Spirits of the *Bon* Festival I," (4) "Dreams of the Dead; The Sleep; The War," (5) "The Spirits of the *Bon* Festival II," and (6) "Statues of the *Rakans.*" In his film, Arai prefaces the dance performance with scenes of Tokyo at night, "Tokyo Nights, Tokyo Delights," as he projects huge filmic images of Hijikata's butoh on the front of shiny skyscrapers in Shinjuku, the glittering center of Tokyo. These large mirrored images of Hijikata's strange dance above Tokyo nightlife are disorienting, catapulting onlookers back before World War II, back to the agrarian roots of Japan before its rebuilding and modernization after the war. Hijikata and his company of "Dark Spirit Dancers" are nearly naked on the buildings, wobbling on their infant legs, discovering how to walk.

Most Japanese have not heard of butoh, and it took those of the intellectual and theatergoing elite many years to understand Hijikata's desire to rescue the Japanese body from what he feared would be its demise and from Western dismantlement after the war.[1] Over time and through translations of Hijikata's own writings, dancers and scholars have understood the source of his chilly, huddled movement. Hijikata sought a way to embody the painful confinement of infants kept in rice warmers while their parents worked in the fields, and the hunched-over postures of old people in farming villages also motivated him. His dance excavates strata of bodily experience in prewar rural Japan. It also represents Hijikata's desire to capture the early raw Kabuki before it was purged of Western views of vulgarity, and it shows his flair for the colorful abstraction and relaxed postures of the ukiyo-e wood-block prints that so fascinated Western connoisseurs. Add to this Hijikata's own fascination with European surrealism, his study of German Expressionism, and his shamanist proclivities. We experience a fusion of all of this in the alchemy of *Summer Storm.*

In the first part, we see Hijikata as the Girl—so small and tottering—his figure shrunken in his loosely wrapped dress and slippers. His form is fluid, nevertheless, and delicate. This girl is not carefree, as we might hope. She is imprisoned, both young and old. Hijikata, as the Girl, cranes his head forward, as he often does, and the fingers of his hands curl tensely in a truncated form—a detail of the hand so etched in his dance that it has since become a cliché with others. His dress seems made of a painter's drop cloth with red smears that look like blood. When he sits and looks down between his folded legs, his crotch is innocently exposed. In a detached manner, his eyes shrink away from view into hollow sockets, rimmed faintly red in the white pallor of his face. The Girl Hijikata becomes kneels and hunches with her hands and arms held tensely close, sometimes tumbling lightly out of the hunch and onto one foot, balancing there before standing up. She comes up to standing through a one-footed crouch several times, creating an easy feeling for this difficult squatting movement, part of the technical virtuosity of Hijikata's dance.

The Girl builds speed with small recurring gesticulations, but they don't become frantic as they develop, just a little more staccato. Maintaining an inner calm while he accelerates, Hijikata doesn't ask us to pity this girl. Is this sad catatonic figure his invention from memory of children in the harsh countryside tied to posts while their parents worked in the fields? In his speech "*Kaze Daruma*" (Wind Daruma), given on the night of the Tokyo Butoh Festival in 1985, one year before his death, Hijikata talks of the infants kept in rice warmers and the small children tied to posts in the Tohoku of his youth. He remembers how they scratched at their faces and how their howls reached to the heavens. There is an ache in this little girl Hijikata becomes. She is helpless to stand, trying and falling, slowly turning on her butt, and rising from sitting on one foot, broken.

Then as the dance shifts, we see pretty girls picking herbs and a country scene with girls mincing in *gaita*, the traditional Japanese wooden platform shoes with thongs between the toes. Their faces are sometimes happy, but with other expressions pending. They smile with a howl and a cry. Their tiny clattering steps are charming and alarming at once, and they enjoy each other in their plucking motions. One girl rides on another piggyback as they play a unison game of skittering and fooling each other. There are four girls at the end who commence jointed scarecrow-arm movements characteristic of Hijikata. These are derived, as I have experienced in butoh classes, through an image of arms tucked away inside the body. They are not the ones we see, as Hijikata taught, but the arms that have yet to appear or have already died. To stimulate the nervous system in somatic play with this imagery is to experience an eerie sense of surrender: To me, these arms tucked inside are not mine alone; they are the inner arms of everyone, emanating from the heart chakra. In yoga teachings and butoh practices, the arms extend from the heart.

Hijikata was born Yoneyama Kunio in 1928 in Tohoku, the tenth child of eleven. In the Japanese countryside where he grew up, the winters are very cold and the summers are brilliant. His butoh, he explained in his speech "*Kaze Daruma,*" came from his childhood experiences in this poor rural district of Japan. In his short surrealist essay "From Being Jealous of a Dog's Vein," Hijikata remembers endless days of soggy rice crackers and childhood terrors of his alcoholic father who beat his mother.[2] This was written in 1969, ten years after his first avant-garde dance *Kinjiki* (Forbidden Color). In his first essay, "Inner Material/Material" (1960), he writes of his early studies of German modern dance and his struggles with Western ballet. This article already bears his surrealist stamp and intent to turn his dance somatically inward and away from consumer politics. His life had spanned the history of World War II from Japan's prewar buildup to the bombing of Hiroshima and Nagasaki, including the firebombing of Tokyo and the Japanese countryside. He saw Japan in flames after the war and the coming of American occupation, the forging of the U.S.-Japan Security Treaty, and the subsequent rebuilding of Japan in the image of Western democracy. He was too young to fight as a soldier, but his whole life was lived under the sign and siege of war. He died at age fifty-seven of liver disease, having created a new form of dance that spoke not only of Japan but also of the vulnerable body we all share.

I experience nostalgia in *Summer Storm,* Hijikata's mixed feelings for a Japan held mostly in memory; I read it as a personal ethnology in search of a moral ethos. Because we experience pain, we know instinctively that it is wrong to hurt others. War reminds us of our vulnerability and always poses moral dilemmas, as Hijikata's dance attests. Not seeking to express anything, he sets the stage for a truth to emerge between the dancer and the witness. Hijikata's search is not so far removed from the intent of modern dance as it originated in Germany and America and spread its creative spirit throughout the world. As I learned through my studies with Mary Wigman, dance is not self-expression but a means toward self-understanding and a way of constructing the self. The existentialist project holds that we construct our own reality. Our fate is not necessarily given or imposed from outside but is the result of our deeds and works. Wigman and Hijikata both seemed to understand this. In Hijikata's case, he used dance as a means of self-architecture in the face of difficulty. He moves inside himself to gather the "Inner Material/Material" (the title of one of his first surrealist essays) that he envisions and manifests in an unmistakably original form.

In "Spirits of the *Bon* Festival I" Hijikata's structural voice becomes more apparent choreographically. Here the company appears together, not in obvious celebration but as a skeletal festival in the abstract. Several dancers have the signature shaven heads of butoh. The informal wearing of red robes suggested in wraps and drapes intensifies their spare Buddhist monklike look. In this we are reminded how the popular international butoh group Sankai Juku has elevated sheer shaven looks of near nudity to high art. Their polished minimalist movement with jointed arms in constant discovery is visually intensified as they drape and robe their whitened nudity and cast their dance against highly stylized geometric sets. They are not as raw and full of pathos as Hijikata, but the germ for their work was present in his.

Part four begins with dancers wearing weathered cotton kimono, old *yukatta*, and sitting cross-legged facing the audience. They occasionally lift their legs, one then the other, not to show a fine design with the body, but more in a mode of experiment. Western dance, Hijikata said, begins with its legs planted firmly on the ground, but butoh begins with the discovery of legs. In his teaching, he used this kind of language to inspire unfinished movement and to draw upon improvisatory aliveness in choreographed forms. Squatting low, the two dancers who begin "Dreams of the Dead; The Sleep; The War" remove their *yukatta*, exposing their breasts. They are nude and powdered white, except for the signature loincloth or white thong often worn in butoh. The neutrality of the all-white figures imparts a universal feeling; the body mask turns the dancer into "everyone" and "no one" in particular. This is a characteristic butoh look, all-inclusive, purified, and Japanese in style. In the dim light, the white bodies are shaded, and they cast shadowy shapes on the backdrop. There is an impersonal aura of abstraction apparent in the dance. The sitting dancers roll onto their sides ritualistically and then cover their heads with the *yukatta* before putting them back on, all in a mode of discovering their bodies and poking the space around them. They carry on what seems like a conversation in very slow motion, punctuated with sudden assertions.

The dance morphs to another register as other dancers enter with giant headdresses, massive museum pieces of ancient warlords designed to frighten enemies with their horny mantels. As the dance proceeds, Hijikata himself speaks, a rare inclusion of text for his theater of darkness: "He got his first pair of leather shoes," he says, suggesting his early introduction to Western ways. Then he adds many phrases lamenting the war. I catch a few of them, sometimes just words, but it is clear that Hijikata grieves: "It happened before," he says, "staggering pain. . . . The world tilted. . . . Sleep; oh sleep on with the souls of the dead. . . . Oh send a good mighty storm our way. . . . Wars, Wars. . . . War is the dripping of blood. . . . Vision of collective hunger. . . . The ultrasexy. . . . Vanish; oh go away horror and greed. . . . Bless us with fruits, with one thousand days of sunshine and peace."

Hijikata's prayer, the whole of *Summer Storm,* is danced with quiet struggle and compassion. The somber tones in "Dreams of the Dead" are clearly antiwar and a memorial, remembering the dead through the names of places where many died in World War II. Hijikata speaks over the dance: "Sleep oh Sleep . . . Iwo

Jima . . . the sea of Midway." (The battle of Iwo Jima was one of the worst battles of the Pacific campaign of World War II, and the battle of Midway Island is one of the most famous naval battles in history.) "I offer this votive candle to the God of Oki." (He speaks of the Oki Islands, a group of small Japanese islands in the southern part of the Sea of Japan.) "War is the dripping of blood. . . . From Oki, let us find a favorable wind with one thousand days of sunshine and peace."

"Statues of *Rakans*" is the final part of *Summer Storm* and is divided into several sections: "Dances of the *Rakans*," "Leprosy 1," "Slackness," "Leprosy 2," "Ice," "Three Fly-Girls," "Dance of *Gibasa*," and "Three Bellemers." "Leprosy" in its two parts is a dance that stands on its own, contextualized by surrounding dances. "Statues of *Rakans*" is based on the statues at Kita Temple that represent holy people who deserve offerings. The very famous *Rakans* were made in Kyoto and later brought to the city of Morioka in Hijikata's homeland in the Tohoku region, where they are kept in Hoonji Temple. The temple's notable feature is the Rakando (Statues Hall) built in 1735 and rebuilt in 1858. Within the Rakando are five hundred *Rakans* kept on five rows of shelves that stretch around the hall. The Rakando is now known as a Zen training temple for monks. From the Muromachi age (1336–1573) onward, Zen Buddhism grew in popularity in Japan. *Rakan* comes from the Sanskrit "arhat" and pertains to enlightenment. It is believed that the statues of *Rakans* represent the religious austerities of Buddhism. *Rakans* also have spiritual significance as sculptures of expressions and gestures that reveal essence. I have seen such figures in a shrine in Kyoto that capture the basic nature of departed souls swept away in natural disasters. Even in stone, they are full of dance.

Hijikata's poignant "*Rakans*" begins with sitting dancers who develop morphing facial expressions. They are mourning, perhaps, or frightened. Expressions of ecstasy and foolishness pass through them as they squat in a low walk, moving through space and morphing their facial expressions. What circumstances animate them, I wonder? They stand up and remain in the dance on tottering legs; they put on plain kimonos while they lift one leg then the other, sometimes squatting, only to rise again. Hijikata appears in the darkness along the side and becomes increasingly more visible, even as his dance of "Leprosy" remains shadowy in the half-light.

I am aware at first of how emaciated he is and that he seems both man and woman with his bearded gaunt face and his wrapped dress hanging in rags. He reminds me of paintings of Christ in the dark manner of Spanish artist El Greco (1541–1614). Like El Greco's works, Hijikata's dance blends passion and restraint and is greatly fused. "Leprosy" doesn't develop toward any culminating point; it is simply there on the stage, not as a visual invitation but as a figure to contemplate. Hijikata's wobbly legs are able to support him, tenuously. Yet his dance doesn't seek pity; it is only faintly present, like the distant lonely voice in the background music. His face searches, and the music morphs to a thin, plain melody of Zen *shakuhachi* flute. From his rocky sitting positions, Hijikata stands up slowly and deliberately, shaking somewhat, drawing all of his limbs softly inward.

The performance transforms as Hijikata's mouth elongates, straining to one side. He creates intense, unusual colors within the pallor of his face. His eyes never completely open; they remain blurry, smudged lightly round with red. Like the paintings of El Greco, his dance is masterfully colored, somber and saintly in spirit. To me "Leprosy" is an icon of butoh, showing the sacred intention of Hijikata's impossibly tender dance. He draws us irresistibly into a pictorial serenity and into a cave of affliction in "Leprosy," his long hair hanging in tangles around his face. Then as with a flutter, his dance is interrupted with three women wrapped in skirts, their breasts bound with white cloths. Hijikata calls this part "Slackness."

The dancers move strangely in a papery way until Hijikata appears again, continuing on in "Leprosy." A baby cries far away in the distance, and Hijikata's mouthing shows his connection; nevertheless, he draws away from his own countenance. This dance doesn't ask to be watched, but rather it asks for us to see leprosy. Hijikata's dance is the antithesis of show, as this solo indicates. The dance of the wounded child, the Girl in the beginning, continues to resonate throughout *Summer Storm,* especially in "Leprosy." But Hijikata never asks us to pity her or leaves us to our own devices. His dance is a guide for the heart, holding us right.

Still, I am left with a question in the midst of this film.

Is a dance about leprosy too obtrusive? Does it take advantage of illness? Hijikata's is a dance about real suffering and long-held prejudice in the face of sickness and disfigurement. And as every dance does, it manipulates theatrical elements. Even as we sometimes don't understand the shift between the performer and his subject, there is always an element of control that separates the performer as who he is from what he is becoming onstage. Hijikata's psychic control is not apparent, although I have no doubt as I watch him that he must exert control to a certain extent. He himself does not have Hansen's disease (leprosy), yet he takes us into his empathic embodiment of the condition, and this is enough. His legs are apart most of the time, bowed, and his feet take weight on the outside border, so his butoh walk (ancient walk) is silhouetted large on the background. As we hear chanting coming from far away, Hijikata's bare legs explore the air around him. He sits down gently and rises from squatting to stand on one leg, uncannily impossible.

Who are the almost naked women in "Ice"? And with such large heads? They wear bulky white headdresses, stand and kneel in side view, leaning their heavy heads forward at odd moments. As the lights come up, we see their wrap skirts of white and gray. They advance on wobbly legs. Their knees are flexed in a typical butoh walk, and we see how they lean over to the side and then come to center, backing up and facing the side again. As their faces pass by us, we can see their life force melt, as in a painting. These ice maidens squat on half-toe with their heels up and finally land in a characteristic sitting position for women and girls in Japan—with the lower legs folded to the back and outside of the upper legs. Hijikata is barely visible in the background.

"Three Fly-Girls," in the last part of "Statues of *Rakans,*" begins with three women in ethereal metamorphosis. They are tightly wrapped in black-and-white fabric: standing, sitting, and bending over, weaving their arms and stretching their necks as they grimace. They continue this manner of transforming through positions and gestures in body and face. Slow rattling movements unravel through the dance at the end, and the dancers' hands transform into animal hoofs. Three men with shaven heads powdered white and wearing red robes overlap this dance, while Arai's film takes brief creative license, shifting to the harvest of sticky seaweed called *gibasa* in Japan. We see the floating weed underwater and how it is pounded into a deep green, sticky mass.

The "Dance of *Gibasa*" features two nudes in loincloths with flowers hanging from their heads. They flow together looking pleased; then curiously, meagerly, they crawl away on all fours like hand walkers who never learned how to stand upright. Intersecting this, the monklike figures in red return to hold quiet shapes, as "Three Bellemers" begins with light, fast, percussive movement. Pulling backward, young women in chemises with flowers attached to their dresses dance and bunch together. Their long pigtails make them look young and quizzical. Are we innocent, their faces ask? Are we prostitutes? Are we birds perching and flying, their arms inquire? The Bellemers walk away softly to the side, as yet another scene overlaps with women in short red dresses and the long-forgotten shoes we saw toward the beginning. They clatter about in their platform wooden thongs, tipping playfully into toe walking. They disappear, winging their elbows, echoing the flight of birds, their outlined eyes glowing darkly in white faces. Finally, they hunch forward and continue a fragile walk.

Many features of *Summer Storm* are repeated in later butoh. We see them today, the chest and ribs hunching over a forward pelvis with legs in a wobble. This abstraction of movement, its exaggerations, the makeup, and the faces looking up in sudden surrender with upturned palms were all stylistically new with Hijikata, but they have sources in Japanese art and theater. His gritty movement themes have precedent in Kabuki and ukiyo-e. Hijikata drew from human and animal gestures and from Japanese ways and stylizations, but he abstracted these skillfully.

As *Summer Storm* concludes, other dancers enter wearing white, and we hear electronic airy zings like fireworks or sirens when the dancers begin their bow. Soft music ensues for this understated bow. Its choreography is not grandiose, as many dance bows are. At one point, the men lift the women gracefully to one shoulder and walk forward with them respectfully. Hijikata enters the line, wearing a flower in his hair, his face content and unprotected.

Arai's film fades from the dance to show snowflakes falling across the screen and melting in summer. Then pulling away from the dance and snow in sunshine, it fades gently to the sea and land of Japan, showing Tohoku from the air in stunning views, its farms and rice paddies a patchwork quilt of green and brown. The film draws upon my own nostalgia and mixed feelings of growing up in a depressed area of rural southern Utah, and I remember how my village looks from the Rocky Mountains, so far away in my imagination. I see it most clearly when I think how the land is materially convincing, made of the same substance as my body and the storm clouds above me.

The less I understand it, the more I love Hijikata's *Summer Storm,* gleaming with unresolved mysteries that do not feel alien to me. No other of the great butohists who followed him carried Hijikata's manner of dancing further. How could anyone imitate him? Future *butoh-ka* would need to find their own way forward:

Forewarned

Swelling with sores, and afflicted.
Forgiven their sins, declared dead.
Shunned.
Forced to wander and beg,
Witnessing their own funeral
And burial.
I warn others of my presence with a clapper, and repent
My witchcraft. No one shall come near me,
Or even think of being close to me.
All my fingers and toes are gone, and I am abandoned
Here in this cave.

Whole World Friend

Ohno Kazuo in Tokyo (1993)

> The saintly character is the character for which spiritual emotions are the habitual centre of the personal energy; and there is a certain composite photograph of universal saintliness, the same in all religions, of which features can easily be traced.
> —William James, *The Varieties of Religious Experience*

Ohno Kazuo, a well-traveled, world-famous performer by 1993, was presented as a treasure of Japan for an international audience in Tokyo at the JADE festival, which drew dance scholars and performers from Asia, America, and Europe. The final ceremony and performance of August 7 featured six of Japan's celebrated elderly dancers, and the last one was Ohno, the only nontraditional performer. The program says, "There are not many examples in the world of performances to welcome elderlies with admiration or to worship them." In Japan they have such celebrations in dances called *Okina Mai.*

Ohno calls his dance on this program *Dance for Blessing the Elderly.* He himself is just two months short of eighty-seven in this work. He dances simply in a yellow kimono, beginning early as he waits for his entrance on the side of the backlit stage. Ohno's glowing ambiance in the background overlaps with *Rojo,* a temple dance performed by the priest of Motsuji Temple, Raiken Nanto. Ohno's entrance is eternally slow, providing the scenery behind *Rojo,* well known for its symbolic and tense beauty as part of *Ennen,* a traditional ritual performance of celebration throughout Japan.

It is instructive to see these two dances together, one traditional and the other metamorphic, one part of a ritual celebration, the other a piece of spiritual poetry. The temple dance features Raiken in movement slow and close to the ground with gliding steps broken into percussive rhythms. He wears billowy ritual pants with a short kimono jacket, decorated simply in plain tones. His dance has delightful surprises, with small hops into the air coming suddenly and without preparation, and the mask he wears formalizes his movements, as does his fan. His dance is smooth with softly bent knees, and his repetitive steps are punctuated with staccato at times. He bows ritually at the end of the dance. Like Ohno's, Raiken's dance conveys the poetry of his body and spiritual character, but it is less intentionally creative and more ritual in context. Ohno's dance is also smooth with an occasional percussive gesture, but it is structured as improvisation and not formal by design. His improvisation is warm and gentle.

Ohno becomes progressively visible on the stage as Raiken leaves; we see his aging, graceful body trailing a yellow kimono in its wake and that he carries a long staff or walking stick. Genderless, even as the kimono is worn by both sexes in Japan, he descends to the earth in his old age, caressing it, and blossoming like a golden flower in a window of sun. His performance is delicately detailed with facial and hand gestures, his large hands beckoning an unseen presence. The themes of Ohno's dances matter less than his dancing: ever fresh, ever young and withering. The stage setting has golden trees in the back and children's cut-out paper creations hanging in long lines overhead. There are many of them, another nod to traditional Japan and a complement to Ohno's golden dance.

As ever, Ohno is highly theatrical while managing to be himself as well. His white makeup and black-rimmed eyes exaggerate his natural features, and he wears a black wig with a long feather of white. As his kimono drops away, we see his body in white briefs; his bare chest, arms, and legs are powdered white. Thunder and rain provide the music for his dance; eventually this morphs to soft electronics with mournful sounds bleeding through, obscured cries or laments from far away. Ohno does not project his dance outward; rather he lets the audience in, cultivating a soft absorbent focus, especially when he uses his staff to listen to the floor, then places it down and reclines beside it, relaxed and alert. He mirrors the staff and then rises without effort, pressing up from kneeling through the power of one leg while using the other lightly behind, this man of eighty-six. His body doesn't falter as he comes to stand. Every moment of his dance makes a wonderful snapshot. Ohno never takes a bad picture because he is always present to the moment and in flow. The silk kimono sleeves hang in perfect squares when he bends his elbows out to the sides and lifts his hands upward. He is clearly conscious of the line and shape he makes, but not simply as a design.

I make quick line drawings of his dance, reducing it (and not too well) to original calligraphic marks. His dance is clear, easy to draw and remember, so I morph my drawings into haiku, quickly without editing:

> Row, plow to the edge.
> Edge your way along, pilgrim.

Don't give up.
Bend like bamboo
Yellow with age, lean
Don't break.

Ohno kneels with ease, leans on his staff, then squats back on his heels. Age like a butterfly, his dance says to me.

Light, light, and lighter
Move ever up,
So desuka. So on. Fade.

As he exits, Ohno lifts his kimono with his staff, wrapping his body and framing it like a child against the golden trees. His dance holds struggle in repose and is not heroic. He gets smaller in the distance as he leaves and shrinks his body, crouching lower, folding in, holding delicately on.

Fallen Western Dancers

Is Ohno "a fallen Western dancer, expelled from Japan, and then rediscovered," as explained by Japanese dance critic and scholar Gunji Masakatsu? In his interview at the 1993 JADE Conference we have been exploring, Gunji notes that butoh began with Ohno and Hijikata Tatsumi, who were not traditional Japanese dancers at first but modern dancers in the style of German Expressionism.[1] Gunji's is an apt, pithy summary of the history of butoh, I think, taking account of Japan's rejection of butoh in its beginning phases. *Butoh-ka* (dancers) are indeed "fallen Western dancers" who create a global way forward. Originally, they used Western creativity with its emphasis on the power of individual expression to reinvent Eastern nativism, and in so doing they fell away from, or transcended, the styles of Western dance they had studied, including ballet and modern. On this point, however, Hijikata and Ohno diverge, as they often do.

Ohno is never hostile to the West; Hijikata often is. But even as he criticizes Western commercialism, the intellectual and aesthetic avant-garde of the West inspires Hijikata. It would be difficult to call him anti-Western in the sense of what that means today. He was speaking and dancing after World War II and during the turbulence of the 1960s at a time when Japan was rebuilding, rapidly modernizing, and had perhaps a bad case of indigestion, or as he put it, "heartburn." There are possibly several ways to hate the West, or the East for that matter, and antipathy can grow from outside one's own culture or from within. In his book *Occidentalism* (2004) written with Avishai Margalit, social historian Ian Buruma gives us some idea of the complexity of Occidentalism—the dangerous hatred of the West that fuels movements such as al-Qaeda.

Hijikata's terrorists (as he sometimes called his dancers) were poised in his mind to undermine capitalist democracy with its emphasis on mass production and to take on notions of modern progress. Hijikata's nativist counterrevolution, however, was heavily in debt to Western ideas and modernism, especially to early modern dance. And his butoh eventually connected in its own way to postmodern eclecticism in the West. Buruma states the dilemma of modernity in Japan this way: "Coiled like an anaconda inside the modern transformation of Japan was a nativist counterrevolution, which sought to save the spiritual purity of an ancient culture from the soulless modernity of the Occident. . . . Western-style modernity and nativist revolt existed in the same establishment, and often in the minds of the same people."[2] The modern, in any case, is a slippery concept. In prewar Japan, it meant the West, and often it referred to colonialism. The West is also a slippery slope, as are generalizations about the East.

Hijikata had strong ideas about what he was against in the West, and it didn't include the Western intellectual life in which he participated. He used it, waging a guerrilla war against Western materialism. His revolutionary means became known as *Ankoku Butoh,* an original shamanist dance. It is important to recognize that in reviving native aspects of Japan in his butoh, he was not guilty of romantic notions about the purity of the Japanese spirit. His focus was local, and it also had global implications. His dance was not about national purity, but about darkness, the weak body, and the dispossessed. His stylization came from his somatic association with mud and wind, old people, illness, and crippled children, and he asserted that his rural roots could be found in every culture: "Tohoku is everywhere," he said.

Like Hijikata, and perhaps even more, Ohno had experienced the West and danced in full view of it. Yet he never showed any animosity toward the West, even though he fought against it as a soldier. We remember that he was born in 1906 when Japan was still coming to terms with Western influences that had overtaken it in the late-nineteenth century. From the 1850s to about 1910, Japan had been assimilating everything Western, from natural science to literature. The Japanese developed a taste for European fashion, changing the kimono for top hats and tailcoats. They pursued Prussian constitutional law, French culinary art, American cinema and dance, and studied British naval strategies. Then came the move against Western imperialism and colonialism. As Ohno became an adult, the West came hotly under fire in Japan. He could not have escaped his country's ideology of Japanese purity and superiority and the romance of state-supported Shintoism. The irony is that today Japan and the West are both seen by Islamic extremists as prime sources of greed, corruption, and immorality.

I agree with Buruma when he says that distaste for, or even hatred of, the West is not a serious issue, unless it is harnessed to political power and the tactics of

FIGURE 9. Ohno Kazuo prepares to dance while his international students watch. Photograph taken at the exhibition of photographs in homage to Hijikata Tatsumi at the Parko art space in Tokyo one year after Hijikata's death. The photograph suspended in the space is of Hijikata rehearsing with his student and company member Tamano Koichi. Photograph by Nourit Masson Sekine, © 1987. Used by permission of Nourit Masson Sekine.

terrorists.[3] Hijikata's terrorists didn't carry guns; his was a war of ideas and aesthetics, the kind of war that keeps people honestly engaged in soul work and definitions of identity. "Who am I?" is the existential question at the heart of such critical work, and "How shall I live?" Ohno's existential questions are embodied in his dance poetry (his *butoh-fu*) in which his attention goes to matters of birth and death, nature, art, and family.[4]

What one needs to avoid in cultural criticism and cross-cultural art is the spread of bad ideas. In this respect, the elegant friendliness and gentle spirit of Ohno Kazuo's butoh speaks for itself. His mother instilled in him a love of Western literature, art, and music, which contribute in part to the abundance of his work. Ohno's ethnic difference with the West spurred his curiosity and study of Western modern dance in particular, and the music for his dances spanned from Japanese flute to Argentine tango—Frédéric Chopin and Johann Sebastian Bach to Elvis Presley and Pink Floyd. Eventually, he became butoh's first ambassador abroad. Hijikata never left Japan.

The Gym Teacher

Butoh first gained wide attention through the international tours of Ohno Kazuo. Nakajima Natsu, a female performer who was a student of Ohno and Hijikata, also carried butoh from Japan, first through her performances and teaching in Europe, the United States, and Canada. Tanaka Min, a disciple of Hijikata, and the highly original dance company Sankai Juku also gained international recognition in the early days of butoh. All of these artists were tested abroad before they were accepted in Japan. But this is not unusual. Most genuinely new aesthetic movements are not accepted at first. Eventually their international tests make them more tenable on home grounds. Ohno took his dance to twenty-nine countries in his mid-seventies when most men, especially dancers, have long since retired. His poetic dance style gained world attention and admiration.

It might be a mistake to call his work butoh. Certainly he learned from Hijikata, and his dance changed in reference to this, but he also moved beyond Hijikata and into his own style, not bound to the past or even to the term *butoh*. There is no other dancer like Ohno; he carries the entire history of modern dance in his body, from its twentieth-century beginnings into its twenty-first-century developments. His journey embraces butoh and extends dance history in the process. Whatever Ohno touches turns to gold.

He makes audiences cry through his age and vulnerability, and no one asks whether his dance is Japanese. Rather, he is our human representative as a survivor who has developed world-friendly characteristics. Ohno could have become callous and bitter through his nine years as a soldier in World War II, the last two under harsh conditions as a prisoner. Not turning away from what he calls the "messiness of life," he learned how to use difficulty and suffering in his life and art and how to expand his naturally gentle character with rare qualities of compassion, not easy to find in our modern fast-track world.

In Ohno's butoh, as in his presence, one learns how to slow down and pay attention to somatic attunements of feeling. Now that he is a centenarian, he himself lingers, perhaps, in *konpaku*. He sometimes speaks of this place in his workshops and asks students to dance there. As he explains it, *konpaku* is the riverbank "nowhere out there" where the living and the dead come and go in peace. It is a Buddhist word and spiritual concept that startles even the Japanese. But Ohno doesn't startle easily. He has made friends in strange places, even sometimes wallowing with pigs during a ten-year reclusive period of his life before his return to the stage in his signature dance (on the opposite side of pig filth), *La Argentina Sho* (Admiring La Argentina, 1977). The evening-length performance is a tribute to Mercé Antonia, a Spanish dancer known as La Argentina whom he had seen dance fifty years earlier and never forgot. Ohno's dance accomplished a dual purpose, one of emulating the famous Argentine tango dancer, and the other of entwining her character with his, autobiographically. "I am her," his dance says, cycling feminine beauty through masculine warmth and incomparable theatrical flair.

Ohno premiered the solo *La Argentina Sho,* directed by Hijikata, in 1977 and won the Dance Critics' Circle Award for it. As the elder is celebrated in Japan, Ohno is the firstborn of butoh and harbinger of metamorphic dances still influenced by this form. The morphology of Ohno's dances moves across cultures and across gender, as *La Argentina Sho* demonstrates vividly.[5] In this dance, Ohno transforms his body, dancing throughout the center section in a ruffled skirt with the ornate gestures and steps of La Argentina. One might imagine her subtle hip movements silly on Ohno, but they are not, neither are her elegant arms. His close identification with her is most evident, as he embodies the same love of dance and the same sadness and fire that I have seen in movies of La Argentina. When I see Ohno dance for La Argentina, I see her gentle joy. And in "Daily Bread," the last part of this episodic dance when Ohno transforms back into himself, I also see the difference he draws. As himself, he calls upon his masculine angularity and tensile strength. Wearing only black trunks, he appears as lithe and athletic as the gym teacher he once was.

"Daily Bread" is performed in silence. Ohno moves minimally, descending into a squat and turning as he crouches to sit down cross-legged. He gets up again by pushing through one leg, gracefully leaning directly forward. When he comes up, he frames his head with his hands above it and looks out matter-of-factly, still in silence. "The Marriage of Heaven and Earth" follows this as he morphs into the actor, backing up against a grand piano, head thrown back and arms outstretched. This might seem overly melodramatic on someone else, but Ohno catches a mood and fastens us there, drawing the audience in through his open mouth. He doesn't give this power away, but commits to the gesture, his arms with elbows and hands pressed back behind his shoulders. His entire body hyperextends oddly from the shoulders and hangs from their angularity, as from a bent coat hanger.

Soft repetitive motifs in a Chopin prelude play in accompaniment of this version, but I think the music sometimes changes for Ohno's dances over the years. His body holds tension in contrast to the flowing piano music; his knees buckle together, and his feet turn in. His head is thrown back as his mouth opens wide. His whole body gestures into the gestalt, morphing down and to the inside as he heaves through his open mouth. Here Ohno morphs from La Argentina to himself, dancing with death, with sacrifice and fatigue. His open mouth gestures, perhaps toward spiritual nourishment and his mother whom he idolized.

La Argentina Sho depicts the fullness of Ohno's dance, including his studies of *Neue Tanz* with Eguchi Takaya and the influence of Expressionist Harald Kreutzberg, whose mysterious dance inspired him. Certainly we see Ohno's embrace of butoh through Hijikata Tatsumi and not least his study of Spanish dance and tango. The global spirit of his butoh is unmistakable, and he also represents the last glowing embers of expressive modern dance. Dore Hoyer, arguably the last to carry the legacy of Mary Wigman's German Expressionism directly forward, committed suicide on the eve of 1968. Hoyer's art and the profundity of her dance were tied closely to the times immediately preceding and following World War II in Germany. By Hoyer's time, Expressionism was slowly dying out. Or was it merely submerging? Soon it would resurface in the Neoexpressionist *Tanztheater* of Pina Bausch and in the butoh of Ohno Kazuo. Ohno's Expressionism survived the vagaries of war and morphed to a new register through butoh, still moving into the twenty-first century. Ohno's spirit of exploration also broadened Japan's gender-bending dance techniques, central to the transformative aspects of Kabuki.

Ohno's gender reversal in *La Argentina Sho* is part of the aesthetic glue of the work. In his interview at the JADE performance we discussed at the beginning of this chapter, Gunji Masakatsu explained the importance of reversing gender in performance. It accomplishes at least two things. First it allows one to become what one cannot be in real life, and second it intensifies gender in the reversal, as the process of change itself makes the new gender more vivid. The idea of gender transformation is not novel for the Japanese, Gunji says, because in Buddhist thought "all is inevitably transformable."[6]

Looking for a Saint

Darkly through spirit and sinew, Ohno developed his metamorphic dances. These grew from his extensive dance experience, from butoh innovations, and as much from his acquaintance with Western aesthetics as from his Asian background. His dances of heraldic colors combine in transformative patterns across cultures; as such, they anticipate our increasingly global world. And just as Ohno says that the back of the body communicates more than the front, we can't forget what his own back carries—that much of his life was lived under the shadow of militarism and war. His poetry speaks of communion with death; in his workshops, he teaches respect for ancestors and those who have died for us: "Listen" he says, "they are talking to you. . . . Their emotions dwell in you, and then fuse with yours. In this way life is retained, and so are emotions. When I felt the emotions that permeated through me, tears flooded my eyes. The emotions of the dead actually come into contact with mine."[7] His works, like his being, are illuminating, never pious or didactic; yet seeking inner harmony, they bear an indelible spiritual stamp.

It would be easy to fall into romantic rapture about Ohno, and I don't want to make that mistake. I would rather make the mistake in another direction: the case for virtue, not just in terms of its moral meaning, but also its related con-

FIGURE 10. Ohno Kazuo dances "The Marriage of Heaven and Earth" section of *La Argentina Sho* (1977). This section shows Ohno as he becomes himself after morphing through several states and transforming from female to male in his homage to La Argentina. Photograph of the premier performance of *La Argentina Sho* by Ikegami Naoya, © 1977, courtesy of the Ohno Kazuo Archives.

notations of beneficial effort and efficacy, or the ability to act. The question of virtue for Ohno is how to carry a complex autobiography from the back to the front, capaciously. I don't know him well enough on a personal level to make any moral claims on his behalf, but I do know that as a teacher and a dancer he encourages virtue. Audiences and students want to bask in his aura. His workshop words are shaped by a felt knowledge of humanity emanating from his relationship to nature and God, or call this Nature within.

Ohno is not a saint, nor has he pretended to be, but he is a sage; he is also a philosopher and outlandish gender-transformation artist. Having no real peer, not even Hijikata, who was his polar opposite and revered him, he seems to rise out of nothing; yet he is very much a part of his times. In response to suffering, Ohno's works are meditations on sorrow and happiness and how to reach a better life. This is his virtue. Until recently, questions of happiness and its body-mind entanglements remained a philosophical topic. Now we see the sciences grappling with it through matters of consciousness, especially cognitive science and the neurobiological studies of Antonio Damasio and others. Most significantly, we see the investigation of consciousness in the arts per se, especially in butoh. As a butohist, Ohno has had to press deeply inward, reconfiguring his soma and transforming his consciousness in the alchemy of his dance.

I see that he represents aspects of the steadfast life and spiritual center of gravity described by William James in his work *The Varieties of Religious Experience,* quoted at the beginning of the chapter. This book is a classic study of the psychology of religion by an American psychologist and philosopher, first published in 1902, four years before Ohno's birth. In it, James searches his Western mind for order in legitimizing the role of silent mystics (not so much a question in the Eastern mind) and outlines saintly attributes that he feels are not bound by culture or religion, but universal qualities to be cultivated. His outline is still relevant. I read it as a template for virtue, especially in relation to feeling, sense, and emotion, or what we commonly call affective life, which is also the central somatic subject of aesthetics and art:

> (1) A feeling of being in a wider life than that of this world's selfish little interests; and a conviction, not merely intellectual, but as it were sensible, of the existence of an ideal power. . . . (2) A sense of the friendly continuity of the ideal power with our own life, and a willing self-surrender to its control. (3) An immense elation and freedom, as the outlines of the confining selfhood melt down. (4) A shifting of the emotional center toward loving and harmonious affections. . . . Having the practical consequences of (a.) asceticism, (b.) strength of soul, (c.) purity, (d.) charity.[8]

The beauty of James's outline, seen from today's perspective, is that it contains a foundation for virtue, which in the owner could lead to happiness, crumbling barriers of loneliness. Ohno's transformative dances represent such strength of soul, just as soul retrieval is the heartbeat of butoh. Contrary to some butoh, Ohno's works do not dwell on ugliness. "There is enough ugliness in the world," he says. Neither are good and evil juxtaposed in his dances, nor is soul revealed by design. Good and evil, ugliness and beauty are discovered individually as they bind themselves "in a way" to his dances. "In a way" means affectively awakened in the experience of the witness. When I first met Ohno and asked him about the meaning of his dances, he told me he was more interested in what audiences experience in his dances than in his own interpretations.

How about Ohno himself? What inspires him? We know that he considers flowers the most ideal form of existence, that he squeezes tears from stones, and that nature inspires him. It is also clear that religion is important to him. Ohno has lived a quietly religious life; his dances and teachings often draw upon his conversion to Christianity and continuing devotion to Buddhist teachings. Religion is not a sometime thing for Ohno; he lives through the light of Christ as part of his commitment to brotherly love and dances through the compassionate eye of Buddhism. When I visited him in his hundredth year, he was weak but had no serious illness. His bed, where he is often resting, faces his Christian altar, and his Buddhist altar is in the room nearby. He was a young high school gym teacher when he converted to Christianity through the Baptist faith and has not departed from that path. Ohno's religiosity is never preachy or pompous, however; he simply lives his beliefs and provides examples of what James calls "harmonious affections" in his dances.

His son, Yoshito, says that his father really lives through his dances and comes alive whenever anyone asks him to dance. So many of his performances don't have titles; they have been done spontaneously on the asking, under trees, with flowers, in dining rooms, in concentration camps, and in Zen temples. His dances are not physical feats of athleticism, but rather are a result of his self-surrender and strength of soul wherever they take place. Sometimes audiences sit in silence after his dances, not wanting to applaud. I myself have thought silence, full and shining, the best appreciation for Ohno's unfettered ease and virtuosity—his virtue—in dance.

3

History Lessons
Joan Laage in New York (1994)
David Grenke in New York (1998)

Scratch butoh, and you will find the original modern dance movement underneath. We have already observed that butoh founders Ohno Kazuo and Hijikata Tatsumi both studied modern forms, especially as represented in German
Expressionism. Although they departed considerably from this early source of
their dance training, it nevertheless informed their work. If one looks carefully
at the aging photographs of Harald Kreutzberg, the German dancer who inspired
Ohno Kazuo to take up dancing, one will see the inner calm and flow of Ohno
himself as well as his special flare for the dramatic. Ohno didn't study directly
with Kreutzberg, but seeing him dance provided the example he needed.

There is a difference between Ohno and Kreutzberg, however, between butoh and Expressionism. The Expressionist modern dance of the 1920s and 1930s
conceived of space and time solidly in concrete terms. In contrast, butoh condenses and evaporates and is not so clearly defined spatially. Historic modern
dance conveyed time, space, and force through the influential movement theories
of Rudolph von Laban originating in Germany. Images in the mind and heart
found their way out in the spatially dramatic forms of dancers Mary Wigman,
her student Harald Kreutzberg, and American Martha Graham. The gestalt in
space, the form in space, defined modern dance for the eye, and the outer vision
was determined by the inner. In Germany and America, the emerging modern
dancers of the 1920s and 1930s cultivated individualism through externalization
of inner dances as they sought to validate personal experience and contempo-

rary life. Their themes were drawn from around the world as trade and travel advanced cultural sharing and tempered individual conscience.

Joan Laage's *Nothing Lasts but Memory* also moves from the inside out, but it choreographs the body in the metamorphic and spatially ambiguous terms of butoh. Her dance travels back historically to Germany as it comments on World War II, and it bridges between Expressionism and butoh, though not necessarily by design. Laage, who has studied Laban's theories and is certified to teach Laban Movement Analysis, has long been intrigued by early German modern dance and the connection between Ohno and Wigman, she told me, but her art takes another turn. With its hanging motifs, surreal costuming, and verisimilitude of solidity—withholding as much emotion as it supplies—her dance provides a prime example of butoh through the surrealistic prototype.

André Breton defines this model in his famous surrealist manifesto of 1924: Surrealism is "a pure psychic automatism by which it is proposed to express, verbally, in writing, or in any other way, the real function of thought."[1] Martin Esslin writes that although in Germany the impulse behind Dadaism and Expressionism had flagged by the middle 1920s and the whole modern movement was swallowed up in the intellectual quicksands of the Nazi period in the 1930s, the line of development continued unbroken in France.[2] As we have seen, it was to France that Hijikata turned for inspiration beyond his study of Expressionism, especially to the work of Jean Genet, who gave voice to those on the margins of society, and Antonin Artaud, who envisioned a theater of conscience that would reveal the physicality of life.

As it probes limits, butoh from its beginnings in Hijikata until now is often surreal and displays elements of physical theater and the theater of the absurd. But most originally, it presents a physical and subtle poetry of telling images continuously transforming. One doesn't know what might happen next in the exaggerations and stylizations of butoh. Its emotions, however raw, are nevertheless objectified in their dramatic context, and butoh styles may be as tender as they are tough, like the beautifully still faces that appear in Min Tanaka's dances, just as the early Kabuki finally cultivated a refined soft-style *wagoto,* the flip side of its rough-stuff *aragoto,* and was closer to the folk than later styles. Butoh and butoh-influenced dance represent a wide range of expressive possibility, continuing a long line of socially responsive surrealist work.

Although he wouldn't necessarily be classified as butoh, the Japanese theater director Shimizu Shinjin uses butoh's surreal physical techniques in spare dramas for his company Gekidan Kaitaisha (Theater of Deconstruction). Along with Japanese Obsessional Art and European theater of the absurd, Shimizu uses movement to address social conditioning and cruelty. He is critical of what he sees as a trend in Japanese theater to replicate power structures rather than critique them.[3] Testing an audience concerning coercive cultural politics is a valid strategy of the avant-garde, one that can be confused with complicity rather than critique. The line between these is sometimes a thin one, as some of the first feminist responses to the work of Pina Bausch demonstrated. Do her works reinforce violence against women, or do they make it visible? Or is the question of culture and gender one that rests with the individual viewer, and not necessarily with scholars and critics? I think so. The question for me as an audience is one of perception and response. What do I feel in the presence of this work? How do I change? What do I understand or learn? What critics discern will also be based in their own experience, ultimately.

Shimizu combines dancers, actors, and performance artists in his 1996 work *Tokyo Ghetto*. In one scene, a man slaps a woman's back; she then presents her knees to be slapped, and he slaps himself in return. The violence escalates. The actor/dancers seem conditioned to give and receive pain without reason or comment, a way of looking at the violence that we take for granted in society.[4] His *Bye-Bye: The New Primitive* was performed during Prime Minister Junichiro Koizumi's controversial visit in 2001 to the Yasukuni Shrine, a Shinto monument to Japan's war dead that is closely associated with emperor worship and militarism. The visit reminded many Asians, including Japanese, of Japan's refusal to acknowledge its World War II crimes. Many would like to see Japan acknowledge the invasion of Nanjing and the tens of thousands of women, especially Koreans, forced into sexual slavery for Japanese soldiers. Twenty young Koreans chopped off the tips of their little fingers to protest Koizumi's visit to the Yasukuni Shrine. Their act itself seems a direct form of Obsessional Art or an orchestrated event of reality theater. Artaud's call for a theater of cruelty, we should note, was not about being cruel, as is sometimes believed, but rather about bearing witness to cruelty and injustice.

For more recent crimes, one can look toward China's invasion of Tibet, its slaughter of Buddhist monks, its destruction of religious shrines, and its rein of terror that has forced the Dalai Lama into exile in India. With the attack on New York City and Washington, D.C., on September 11, 2001, there is a new awareness of religious intolerance. We witness the Taliban's mass destruction of Buddhist shrines in Afghanistan and its beatings of women who expose even one inch of flesh or of men who don't grow their beards long enough or pray hard enough. Now America in the wake of its invasion of Iraq is forced to look at its policies in terms of torture of political prisoners. Intolerance and beatings of homosexuals mar America's vision of freedom for all, as did the incarceration of Japanese American and Japanese Canadian citizens during World War II in their own homelands. All is not utopia.

Butoh artists challenge a utopian vision of the modern world to focus instead on intolerance and senseless suffering. Much of butoh has been an attempt to rescue the human spirit in the face of war and to seek somatic solutions toward peace through bodily expression. We should not flee from our pain, their works seem to say, but stand in its power. "Remember those who have died for us," says Ohno Kazuo. He is not simply speaking about his own country, but about all the dead who have suffered in war and made sacrifices. His view of ancestry is global. As a butohist in the lineage of Ohno, Laage's view also transcends cultural boundaries. She is an American who has danced in many American venues and in Europe, Japan, and other countries. While living in Korea, she created *Earth Mouth Open,* a dance inspired by the suffering of "Comfort Women," those Korean and Philippine women forced into sexual slavery for Japanese soldiers in World War II. Shortly after the September 11 attacks on New York City, she created *Falling Souls.* The image that drove the piece, she told me, was one she couldn't get out of her mind—her feeling for months—"that so many bodies were reduced to merely particles, they never could land, never could join the earth, so they would be falling eternally. During that whole period, it seemed the world was suspended." As in many works of butoh, Laage's *Nothing Lasts but Memory* grieves the aftermath of war and its human casualties, yet it at the same time accepts suffering in human life. This work reflects her soul-searching study of butoh with her mentor Ohno Kazuo as well as her training and performing under Ashikawa Yoko, the principle protégé of Hijikata. But Laage's dance emanates primarily from her own conscience. I revisit her butoh on World War II:

The Hanging Body
The Body Adorned,
Details of anonymity and perfidious age,
randomly placed white gloves,
the clatter of blocky, black shoes.
Unsteady posture and fading
grimace
A grand annihilation.
nothing lasts
but memory.
Under a pile of dead leaves
and a rope-linked
ladder to the stars,
a white arm reaches upward
out of the pile.
Then, just as we inhale,
the whole figure rolls over on its side,
light and empty as the ashes of Auschwitz
the old woman in the flowered dress rests and drifts.

• • •

In reprise: her drab body transforms
and enters, nearly naked, a blue strip of light,
her back powdered white and marked with
strikes of black. Painted numbers,
imprints, or brands.
The dancer bathed in
silvery stillness,
whip-wraps her body in
Red silk cords
she pulls from the ceiling,
as tracks of blood lace through
her human calligraphy.
In the tragic shadow
there is light,
a search most glaring in the
string of shoes,
bound together
in the dancer's arcs.
And we cry because they are not dancing—
the string of empty shoes
in which were discovered bits of
ribbon,
and notes of those who walked
in the crisp light of a secular morning
too early to their death—and so much silence.

Laage is aware, as she told me in 1994, of a double focus, of not being in "this world" when she dances: "At the same time, I want to face the world as it is."

Her work continues to expand in the twenty-first century. In 2004, she performed five related dances, beginning with a creepy *Black Widow*. Wearing a black dress and hat with lacy tendrils drifting over her face, she stands almost in one place on a leopard-covered box in this dance. *Voicing Blue* is also part of this series. She performs this in a wedding dress with a blue ribbon in her mouth, creating an aura of sadness that confounds the usual expectations of weddings. *Road to Nowhere,* a dance of absurdity and androgyny, comes next, followed by *Umi,* performed in a patchwork kimono. Searching, squatting, and diminishing, Laage's *Infanticity* completes these dances, very young, very old, very butoh.

She danced her works in Poland, the United Kingdom, and France from 2004 through 2007, adding *Salt Sea Grass* (2005) and *Chopin Dances* (2006). The first is transparent in its style and holds amazing stillness, the dancer's movement alternately trickling like drops of water forming through mist and hanging from tenuous threads. In this Laage reflects the style of Hijikata in his more vulnerable moments and that of Ashikawa in her transparency: Laage's dance assembles and disassembles in short waves, appearing and disappearing in stage presence. It's not that she stops performing or falls into a mundane mode; rather, she morphs through *ma,* letting herself go into the mysterious in-between spaces, drawing us with her, passing through.

My favorite is her *Chopin Dances,* first performed in Kraków, Poland, with a grand piano onstage. In this work, I see traces of Mary Wigman's farewell dance in her long, heavy satin dress.[5] Laage wears a similar but shorter one, and she

FIGURE 11. Joan Laage in *Chopin Dances* (2006) first performed in Kraków, Poland, with a grand piano onstage. Photograph by Paweł Gula, © 2006. Used by permission of Paweł Gula.

FIGURE 12. Joan Laage in a dance of the face in *Chopin Dances* (2006). Photograph by Paweł Gula, © 2006. Used by permission of Paweł Gula.

also uses her body like Wigman in spatially tense and sometimes lyrical shapes, fully realized gestalts that Laban would have liked. But then comes butoh: Laage's falling apart in ways small and large, the absurd faces, and the mystery. In her teaching, Wigman spoke about mystery and was drawn to the idea, as were Expressionists like Emile Nolde in the visual arts of her day, but the mystery of the East that butoh embodies is more subtle. It is cultivated in the body through explicit techniques of meditation and modes of art that leave out as much as they show. When I look at my books and films of German Expressionism now, it seems blocky and maybe too dramatically explicit. But I try, even so, to see Expressionism for its originality in its own time and its daring plunge into the human psyche. It holds this in common with butoh. Laage's butoh is more slippery than its Expressionist cousin, and her mystery both reserved and ingenious.

Degenerate Art

All the king's horses and all the king's men
Couldn't put Humpty together again.

David Grenke's dance *Degenerate/Art* refers to this label assigned to modernist art and dance in Adolf Hitler's Germany. I saw his work in January 1998 and revisit it here a decade later as a dance that contains historical residue. Grenke is not a butoh dancer or choreographer, but like Laage he delves into the Expressionist roots of modern dance that underlie butoh. I include his work here as an American twist on German Expressionism. Because of my study with Mary Wigman in 1965 and the branding of her work as degenerate by the Nazi government, I paid special attention to Grenke's dance. Isa Partsch-Bergsohn's research provides one view of the circumstances behind it:

> [Gret] Palucca and Wigman performed and choreographed for the Olympic games in 1936, presenting large group arrangements for the outdoor performance on a newly built outdoor stage. Wigman's version of a death dance (*Totentanz*), however, displeased the Nazis. As soon as the Olympic games were over, the Ministry of Propaganda placed both Wigman and Palucca into the category of "degenerated artists," along with the artists of the Weimar era to whom they were closely related.[6]

Susan Manning's research presents the complications of this view. She sees a break between Wigman and the Weimar artists and questions whether Wigman's work benefited from the Nazis.[7] My view is that lives are complicated and many stories could be told about any of us. We know that Wigman suffered while struggling with a repressive regime and that she continued her work in impossible times. Did the Nazi regime assist or resist her work? Maybe some of both. And did she cooperate with the regime or resist it? Perhaps some of both. When I lived in Germany and studied with Wigman, she was seventy-nine. This was 1965 and twenty years after the end of the war. Her formidable intellect and experience was obvious to me, and I could also see that she had forged her art partly through international acumen, from her reading of Shakespeare to her knowledge of Western and Eastern philosophies, not to mention her extensive knowledge of music and several languages. If I try to understand Wigman simply through her choreography and teaching, I sense mostly the daring and the talent to find an original way forward in dance in the 1920s and 1930s—as butoh artists would also do three decades after this, beginning in the 1960s.

For me, Grenke's dance holds elements of history loosely together in an uncanny way, especially the duet on *Waltzin' Mathilde,* a popular song during World War II. My principal teacher at the Wigman School was a real-life Mathilde who survived the firebombing of Dresden, Frau Mathilde Thiele, an Expressionist dancer and soloist in the companies of Gret Palucca, Mary Wigman, and Dore Hoyer. Thiele was born in 1907, one year after Ohno Kazuo, and she survived well into her nineties. As an elder, she lived not far from me in Western New York. I visited her often and listened to the many stories of her life in dance and war. When she joined Wigman after the war to start the new Wigman School in Berlin after the first one in Dresden had been destroyed, they were near starvation and smoking cigarette butts from the street. Thiele had been living on sugar and suffered a heart attack. She appreciated that Wigman allowed her to teach in her own way and didn't insist on a specific "Wigman technique." The idea that one might find one's own way in dance was part of the early modern dance ethos, one that stuck in the creative ferment of butoh, as Hijikata and Ohno had both experienced the creative permission and experimental style of German Expressionism, as we have seen.

Grenke, who danced in the Paul Taylor Company for many years and now directs his own company, is creating an American theatrical dance that revitalizes the Expressionist beginnings of modern dance in Germany. These took effect later in the United States through Hanya Holm, Alwin Nikolais, and Joan Woodbury, the latter two becoming more abstract through their employment of multimedia technology. Grenke's section "Mathilde" quotes problems of decline and degeneration, and true to Expressionist art, it looks beneath facades. Through Grenke's treatment of the feminine in "Mathilde," I sense a rag-doll death and the crying of a little boy, hugging an afterimage of his mother. The work is not didactic and solves no problems; rather like Expressionist art in general, it copes with darkness rather than denying it. Its American spirit draws a wry and saucy edginess, prying childhood memory from an adult world, first in a section on "Humpty" and then with "Mathilde." Falling down, it seems to say, is tactile and mythic, both an action and an experience, harsh and raw. Here I reconstruct the rhythm, rhyme, and irony of Grenke's "Mathilde" in *Degenerate/Art*.

Degenerate Duet

He sat and he spat
as he tumbled round
entwined with her.

She didn't wake up
but lay there askew.

I want to be hap-
py-he played and he swayed
and he threw himself
upon her corpse.

I'll come a waltzin'
Mathilde with you.

But I can't be hap-
py-he drew and
he threw her

Upon a pull to fall apart.
I'll come a waltzin'
Mathilde with you.

Will she fail or derail,
or does she feel at all
his grabs and hugs.

Till I make you hap-py too.

But, should she rip
from her tug-abouts
and whereabouts,

She'll not be waltzin',
Mathilde *adieu.*

4

Crocodile Time
Furukawa Anzu in San Francisco (1999)

Furukawa Anzu has studied modern dance, ballet, and butoh, as we see through the blend of styles in her solo dance concert *The Crocodile Time*. Her nonliteral characters, or anticharacters, transform continuously and collect emotion through time and interpretation. One cannot name them; they are signs and transparencies.

The Crocodile Time that I saw in San Francisco in 1999 represents forty years in the growth of butoh, but it is very different from Hijikata Tatsumi's butoh beginning in 1959. Like Hijikata, Furukawa is a highly skilled mover, an inventive choreographer, and user of surrealist tactics. Her movement pallet is not frozen in past butoh, however. Her unpredictable movement comes directly from the heat of her personal voice and sparkling style, energetic and highly original. Concerning Furukawa's choreographic orientation, Ephia Gburek, who sometimes danced in her group works, says that "humor played a central role in Furukawa's approach toward butoh; Charlie Chaplin and Fred Astaire were perhaps more influential than the white-faced phantoms of Japan."[1]

Furukawa's performance of *Crocodile* creates furtive characters that glide and flip-flop across the stage. She maneuvers them in a romantically conceived moss-green velvet gown extending into a scaly-metallic crocodile tail. As she flips through stealthy twisting patterns and drags her long tail across the floor with heft and abandon, she paints the lines of the dance over and over again, her tracings etched colorfully in time and repeated many times, each time with slight discrepancies, like her deliberate eyeblinks. She performs a seriously silly solo in the center of the stage to begin, "The Crocodile Eats an Alarm Clock," then develops

FIGURE 13. Furukawa Anzu in *Crocodile Time,* photographed in the environment rather than its theatrical setting. Photograph by Shoichi Okano, © 1999. Used by permission Shoichi Okano and Hiromi Yokoo.

melancholy, disjunctive afterimages. Is she referring to the clock in the crocodile in *Peter Pan*? Or maybe the melting watch of surrealist Salvador Dalí?

She races back and forth from center stage to sit, and sometimes leap, on the handsome French provincial desk in the downstage left corner close to the audience. She crouches on the desk beside a glowing candelabra and gestures with her mouth, waiting, looking out from under heavy lids before lurching forward again. She gets eaten herself, twists and writhes through space, as if being digested (I think). A ghost, that favorite Japanese apparition, enters into her dance, as indicated in Furukawa's notes and the supernatural aura of her movement. She ends the dance hypnotically, losing herself in the soaring tones of *La Traviata* and ecstasy—standing on the desk, a Dada dancer, reaching for the high notes, her whole body vibrating with the passionate vibrato of the soprano. In her notes on *Crocodile Time,* Furukawa explains the soporific time and physical tension mirrored in butoh and her absurd "study of a tick tock crocodile":

> In the time that slipped down from our time, a crocodile is occupied easily in sleep, on the way to eternity; there is no beginning, no middle, and no end. So there will be a dizziness of crocodile handbags. . . . Sometime just stop your breathing, you will get a red face, and taste the crocodile time.

The butoh aesthetic is avowedly dark, but as in Furukawa's ridiculous *Crocodile,* it can also impart absurdity. In my 1999 interview with Kasai Akira, who danced with Hijikata early in the development of butoh, I learned that surrealism in art and theater of the absurd were important motivations for butoh, beginning with

Hijikata, who was particularly inspired by the literary existentialism of Samuel Beckett, an Irishman writing his plays in French. As Kasai puts it: "Hijikata congealed the esoteric absurd in dance movement."[2] Like butoh, the aesthetics of the theater of the absurd is also opaque. Martin Esslin gives an example of Beckett's plays in the latter half of the 1940s:

> Things happen in *Waiting for Godot,* but these happenings do not constitute a plot or story; they are an image of Beckett's intuition that *nothing really ever happens* in man's existence. The whole play is a complex poetic image made up of a complicated pattern of subsidiary images and themes, which are interwoven like the themes of a musical composition.[3]

Esslin finds antecedents for the theater of the absurd in the mimes of antiquity, commedia dell'arte, the French harlequinade, the English music hall, American vaudeville, the Expressionist and surrealist drama of the early twentieth century, the Keystone Kops, Dadaism, the Marx brothers' movies, and Bertolt Brecht's epic theater in its use of music hall knockabout and its preoccupation with the fluidity of the self. Esslin traces relationships through the Dada movement and German Expressionism to early Brecht and surrealism, and he notices how the puzzling irrationality in the procedures of the theater of the absurd closely resembles the Zen koan riddle in its resistance to reason.[4]

I do not suggest that butoh resurrects theater of the absurd, but it does contain historical residue. Butoh, however original, has a kinesthetic memory, imagistic as well as methodological. Its absurdities, riddles, and shape-shifting have a reason. If theater of the absurd often saw the universe as bleak and meaningless, butoh does not. It shares a Zen Buddhist, surrealist, and Jungian belief in the healing potential of the unconscious mind. Darkness in butoh, like the nothingness (or emptiness) of Buddhism, can clear away personal history to allow being (itself) to shine. But butoh is not Buddhist by design; it operates more theatrically.

We see this clearly in the absurd elements of Furukawa's works, especially her incongruous style, playful and bizarre but carrying serious import. *Crocodile* is playfully tense, while her work *Goya,* as we explore in the next essay, is darkly serious. Furukawa's highly visual dances—political, strange, and comic—reach behind surrealism and theater of the absurd to their historical sources in Dada. I see her butoh as culturally eclectic and original as *Dance Dada.* In its improvisatory expressiveness, her dance bears a methodological similarity to surrealism. In its antiart, antiwar sentiments, it renews Dadaism, the passionate cultural movement that began in neutral Zurich, Switzerland, during World War I and reached its high point from about 1916 to 1920. Dada's antiwar activities included poetry, visual art, public gatherings, demonstrations, and publications. This movement influenced later styles of art, including theater of the absurd and surrealism, and it ranged in its expressive modes from social critique to absurd and comic forms.

In Furukawa's conceptual approach, she reminds me most of the important bridge between Dada and surrealism, Marcel Duchamp (1887–1968), a French-born American artist whose work played a major role in the direction of twentieth-century art, also influencing the late modern and postmodern dance. Duchamp helped introduce Cubism and Dada to the United States and was influential in the surrealist movement of the 1920s and 1930s. Through his emphasis on the intellectual aspects of art, his influence extended to 1960s conceptual art and to the late modern work of dancers like Merce Cunningham. Even later, the tendency of postmodern dance in America toward the use of nontechnical everyday movement might well be traced to Duchamp's ready-made art—found objects such as his bicycle wheel turned upside down and mounted on a kitchen stool (1913) and the urinal entitled *Fountain* (1917) that he displayed as sculpture.

Duchamp functioned in between Dada and surrealism with these found objects that became known as "readymades" and his masterpiece called "The Large Glass," or *The Bride Stripped Bare of Her Bachelors, Even* (1915–23)—an abstract bride imprisoned in machinery. If he took inspiration from found objects, the final display was not left to chance or improvisation, and his *Bride* was intricately conceptual and concrete. Furukawa's work is also clearly focused for the eye, and her improvisatory vivacity occurs within tight choreographic structures. It is apparent that her dances, however eccentric, can be repeated and are not simply open fields for experiment. At the same time, her cross-referenced structures, from reptile tails to candelabras, leave room for the improvisatory moment of awareness. Her ricochet of sight and thought, the changing center of eye and mind, like the phased shifts of Duchamp's *Nude Descending a Staircase* (1912), give fresh sense to the time and space of dance. Similar also to Duchamp with his readymades, Furukawa's dances negate art as commerce. I have seen people leave her performances in disgust, or maybe just because they expect a finish.

The time element of her butoh is tactile and endured, using eternally slow time and stillness against wildness and frenzy. The cathartic endings so typical in butoh do not arrive in Furukawa's work; such endings often produce spiritual tranquility at the finish, as in Natsu Nakajima's prophetic transformations—from a grinning insect, to a ghost, to the Buddhist goddess Kannon at the end of her dance *Niwa* (The Garden). Furukawa's dance provides an exception to butoh transformations. Her unfinished, highly detailed dances leave us curious, emotionally spent, and still vibrating.

Furukawa's vision crosses stylistically between two worlds. She turns European and American appropriation of the Far East on its head, incorporating the historic avant-garde of the West in her dance—from the Impressionists to Dada and the surrealists—which reflect Japan's virtue for detail and abstraction that we explored in chapter 1.

5

Goya La Quinto del Sordo

Furukawa Anzu in San Francisco (2000)

Absurdity and the grotesque mark German Expressionism and butoh—as well as Pina Bausch's Neoexpressionist work. Surpassing Expressionism, however, the dark side of butoh is a yin-yang transformer of reality. Butoh helps bridge the shadow self with the ego as it makes the unconscious conscious, risking bedlam and testing the erotic nature of the body. Trusting uneasy bodily states, butoh shadow figures display awkwardness. Shaking and twitching through the body, off-balance, wounded movements often portend an uncanny humor. Butoh aesthetics embody these somatic *qualia* for a reason, as from mud and darkness the lotus rises and from burnt wood a tiny green sprout appears.

In this essay, as in the previous one, I explore the distinctive butoh of Furukawa Anzu with her adopted home in Berlin, Germany. Furukawa extends the cultural backgrounds of butoh, preserving its pagan spirit and Japan's attempt to cross from atomic fallout to new beginnings after World War II. She remains close to the Japanese source of butoh, but her modern dance training is not denied. Nevertheless, the work I describe here is tethered in butoh and Expressionist sources, as a theater of psychophysical motivations where movement proffers the alchemy of human experience.

Furukawa's all-female company Verwandlungsamt, based in Berlin, Germany, performed *Goya La Quinto del Sordo* at Theater Artaud in San Francisco on August 5, 2000. Verwandlungsamt, a German wordplay that means "Transformation Bureau," commutes murky mind matter in bodily cauldrons. Jerky, sliding time-space bodies root in turbulent movement stemming from Furukawa's performances with the butoh spectacle theater *Dairakuda-kan* and the first female butoh group Ariadone. Furukawa slides across cultures as well, reaching back to her training in ballet and the choreographic designs of modern dance.

Goya moves through one day: morning, midday, and evening as a sequential map of World War II. Text from Franz Kafka is woven into this butoh theater piece of the year 2000. In the beginning, it's *Morgen* in Germany and morning in America before the outbreak of the war, the one that affects us still, perhaps the last credible contest of good and evil in war. Other ones came, the no-win ones fought in dense jungles, in desert sandstorms, on oil fields in the name of making the world safe for democracy, and on home grounds against drugs and the terror of unseen enemies. This tellurian war of Adolf Hitler's *uber alles in der welt* is stamped in the innocent imitative salutes of my childhood, as the first five years of my life coincided with the last five years of Hitler's "final solution" for his "Jewish question." I was neither Jewish nor German, but the war consumed the America of my early childhood. I remember clicking my heels together with my friends when I was five and understanding evil in the act. My child self in the aftermath of war remembers newsreels of Hitler's ranting and the cloudy photos of muddy graves.

Furukawa's dance is one of the metaphysical remains of this war, as are early butoh artifacts like Hosoe Eikoh's film *Genbaku to Hesoo* (Atomic Explosion and the Navel) including dance by Hijikata Tatsumi and his wife, Motofuji Akiko, in the 1960s. Later, Hijikata's mature work *Summer Storm,* choreographed in 1973 and produced as a film by Arai Masio in 2003, also addresses war. It is significant to the development of butoh that Hijikata grew up during the war and initiated his art during its aftermath. The firebombing of Tokyo and the atomic destruction of Hiroshima and Nagasaki were unprecedented tragedies. Contemporary butoh teacher and performer Nobuo Harada states the advent of a central butoh aesthetic when he speaks of the "melting of the human body" shaking Japanese identity in the atomic destruction. Melting figures permeate butoh.

Act 1. Morgen (Morning)

Corina Krutti, Yuko Kaseki, Juschka Weigel, and Ephia Gburek join Furukawa in *Goya* with Tomski Binsert as lighting designer. Four performers are strapped to their chairs in permanent sitting positions for most of the dance. Their sitting is labored, however, because the chairs are missing their front legs. The dancers clatter about and strive for balance using their own legs to make up for the lack-leg chairs. In red and blue girlish dresses, they clap insanely and clump together. Red, white, and blue are the patriotic colors of act 1.

The dancers sit in a three-sided box formation strapped to their two-legged chairs; they clap their hands, clatter about, and struggle as if viscerally gagged. A small, graceful white clown in a puff flips over them, one by one, leg over leg in backbends and light landings. Steve Reich, in the music of his *Different Trains,* spins out the clown in our world before the war and sips its dangling legs in sound. Pictures play in awkward arrangements that accrue from the inching and heaving bodies, as dancers fall over in their chairs only to sit up, time and again, their blank faces a canvas for change and grimace. Talking and bouncing above us, a dancer has managed to climb the rope hanging at the front of the stage with her chair clinging to her body. She looks down from her seat; I observe how her elbows and knees downslide the diagonals of her leaning in the chair. The chair dance below travels across the stage in a train-driven trance, reclines and murmurs, gurgling an unknown language. It squeaks and speaks a prelanguage of one-legged stools with crude counting.

What does the dancer high up the rope see, I wonder? A sfumato shadowing of seated figures that dissolve linearity, as Francisco Goya's pictorial art did? Goya (1746–1828), I remember from my visit to the Prado Museum in Madrid, was painting in the baroque era. I also think about my baroque pearls, and that baroque means uneven and imperfect, even rough, despite the many florid products of baroque art. But the baroque had its dark side.

La Quinto del Sordo, for which Furukawa's dance is named, was Goya's country house just outside of Madrid, home to his dark and brooding wall paintings, anticipated in such works as *The Incantation* (ca. 1793). In this tactile gestured painting, Goya shows an Expressionism as dark as any. A group of black witches surrounds a frightened woman who kneels in her chemise before them, while the central figure in yellow is casting a spell in the twilight. One of the witches holds a basket of infants, one torments them, one gestures hideously, and another reads the incantation by candlelight. It is believed that Goya executed this during the period of introversion he underwent following his grave illness of 1793.

The Witches' Sabbath (1821–22), an expanded composition lining the walls of La Quinto del Sordo, develops an expressively dark scene in which the surrounding elements disappear. The external environment gives way to the shapes of a he-goat personifying Satan and a white-hooded witch who is seen from behind. Color is reduced to patterns of black, gray-brown, and muddy white, with intervening sepias. Masses form where female figures are seated. They are crouching, as is often the case in butoh, where humans squatting on their haunches seem to approximate animal life. Horror and the power of the unknown abide in this work. Blobs and broken lines create the elemental mud of the painting, its violent brushstrokes accompanied by delicate smears. The hands, the toes of the bare feet, the lines of the cheeks, and intimations of noses stir in the figures; their turbulence spirals inward toward the central assembly. *Preaching Monk* (ca. 1820), also known as *Women in Prayer,* is likewise dark. Women seated and kneeling appear in the blotchy foreground below the massive monk. His hands cover his mouth, and his eyes barely visible in the thick gloomy tones neverthe-less stare out of his face. The narrative character of this work illustrates some of the mysteries that tormented Goya during his last years.[1]

My mind moves through reflections on Goya to an earlier baroque figure and another evangelical monk, Abraham Sancta Clara (1644–1709), the Augustin-ian monk in the background of philosopher Martin Heidegger's nazification, threading through his childhood in the Swabian village of Messkirch, which was drenched in Sancta Clara's anti-Semitic lore. Heidegger made one feeble attempt to explain his fascist politics when he spoke after the war on Sancta Clara, the hero of his first written work as a young scholar. Sancta Clara was born in Kreen-heinstetten, not far from Heidegger's home in Messkirch. He became a famous writer and important Catholic priest in Germany during the baroque era.[2]

I think how Heidegger's early Catholic fervor led him to the popular Sancta Clara, a prominent root of Jewish hatred in Germany. I wonder why Heidegger, whose fame outgrew even that of Sancta Clara, never expressed remorse over his active participation with the Nazis when he was rector (and führer) of Freiburg University and why he couldn't rid himself of Sancta Clara? Did he consider it suicide to do so? Was he saving face? Was there a face left to save? Was his later resignation as rector apology enough? He might have rescued his philosophy if not his name from the ruins of the war, as Herbert Marcuse requested of him—to no avail. Perhaps he understood that there was no excuse for his fascist affiliations.

Heidegger's philosophy in his middle period (during the midday of Hitler's war) and late period (the evening years after the war) shows a distinct turn away from cultural and technological hegemony. Was his philosophical turn toward gentle cultural entwinements of the "four-fold regions of the world," his world-friendly views on "building, dwelling, and thinking," and his critique of ascen-dant technologies of mass destruction enough to make up for his early belief in fascist goals? Are we to believe that this great mind didn't detect the evil in fascism early on, as Hitler prepared for war?

I flow back to the dance, still in its morning phase, as it moves to Europe *wahrend des krieges* (during the war). Connected to the floor, guttural motions bend bodies and pulse into hands. The dancers have changed to khakis and shirts as they dance over one another's legs, circling their arms and sinking as though in mud, squatting in stupors, moving brusquely, hitting and slapping themselves awake.

Act 2. Mittag (Midday, After the War)

Steve Reich's music of *Different Trains* continues through midday. After the war, the dancers sport casual clothes; black pants will do as they burst into nervy movement. They gesture toward and past us with the assisting force of the self, given up to the dance. They move with weight and desire, sitting and turning at once, no longer in the grip of the demanding ego and charged with initiative. Across the space, our mind can gesture, too, the mind you cannot see.

Act 3. Abend (Evening)

Evening settles in with Gioachino Rossini (1792–1868) and excerpts from his *Il Barbiere di Siviglia*. The music changes places with the dancers. They tense to let go, seething, as their fingers cup their chins in tableaux and their faces gleam with studied features. They keep turning the dance, changing paces with one another. Verwandlungsamt in its torqued loops and arched backs is baroque but not decorative; grounding the dancers' transformations, the energy of the pelvis holds postures at times and then ripples into the limbs. The sensations that arrive through the body of the dance reconstitute the staccato of percussion and guitar. As the work seeks a closure, less ending than suspension, the dancers carry Furukawa like a rigid slab of dried wood. They search for something in the dark with their eyes closed. (What characters we are! I think to myself.) In a duet, dancers cover each other's faces, repeating the search. (Our self-doubts masquerade while our potentials gather dust in the attic.) They lift each other and let go as we keep in touch with our bellies through our breath. A lone figure sits in the twilight reading Kafka in German, whispering tones into disappearance, as I walk away.

> *In the wet chill of evening streets*
> Strewn with purpled leaves,
> Walking clears my mind
> and lets it rest.
> How my diaphragm drops easily
> toward my navel,
> as my belly swells.
>
> The evening covers me
> with its cloak of light,
> That I shall wear,
> Till night doth carry me
> into its sea of sorrow,
> And I am lost.
> And there is nothing to make
> me weep, or praise the day.
> I will walk till
> stillness overcomes me,
> And I am awake.

I am sorry to inform you that Anzu Furukawa passed away early this morning. She had been sleeping for more than 30 hours and stopped breathing in peace with her two lovely children holding her hands. She danced at the Freiborg New Dance Festival only 20 days ago. In my memory, Anzu was and is always a "little girl in an oversized dress." She ran through us in such a hurry. I hope you let her live forever in your hearts.

—Furukawa Chikashi (Anzu's "little boy" brother), October 23, 2001[3]

Epilogue on Dancing *Goya,* by Ephia Gburek

Ephia Gburek, one of the dancers in Furukawa's *Goya,* describes the experience of dancing in this work and her memory of Furukawa's butoh:

> *Goya* was a strict choreography. Clapping of hands, stomping of feet, tossing of chairs through the air were all set precisely in musical time. There was a necessary brusqueness in the gestures, an urgency and true precision. The slightest delay ensured a train wreck, and, in the instance of our last representation, a blackened eye for Anzu as she was struck in the face by flying chair. The rhythm was one of a country mobilizing for war, a severe order accelerating toward destruction.
>
> Bodies strapped to two-legged chairs, passengers on a locomotive, our legs sometimes cooperating and sometimes betraying their wooden partners. Hopping, turning, falling repeatedly, always with the seat attached. Suddenly the bottom falls out of an apparently stable situation, and the accidents accumulate. Now, I would like to pose a question to Anzu about this strange physical hindrance, which certainly created many humorous situations.
>
> Anzu first introduced to me a territory of imagination that is quite influential to my current process: the notion of "living space." Today astrophysicists claim in the "theory of field" that there is no empty space. The emptiness is absolutely full, filled with anticipation for interaction with a particle, with a body. We enter a space and we alter its configuration, both geometrically and qualitatively. Likewise this "living space," the primordial matter, also transforms us. Anzu handed down to me an improvisation that apparently originated with Hijikata Tatsumi and was first interpreted by a very young Koichi Tamano: "the space of elephants approaching." Inside *Goya,* I danced this improvisation solo with the imagery of elephants, slow and heavy, approaching the body from all directions, the body resisting these enormous intruders, a grimacing effort, the fire of a bullfighter, the music of flamenco, the biting jaws of a Kabuki lion. I danced the heated passion of one who cannot be crushed, a continual struggle to hold back the intruders and maintain the space of the body. To dance this improvisation was always exhilarating. Anzu's commentary was to remain cool inside this fire, that too much emotion revealed my youth.
>
> Anzu's daily training for the company members was not typical in the practice of butoh, if there can be a typical butoh practice imagined. We rarely spent

time developing internal image-based improvisations. Anzu's work did not often wander into the slow world of ghosts. Indeed, she sometimes led a ballet barre for our warm-up. And the group focused on games of rhythm and spontaneous composition.

Anzu's concepts that have stayed inside me: The fastest possible movement is vibration. The slow-moving body inflates to the size of a universe. A body of skin, an empty shell dances dryly. The open mouth poses a threat. Everything originates from the center.

6

The Sounding Bell
Denise Fujiwara in Toronto (2000)

> To dance is to journey into the secrets of intuition,
> memory, dreams; to encounter and express the mysteries
> of human nature as they are manifest in the body, before
> words. I believe in the ability of art to move people, to
> change people, to put people in touch with the best part
> of their humanity, to remind people of the complexity of
> their humanity and to cultivate compassion.
> —Denise Fujiwara

Sumida River is a haunting dance created especially for Denise Fujiwara of To-ronto by choreographer Nakajima Natsu of Tokyo, one of the core founders of butoh in close association with Hijikata Tatsumi and Ohno Kazuo. Based on a popular *Noh* drama, *Sumida River* could be called *Butoh-Noh,* so clearly does it articulate the synthesis of classical *Noh* with contemporary butoh. In it we see how boundaries both ethnic and aesthetic are crossed. Fujiwara's performance of this work has been featured in dance festivals in Seattle, Washington, DC, Vancouver, Calgary, and Copenhagen and seen on tour in Ecuador and India. In March 2008, it was the featured performance of the Third International Festival of Dance Anthropology in Kraków, Poland.

From her first butoh choreography, *Niwa* (The Garden, 1982), to *Sumida River* (2000), Nakajima pursued a personal and Japanese vision of intimate space known as *ma,* or "the space between." This is the subjective, transformative inter-val where space fades as entity and reappears through identity. Fujiwara dances a woman's spiritual transfiguration in Nakajima's *Niwa.* The dance transforms through the deliberate use of *ma* in a contractive spatial poetics, condensing mental anguish in floods of gesture that coalesce and dissolve in seconds, like ripples in a pool. Nakajima has given Fujiwara a special vehicle for her talent in this classically inspired dance drama, and rare challenges as well. For in Naka-jima's butoh, the face and psyche live an intensity that vibrates with *ma.*

I saw Nakajima's North American premier of *Niwa* at the Festival of New Dance in Montreal in 1986 and started to write about butoh from that time on. Fourteen years later in November 2000, I saw Fujiwara dance the premier of Nakajima's *Sumida River* at Buddies in Bad Times Theater in Toronto and marveled at the choreographer's extension of the still-evolving post–World War II butoh aesthetic, turned further back toward *Noh* on the verge of a new century.

Fujiwara lends a simple glowing anima to this dance. Her performance, based on the *Noh* story *Sumidagawa* (Sumida River) and a mother's agonizing search for her lost child, brings to life a universal tragedy of separation. The son has been kidnapped and taken away to the north by a merchant who hopes to sell him, evidently a popular profession in the fifteenth century when Motomasa created *Sumidagawa* for *Noh* theater. The boy sickens and dies along the way. But one year later, the local people gather along the banks of the Sumida River in Tokyo where he is buried and perform a ceremonial dance in his memory. At just this moment, the boy's mother, driven to distraction by a prolonged search for her son, arrives at the Sumida River where she asks a boatman to ferry her across. The sorrowful experience of travel has deranged her mind. Once aboard the boat, she asks the boatman about the people gathered on the other shore. He tells her the story of the death of a boy, a stranger, exactly one year ago.

From the story, the woman recognizes the boy as her son. She is taken to the grave and joins in prayers for his salvation. Her son's voice can be heard chanting in the background as she is reunited with his spirit and her madness is transformed into deep, transformative sorrow. The play closes with the merged voices of mother, the onstage chorus, and the ghost of the boy:

> Is it you, my child?
> Is it you, my mother?
> And as she seeks to grasp it by the hand,
> The shape begins to fade away;
> The vision fades and reappears
> And stronger grows her yearning.
> Day breaks in the eastern sky.
> The ghost has vanished;
> What seemed her boy
> Is but a grassy mound
> Lost on the wide, desolate moor.
> Sadness and tender pity fill all hearts,
> Sadness and tender pity fill all hearts!

Nakajima has not attempted to narrate the story but has sought to approach the core of the dance, the *Mai,* in a contemporary way. *Mai* in *Noh* is a sacred internal dance emphasizing upper body and arm movement rather than *Odori,* the more common word for dance. Strictly speaking, a *Noh* play is not acted but danced. *Noh* dance is not of the expansive leaping variety but is a sedate dance of the soul, related to the floor of the stage and expressed through the meditative groundedness of the dancer.

As a guest backstage at a *Noh* performance in Tokyo in June 1990, I observed the all-day preparation for a performance, including a luncheon for the actor-dancers, and how the mind of the main performer is prepared as she is sewn into her costume and enters into a final meditation. A man traditionally plays the central female character, but in this case, a female student of *Noh* performed the main role. After the elaborate costuming ritual, she was led into a small room for preperformance meditation. This was described to me most charmingly as "a room for changing your mind," perhaps the nearest English translation, even as it carries a humorous connotation and makes me think twice about what "a change of mind" can mean. Now when I meditate, I feel the room change along with my mind.

Fujiwara performs in this mind-clearing space that *Noh* prepares. For its Japanese audiences, the *Noh* drama of *Sumidagawa* is so well known that a few simple references—to the place, cherry trees in springtime, the boat, the boatman, and the distraught mother—are sufficient to clue them into what they are seeing. The performer carrying long strips of bamboo signals her anguished state of mind. Contemporary urban planning in Tokyo ensures that the Sumida River still threads its way through the great city as part of a revivified waterway system.[1] In the spring you can enjoy a magnificent boat ride along the river, cherry trees in bloom on both banks near Asakusa.

The river is the main anchor for Nakajima's butoh for Fujiwara. In the beginning, we see her inching along the floor under a large wrinkled cloth that will later open into a rough, earthy costume resembling the angular kimono. Fujiwara could be moving along the river's muddy bank or emerging from its depths. She rises up from her belly slowly in smooth increments until she reaches a crawl. We do not see her yet, just her drag of earth and body, slogging up in a mound from the river. Fujiwara moves at a snail's pace under the cloth. It is intriguing how she manages to slip the material across the floor—gliding bonelessly along without inflection. She moves from the downstage right corner to pass through center stage, rising ever more vertically in space until her head appears and the large cloth eventually drapes her with its weight.

As she lifts her arms, her cover becomes a square costume of neutral beige tinged with muddy brown, blurred and fading up from the bottom edges. This opening image of the dance develops deliberate and painstaking steps, walking and turning smoothly in space, often shifting sideways then receding from the audience. Finally, with her back to us, she walks and then turns, slowly showing her face. Her character materializes through this tensional build, then glides as though on water, and runs in sporadic release. Stopping in the powerful center established from the beginning crawl, the mother of *Sumida River* backs up toward us as her arms extend to the sides, turning her garment into a wide, wrinkled canvas.

This beginning continues to unravel a visual dance, tactile and emotional but distanced through carefully drawn stylization that tests reality. Fujiwara is set apart in bright relief from the deep black background through cleanly honed, softly delineated costumes, designed by the choreographer to integrate with the dance. But the genesis of the dance is not in costume; it wells up in the face as drawn through history and distilled in gesture. The dancer's face is curiously intensified even as it is blanked out in white rice powder makeup. Fujiwara's delicate features are not painted back into the stark white of her face. The lips are pale, not red, and the cheeks are not shaded; the eyes alone are rimed darkly so they will carry their expressiveness across the space. Fujiwara's eyes often blink in rapid succession as they look without seeing, allowing an alternative seeing "in-between" to occur. I am aware of how her half-seeing eyes create a state of limbo, suspending me there with her as she conjures the ghostly state of *Sumidagawa*.

Black fans facing each other perch on her head like a regal hat. She takes one fan off and touches it to the floor, walking it along beside her. In the image of the fan, she has a child by the hand and carefully leads him toward us. Her face is serene at first but changes dramatically over time; opening her mouth in a silent scream, she crumples into the canvas of the painting she has been creating.

In the next episode, Fujiwara lifts herself up and enters a new phase of anguish. She runs holding her ears and our hearts, her canvas cloth now a heavy dress swaying with momentum. As her arms appear from under the heavy costume, they are covered with white gauze in several layers, crisscrossed with heavy black string. And as she sheds more of the canvas, we see a rustic apron covering her chest. She slows as her desperation begins to cool and she discovers four long, thin bamboo strips, lifting them into the dark space overhead. They look electric as she waves them in elegant willowy arcs to catch the light. Do they offer hope? Are they magic? They shimmer and undulate in her hands. Their bending and breathing is a pliant extension of her movement, her dance a pensive architecture of body and bamboo.

As the mother, Fujiwara comes to sit and face the audience. The bamboo strips are spread out on the floor. She picks them up, hits and drops them like a woman in a trance. Her eyes blink and lower so that the audience sees the half-moon rims of her eyelids, darkly traced in the white of her face. Gradually, she makes her way up and enters into an exhausting sequence, her black hair gathered in a long tail—trailing, whipping, and wafting. She creates a ritual with the sticks. She skates on them across the floor, along the river, seeking in vain, and staggering through the voyage of a story more lived than narrated.

Blackness covers the stage, and the mother disappears for a time as haunting howls of a lone wolf fill the darkness. She reappears with a chalky gold countenance and off-white fabric gathered around her in a long skirt. She seems to float. Her arms flow and lead the dance obliquely forward, her feet feeling their way carefully, one after the other, first with the toes pulling the forward foot along,

FIGURE 14. Denise Fujiwara in *Sumida River* (2000).
Photograph by Cylla von Tiedemann, © 2000. Used by
permission of Cylla von Tiedemann.

the back foot never catching up. She leans away from the ventured foot as she glides slowly along. Before this painfully slow line of motion is completed, she begins to pull something from her mouth, as though from the puckered "O" of it her innermost being could unravel. When she stills and gains composure, her thumb and first finger touch in a Buddhist mudra. Serenity and "suchness" settle in through the gesture. Nothingness supersedes occurrence in time, and as in *Noh,* the meditative intention becomes clear. I drift into this subtle atmosphere. Then as the dance returns with a lift of the shoulders, I do also.

The dancer's head is covered with deftly arranged dried weeds that feather to the side, creating a reference to nature, its rawness manicured as often in Japan. Fujiwara maintains a concentrated composure, searching and reaching. In one striking episode, she traces figures in the sky with an imaginary kite. This playful interlude takes us back to the connection with the child as she draws the kite down into her body.

Dreamlike, her hands create pictorial shorthand for the soul in an exchange of gestures. She sends them as light emanating from hand flutters and facial transformations, moving into the darkness beyond her material body. The mother's grimace seeps into anguish; her grinning falls into choking, falls still farther, collapsing her chest. The dance drops to a crouch at times and conjures the lost baby. Fujiwara embodies the dance and the infant as she curls up choking in frenzy, scratching the space. She comes back to herself with emotions that seethe inside, morph, and leave on the breath.

• • •

Part of the interest of the butoh aesthetic is how in a short space of time and restricted space onstage an entire lifetime can be exposed. Space is often measured in extremely slow footfalls that stretch time and lengthen the breath. Time is condensed in concentrated steps and gestures, not thrown forward. *Sumida River* distills an imagistic world tuned to human emotions, but it doesn't focus on the bright ones; rather (like Buddhism), it recognizes the universals of suffering.

Fujiwara recovers her pathfinding walk, a motif that returns with variations. Her head vibrates, and her arms undulate as though borne on water; they flow along, and then finally still. The yoga asana of "I Am" coalesces from the floating visage with hands and palms pressed together. Fujiwara gestures from within a contained and ghostly figure, trembling. Her body weeps and kneels as her hands close to her sides flutter like a bird in the white and blinding light. It seems the dancer's soul in flight, her ordeal lifting to another level; then blackness consumes the stage.

When the light returns, Fujiwara in *Sumidagawa Butoh* is pulling a life-size boat made of white paper stretched over a frame built of sticks (a reference to the Japanese festival of Obon). The boat is light and looks weightless. The dancer and the boat are one as they float in golden light. In the ease and emptiness of the image, butoh is joined with Zen through *Noh*. Fujiwara traces a great circle that has no end. The theatrical device is amazingly simple, meditatively smooth, and single pointed. There is nothing added or subtracted from the circling of the boat and the mother.

Toward the end, Fujiwara wears a simple silk kimono with no ornamentation. Its light tea color is caught in the sandy-gold light. The music and the dance disappear in the circling arc of the boat. Darkness once again covers the stage. And as we wait for a renewal of the dance, a brass hand bell sounds offstage. We wait, and a higher tinkling chimes. Mother and child communicate at the burial mound in the call-and-response of the bells—like a call to meditation in the darkness. When the lights come up, the stage is empty. The dance and dancer have vanished into the sound of the bell. Fujiwara, as performer, enters the lighted stage in silence and takes her bow kneeling in a formal Japanese position with hands touching the floor and the head bowed low in respect.

7

Ancient Dance and Headless
Tamano Hiroko and SU-EN in San Francisco (2002)

Tamano Koichi and Tamano Hiroko formed Harupin-Ha Butoh Company in Berkeley, California, in 1987 when they relocated from Tokyo, Japan. They are well known to international audiences, performing with the esteemed Japanese musician Kitaro on his world tour in 2000. His mentor and butoh's progenitor, Hijikata Tatsumi, anointed Koichi the "bow-legged Nijinsky." Hiroko is a noted butoh teacher and has influenced a generation of dancers, musicians, and creative artists. The Tamanos are deeply influenced by Hijikata's style of butoh, but Hiroko takes liberty as well.

In her solo *Anc-ient,* Hiroko dances a free-form style at the Butoh Festival on August 10, 2002, in San Francisco. Her dance is not as tightly choreographed as Hijikata's were. Rather, it seems improvised within well-defined structures using butoh techniques and stylization stemming from Hijikata's concern to retrieve the Japanese body after World War II.

Hiroko's highly theatrical work is full of what the Japanese call *Ki* (and the Chinese *Chi*) or "life force." She begins this work lying on her back in a typical butoh emergent pattern with her legs and arms exploring a heavenward space with an antigravity technique sometimes called "floating power" in butoh. From the stage floor, the back of her head is facing the audience and almost hidden in a frothy pile of light, crumpled paper. The dance is centered here as the pile surrounds her body and sets off her movement. When she finally finds her feet and stands, we see she is wearing a long, red cloth with an opening for her head. It drapes gracefully over her shoulders and is cinched at the waist with a gold-

FIGURE 15. Tamano Hiroko in *Celebration* (2006). Photograph by
Stephan Funke, © 2006. Used by permission of Stephan Funke.

lined band. This tuniclike, simple costume opens up the sides to allow legs and
arms total freedom of motion, as throughout the dance Hiroko uses her legs and
arms erotically, letting her energy and heat animate the space and the audience.
Such freedom is not the case with all butoh, as we see with SU-EN's work *Headless* on the same concert program.

The rising-and-falling upward climb of arms and legs in the first section of
Anc-ient reminds me of the beginning of Sanki Juku's work *Jomon Sho*. Similarly,
Hiroko creates an organic image of limbs growing gradually from nowhere as
they find their way in space; in the weave of her arms, she weaves time as dura-
tion, taking time. This open-ended concept of time that one can experience in
butoh permeates Japanese aesthetics and shows itself immediately in *Anc-ient*.
Time, we gather from the beginning, will not be cut into beats and measures as in
much Western music and dance, nor will it be measured in clocked periodicity,
time units, and accident, as in Merce Cunningham's works. Time flows transiently
past; it waits and wanders away if it needs to, spreads out, then comes back with
energetic power. This is how I experience time in the dancing of Hiroko.

She dances to the sounds of whales and wind, probes the air with her limbs,
pokes through, and finally surfaces to land on her feet and find the ground. Meanwhile, the effect of her limbs emerging from her torso, as from their burial in a

central container, is nothing short of gorgeous. Perhaps it stems from Hijikata's technique of the discovery of hidden arms? If so, it is not shown as a struggle. In Hiroko, the loveliness of the emergent flow of extremities shows a stylized beauty called *shibui* in Japan, a disciplined and spare grace. But her dance doesn't dwell there; rather, it evolves a variety of feeling states and movement qualities.

Hiroko's dance morphs freely through primal movement, more figurative than literal. Her body squats and swaggers, shrinks and swells. She struts her stuff and peeks out from behind history, revealing natural elements and textures from daily life. Hiroko opens a joyful space well lit with sighs and whispers as she moves from the sounds of whales to the sounds of jazz. Mixing Africa with America in jazz, she lets go. Just let me dance for you, she seems to say. See me seeing you.

As sometimes in butoh endings, a sublime smile, half foolish, half wise, creases her face, disappearing in light and spirit and given to the moment. I like the fragility of these butoh endings. Not insisting or forcing anything overt, they allow the face to bloom. For me they hold the secret faces of time and being, looking at each other through a single mind.

These fragile morphing faces demonstrate Martin Heidegger's view of "the ecstasy of time" in *Being and Time* as past and future meet in the present.[1] Heidegger broke from Western linear perspective to conceive time through "the horizon of being." In his later work *Contributions to Philosophy*, he anthropomorphized time and being in an image of sway, "the inmost sway of being."[2] I wonder how much influence Heidegger's reading of Eastern philosophy had on his philosophy of time? I think of this when I see how butoh brings the sway of being to awareness, how time connects to itself, inseparable from space and infinity.

The best butoh, I am reminded, has what the Japanese call *ma,* and butoh pioneer Nakajima Natsu describes in her teaching as "the ability to contract and expand time and space." I understand this to mean that time and space can change with consciousness, as new physics holds (and Heidegger made central to his philosophy). The manifestation of *ma* is possible then for the performer in concert with the audience. When butoh works, it holds time in its hands. I'm not sure Hiroko does this throughout her dance, but certainly her ending does. Her face centers in the fading light, the chin lifts gently as her eyes take the audience with them, floating on her wry smile in the sway of her dance.

• • •

Whereas Hiroko dances with freedom and celebrates her body, SU-EN uses the tight, brooding end of the butoh spectrum, entering into a dark depressive state in *Headless* (2000). Butoh techniques and processes vary widely as we see through the contrast of SU-EN and Hiroko. SU-EN throws herself toward harm, turning the tables on life. She wears only red shorts and a red square of cloth covering her face and head. Her movement is anything but free as she tumbles across the floor in excess, over and over, to make her mark. Landing in impossibly awkward postures, she performs symbolic acts of self-mutilation and dashes her head against an imaginary wall. She dances for a long time over a bare lightbulb on the floor with an object suspended from above—probably a head on a rope. Finally she moves under it and sits behind a puddle of black slime, smearing it ritually on her shoulders, down her arms and bare breasts. She transitions by removing the red head cover to show the blank expression on her face. Matter-of-factly, she puts on a tight red sheath, becoming less androgynous and more feminine but still drained of emotion.

This is a visceral dance: SU-EN seems to embody masochism, not for itself or for shock, but to trace experiential matters. She shares a compulsive inner world with the audience and reflects chaotic pain. So when she bites herself without emotion at the end, we are not surprised. The gesture grows out of the bleakness of her work, as throughout she glazes over any possible feeling, moving without will, like a woman imprisoned with nothing left of joy or spirit.

Unlike the Asian mind of butoh, SU-EN does not transform in *Headless*. Her images do migrate, but they do so episodically as sections of the dance differentiate. Her dilemma is not spiritually resolved or lifted to a higher plane in the dance. She remains passively present; even her disturbing self-cannibalism is performed out of an unfeeling state. She never really "gets a head" in this work. Maybe the odalisque reclining on the floor with a lifted leg or long pauses in the central tumbling motif provide the audience a meaningful entrance, signaling that uselessness that women who never achieve autonomy can feel when they are being used without love and being eaten up by others. Affectively, aesthetically, this could translate as a nonfeeling or headless state. I am reminded, however, that butoh seeks not interpretation or meaning but a relationship with the audience. If I suspend my penchant to interpret, SU-EN's dance still leaves me with a question: How does she move to what she calls "the other side of love" in her program? Is she trying throughout? What she shows is loveless, but I see remarkable courage in her thrown and painful movement toward the other.

Like Hiroko, SU-EN takes her inspiration from the origins of butoh in Hijikata, having studied with Hijikata's close artistic associate, Yoko Ashikawa, who gave her the name SU-EN (also known as Susanna Akerlund). SU-EN is Swedish and one of the first to adopt Japanese butoh and make it her own. It is apparent the she uses butoh training and imagistic process for her existentially stark presentations—showing rather than telling about "love on the other side."

It is a testament to the range of butoh that Hiroko and SU-EN are seen side by side on the same program. Hiroko shows love in presence, the here and now,

FIGURE 16. SU-EN in "Headless Body and the World," a photo collaboration project with Gunnar Stening, © 2006. Used by permission of Gunnar Stening.

even as she links this to ancient fragments, lending continuity to time. SU-EN makes us grovel with effort as prisoners of time without surcease.

The success of butoh in both cases lies in the audience's response to the dance, not in interpretation but in connectivity. Certainly I would rather connect to the joy of Hiroko than to the pain of SU-EN, but in truth, I connect to both. SU-EN shows the suffering and pain that wisdom traditions would have us acknowledge, but in a dancer's way and often through the darkness that was Hijikata's stamp. In her teaching around the world, she encourages dancers to twist their faces like rubber, to become demons, skeletons, and discarded junkyard metal. And as Hijikata taught, she teaches dancers how to embody chickens, but she takes his preoccupation with chickens a step further. SU-EN's *Chicken Project* in Sweden, in which humans live as chickens and present their work in a five-hour event, gives attention to the problematic situation of the treatment of chickens globally.

Just how then does such butoh work reflect the spiritual body of butoh? Juliette Crump, an American who performed in *The Chicken Project* in the Stockholm state theater understands how SU-EN's butoh, however anguished, relates to the detachment of Buddhism. "Paradoxically, butoh embraces such activist material and intent with a Buddhist detachment," Crump writes in "One Who Hears Their Cries," her study of the Buddhist ethic of compassion in butoh. In *The Chicken Project,* the subject of chickens jammed into cages for life is experienced in the lived time of a five-hour performance. The Buddhist detachment that Crump explains is achieved in the event through ritual repetition and progression "with purity and emptiness" balanced with "distortions, broken body movement, and intense scenarios." As a butoh scholar and *butoh-ka,* Crump is reminded through her performance in SU-EN's *Chicken Project* that "compassion occurs within a fleeting world."[3] Whether intentional in its relation to Buddhism or not, globally sensitive butoh brings awareness to the web of life of which we are all a part.

I asked SU-EN how her work has changed over the years, as she has become one of the leading international exponents of butoh and has a long history with it. She states best the perspective of her present work and the changing borders of art.

> The reality of the butoh body is born from the explosiveness of the secluded space of the studio. Then you throw that intensity out again into the world through per-forming it. I see clearly how working with Scandinavia as a base and also being located in the countryside and not in a big city has changed my work. The forest surrounding our studio provides the drama for daily life inspiration. When you live near nature you see the friction and death as part of daily life and it becomes something natural, even beautiful. The roots of my work are clear and firm there but interacting with society, people and nature also forces change. Borders in the world are changing and so is the border of the human outline, and in the artist.[4]

8

Salt

Ledoh in San Francisco (2002)

There can be serendipity in butoh. This is apparent in the work of Ledoh, the director of the performance community Salt Farm in San Francisco. Ledoh was born into the Ka-Ren community, Burma's largest ethnic minority. Since returning to the United States after a period of intensive study in Japan with butoh adept Katsura Kan, Ledoh has performed widely. In his program notes, he says that his choreography and Salt Farm community are "a response to fundamental tensions between technology and the survival of the organic life force." His says his dance is also a response to timelessness in movement: "When I am fully in the body, I experience a sense of timelessness. . . . When fully standing in the moment, the past and the future are easily accessible. I am a filter allowing energy and experience to pass through me."

I saw his work *Pause* on August 11, 2002, at the San Francisco Butoh Festival. His dance begins subtly with the sounds of rain embedded in electronic music, then sweeps through space in downpours. There are three women and a man who perform with him. The impeccable style of Ledoh's dancing captivates me, but the others are not able to hold the electric charge that animates him. They seem to lack his deeply embodied method. There is a difference for me between butoh and step-oriented modern/postmodern dance. Butoh seethes inside always brewing a golden thread of anima, even when the observable exterior is dark. The dance making of the West moves in steps and passions, thriving either on narrative or formal abstractions. Its products are often playful, as seen in re-

FIGURE 17. Ledoh in rehearsal for *Color Me America,* a culmination of Ledoh's time in the United States seen through the personal lens of a migrant from a Burmese indigenous culture. As an American today, Ledoh seeks to expose the internal contradictions of his own national identity by utilizing butoh. Photograph by Kathryn Balasingam, © 2008. Used by permission of Kathryn Balasingam.

lease dancing and contact improvisation, and sometimes they are emotional, as in *Tanztheater.* Butoh cultivates the spaces in between steps and emotion.

In butoh the dancer supersedes the movement and conveys states of being, never overtly emotional and always on the verge of change. *Butoh-ka* invite the audience to enter states of being with them. To be sure, these states have emotional valences, or at least feeling tones, but as soon as one identifies with a familiar one, it has moved complexly. This is not the same thing as dancing an emotion such as grief or love, and dancers who have trained in Western styles that seek to display emotion have a difficult time with butoh, as do those who have trained in postmodern workmanship. I don't claim that the way toward feeling and emptiness in butoh is superior, just that it is unique among dance forms, as we have discussed extensively; and while some temperaments are more suited to its methods than others, like any, these can be learned. Not everyone will be as natural in butoh as Ledoh, however.

His choreography features the "hanging body" prototype of butoh, juxtaposed with floating releases through the torso and arms. The empty hanging images fill up the body and undulate outward into space without punctuation, while the arms hang down and float at once from the low-bending upper body. Tammy

Ho, Chi Hung, Wanda Kraikit, and Lisa Micheli dance tightly in tandem and with freedom in the arms. Their wavelike torsos, bending and lifting, are typical of butoh. Their truncated hands with fingers tucked away and wrists lifted are motifs of animal force, also seen in butoh from the time of Hijikata. When they waft through the air, these hands could be cobra heads or hoofs when they paw the ground. *Pause* is choreographed for spasms to overtake the body from time to time, rippling through to completion or just shaking with a quiver. The dancers draw upon these intensions but are not yet able to realize them fully.

Ledoh's two solos are proof that butoh can grow and change while still remaining vitally connected to its source. If it goes so far away from its origins and impetus, will it become something else, as stands to reason? Many examples of dance are now being called "butoh" that have no source in the spirit or techniques that motivated the original movement. Kathy Rose performed at the San Francisco Butoh Festival, and her work has no association with butoh that I can see. She certainly shows intensity of form and has flair, but that alone does not make butoh. Her work to me is closer to the technology, light, and costume designs of Loie Fuller. The Orientalism of Ruth St. Denis also comes to mind. Rose included an excerpt called "Oriental Interplay" in her festival contribution. But recalling the Orient is not a formula for butoh. The theatricality of butoh gets under the skin, as Ledoh's dancing does.

His solo is stylistically reminiscent of Sanki Juku, his rice-powdered body almost nude except for a loincloth, and his head shaven. He enters from upstage left, making his way toward us and to the center along the diagonal. This is a classical entrance in butoh and makes use of the space of beginnings, called *Jo* in classical Japanese theater. We see the dancer's white, shorn body only from the back, and his head is hidden, hanging forward and away from our view. His crossed arms knit his torso together in front. As the right hand grips the left shoulder, the left arm wraps around to the right so the hand can grasp the right side low over the hip. This self-embrace and protective enclosure renders his back extremely articulate in its minute undulations. Ever so slowly, we see the white, ghostlike figure making its way toward the center, walking retrograde in slow motion like a film running backward. Once and a while, the clean white shape of the shaven head appears above the shoulders only to recede at the next moment. This is a powerful image of the mobility of the spine and ribs, made more so through the support of a quiet pelvis, relaxed buttocks, and bent-knee legs. Ledoh embodies a state between this world and another that invites meditation. His dance transfixes through its pure and neutral presence.

Gradually he turns to the front, and his face fully given to the moment draws us in. This *butoh-ka* is not trying to express anything, nor is he suppressing either. Rather, he shows the audience a receptive face, not doing anything, just being itself. Out of this quiet, Ledoh adds an absurdist comical touch, raising a hand to the side of his face, his fingers miming a tiny wave—or mysterious bye-bye—migrating from the divine to the ridiculous. Instantaneous transformations brush by as the dance passes through the dancer and the audience on a river of time.

Similarly, Ledoh's last solo is a butoh classic. He covers his chalk body with a white, transparent sheath, like the early modern dance sheaths that stretched around and draped Martha Graham. But his costume invites spiritual transparency and light and does not stretch the emotions. He approaches the audience directly. Evolving simply, he moves in light ripples of form. The dancer's feet stay connected to the earth, and as in butoh *hokotai* (the walking body), his knees are softly bent. From this grounding, his body can float upward, or hang, or undulate side to side; and his head can do a slow, intoxicated bobbing and shimmer. Ledoh pauses momentarily in places that catch us off guard. His face catches a beam of light at the end and fills the stage with *ma*. He sees us out there in the darkness looking back and connecting as his gaze takes in the whole, not landing anywhere in particular, but, like salt, glowing there in perpetuity.

9

Da Vinci

Marie-Gabrielle Rotie in London (2002)

Susanne Linke in Tokyo (1990)

> My dance arises from a desire to reconfigure my identity and
> wrestle with the various encodings that are social, cultural,
> and above all gendered. In dance I can become and become
> and never fossilize. In dance I can be insect, leaf, wind, male,
> baby, star, ancient crone, madwoman, animal. My becoming
> is only limited by my inability to listen to my imagination. In
> dancing I can try to overturn centuries of confusion over my
> "sex." I hope to find wisdom, knowledge, and above all help
> heal the conflicts that endanger our earth.
>
> —Marie-Gabrielle Rotie

"Woman is female to the extent that she feels herself as such," says Simone de Beauvoir in her 1949 publication *The Second Sex*. De Beauvoir does not believe the feminine is an unchanging essence.[1] In contrast to this view is Camille Paglia's *Sexual Personae,* published in 1990, which stresses sexual stereotypes. Is sexual freedom and gender liberation a modern delusion, as she asserts? Has feminism "exceeded its proper mission of seeking political equality for women and ended by rejecting contingency, that is, human limitation by nature or fate," as Paglia also believes?[2]

There is a line in dance history on feminist questions of contingency, stretching from Mary Wigman's work early in the twentieth century to that of Marie-Gabrielle Rotie early in the twenty-first century. Roughly ninety-five years connect this lineage. Wigman's first *Witch Dance* (*Hexentanz*) was performed in 1914; it was a shamanistic dance that dared to be ugly and defied both seductive and domesticated femininity. Rotie's perspective on dance and contingency reflects that of Wigman, and this would include her disciple Dore Hoyer and later

Neoexpressionists Susanne Linke and Pina Bausch. If Rotie reflects their work, she nevertheless doesn't copy them.

Rotie accomplishes an interesting connection between three schools of dance—postmodern minimalism, Neoexpressionism, and butoh—as I show in describing two of her dances in this essay. Linke's more tightly structured work provides a good example of the continuity between original German Expressionism and newer Expressionist forms. I explore these connections by looking at four of her works. Traces of Wigman and Hoyer recur in Rotie and Linke. All of these artists have furthered dance as theater, and they have all been concerned to embody circumstances of feminine contingency in the form of dance. What butoh has added to issues of gender and existential contingency is the metamorphic context in which the dance lives. This is apparent in Rotie's butoh-influenced work. In Linke, we see the Expressionist basis out of which butoh grew, the root of which it ultimately transformed.

On Linke

Susanne Linke studied with Mary Wigman and Dore Hoyer and is regarded as one of the great female figures of the modern German dance theater. Along with Pina Bausch and Reinhild Hoffman, Linke belongs to those acclaimed dancers associated with the Folkwang School of Music and Performing Arts in Essen, whose dance department was established by Kurt Jooss in 1927. She develops a style that combines the Expressionist modern dance tradition in Germany with sensitivity to postmodern deconstructive/minimalist tendencies in contemporary dance, even as deconstruction is an outgrowth of existentialism in its refutation of linear thought and rationalism.[3] Her themes remain true to the brooding nature of early German Expressionism and the existentialist's concerns for the individual. "Who am I?" the basic existential question that Mary Wigman sought to answer through dance,[4] is clearly Linke's as well. I first met Linke at the Wigman School in 1965–66 when we were both students there and performed together in tours of our original works.

Linke's dances speak to the human condition that concerned Continental existentialism in Germany and France, the courage to be oneself, and the responsibility of confronting our inescapable freedoms. Making choices is fundamental to human existence. Not to choose is also a choice, in the existentialist philosophy of Jean-Paul Sartre.[5] De Beauvoir further identified freedom and self-transcendence as concerns for women in her enduring text *The Second Sex*. Linke's dances also grapple with freedom and constraint, especially the limitations of feminine immanence, best explained in the words of de Beauvoir:

What peculiarly signalizes the situation of woman is that she—a free and autonomous being like all human creatures—nevertheless finds herself living in a world where men compel her to assume the status of the Other. They propose to stabilize her as object and to doom her to immanence since her transcendence is to be overshadowed and forever transcended by another ego (conscience), which is essential, and sovereign.[6]

Linke's works explore immanence and contingency, key concepts in existentialist thought. Tenuous and fragile connections develop in her dance—nothing seems certain. Her conditions are not fixed, and her limitations not final, in other words. Thus her dances walk a fine line in their feminism. They expose human contingency from the perspective of woman, the female body and experience; like de Beauvoir's philosophy, Linke's dances challenge fixed conditions and stereotypes. At the same time, they hold emotional ambivalence and "not-knowing." Linke's style is shadowed and fatalistic, admitting the limits of ego and rationality. Her dances materialize the dilemma of feminine immanence; they make it matter, and they also voice an existential contingency that all humans share. In fact this seems their starting point.

Dolor, a solo I saw in Tokyo in 1990, is Linke's homage to Dore Hoyer and a bridge between Hoyer's work and her own. It speaks clearly of human contingency, though it speaks very softly, and its feminine beauty is austere. Linke dances *Dolor* in a long, black dress of plain classic lines, beginning with a slow walk to the center of the stage and down toward the audience, hands open with palms gently exposed, slightly breaking the line at the wrists and elbows so the arms and fingers slope downward. In the droop of the hand, a crucifix might be perceived. The exposed wrist makes this a vulnerable image. There is an aura of futility in it as the arms give up, allowing the wrists and hands to fall limp in a single gesture. The face remains serene.

Linke develops *Dolor* as a meditation on death, relying on composure rather than drama. Performed in half-light, its images are greatly distanced and softened. As she backs away from her original approach toward the audience, her arms open slightly to the side, never extending completely. They fall, barely to lift again and again, always receding—moving back into the distance. When she touches the back curtain, the lights drop suddenly, almost to black.

The rest of the dance builds a drone step pattern reminiscent of the *Dreh Monotonie* (Turning Monotony) developed in works of both Wigman and Hoyer. I saw Hoyer dance her *Dreh Monotonie* in Berlin in 1965. Gathering tension throughout this work, she repeats its patterns until they become frantic. But Linke's dance goes the other direction. It decreases by leaving out one step then another, so the pattern becomes ever more contracted in time and reduced in space, its final steps disappearing into the dark corner. The music ends the dance in a reflection on death with Janet Baker's singing of Mahler's "I Disappeared from This World."

Hoyer took her own life on the eve of 1968. She was considered by Wigman to be her closest heir and was indeed the last ember of the original German Expressionists. *Dolor* is the center section of a longer work, *Affecte* (1987), that Linke based on a dance by Hoyer and dedicated to her. I have written about other sections of this dance elsewhere.[7] With the passing of Wigman and Hoyer, contemporary European artists like Linke and Rotie create new Expressionist forms and lived states of immanence.

Linke's dark work on a score by Iannis Xenakis, *Orient-Occident* (1984), portrays immanence in a state of floating suspense, at the same time executing a tug-of-war between opposing directions. There is tension toward resolution, but no literal scenario and no finality. Her struggles take place as part of the structure of the dance and within herself, moving in visceral paths—like the solving of a life problem, if not satisfactorily solved, at least spiritually risked.

Like many modern dancers, especially Ruth St. Denis, Linke finds in the East a fullness of spirit she seeks in her own dance, she told me in an interview. While acknowledging the West in her dances, she deplores the "intellectual" influence of Merce Cunningham, despite his association with Japanese Zen and the Chinese *I Ching*. She feels close to the "honesty" of Chandralekha and Western female choreographers Isadora Duncan, Pina Bausch, Mary Wigman, and Dore Hoyer. Like these authors of modern dance, Linke is adamantly opposed to sexual and social stereotypes and to what she and de Beauvoir decades before her call the masculine "ego."[8] She might put it differently in today's less bifurcated gender milieu, but her early work makes use of dualisms. *Orient-Occident* shows Linke's strength, determination, and spirit to overcome, danced complexly in dualistic splits of temperament.

Leaving behind the overt tension of *Orient-Occident,* her dance *Flood* turns toward an existential void, making it beautiful. With its air of inevitability, however, this dance is also fatalistic. Indeed the most breathtaking moment is the complete withdrawal of the dance at the end, when the blue silk the dancer has laboriously unraveled as a watery floor for her elegant arabesques and descents is sucked like a fluid fog into the wings, leaving her alone and more aware, having undergone her flood. The final maturing, however, is given as emptiness, not fullness. Linke walks off, as if submitted to (or flooded by) an inner truth given and not asked for. The audience watches the empty stage, still listening to the recording of a rehearsal with Pablo Casals as conductor of *Elegie* by Gabriel Faure.

Linke lets the emptiness speak. She describes her dance in program notes as "that moment of dismay in which all horizons start to disappear." In her note,

I hear the German root of existentialism in Friedrich Nietzsche as he laments the death of God: "Who gave us the sponge to wipe away the whole horizon,"[9] he asks incredulously. Without God as its ordering principle, Nietzsche sees life cast into an "open sea."[10] Similarly, Linke's *Flood* uses the instability of water as a metaphor for existence—tilting, balancing tenuously, and using space to no avail. Like Nietzsche, she seems a wanderer in a watery abyss. What he says in *Joyful Wisdom* could easily describe her dance:

> Whither do we move? Away from all suns? Do we not dash on unceasingly? Backwards, sideways, forwards, in all directions? Is there still an above and below? Do we not stray, as through infinite nothingness? Does not empty space breathe upon us?[11]

In 1980, Linke choreographed her first famous work, *Bath Tubbing,* to Erik Satie's *Gymnopedies* and brought a poetic and chiseled expressive imagery to female solo dance, not seen since the early innovative period of the 1920s and 1930s. The solo dancing of Linke, like that of Hoyer and Wigman, accomplishes an inner plot and communicates through plastique, or a sculpting of the body in space. Time for Linke is conceived emotionally in its lived dimensions or according to the ripening and fading of gestural movement. *Bath Tubbing* lives in gestural time and is an original interpretation of Satie's music, which has served as background for many dances. Linke's shaping of her body within and around the oval, small, and Germanically clean bathtub must certainly be the most original juxtaposition of dance with Satie's music, riding its hypnotically slow rhythm without actually dancing to it. She embodies its containment and then grates against its repose in agitated moments. Throughout, she strokes and caresses the tub, sustaining the repetitive ground bass of the music.

When she suddenly overturns the tub and tips it toward the audience with the inside squarely exposed, she manages to place herself instantaneously inside, remaining motionless for a while in one of the stony shapes that come and go throughout the work. The bathtub frames her, supports her, and presents tasks to be accomplished in a postmodern, mundane sense, real tasks, like polishing with a cloth, and abstract ones, as when she postures against it, using it as a background to enhance a shape, or dunks her head and upper body inside unrealistically. The dance is of reality (she polishes the tub) and unreality (who dances with a bathtub?). Most of all, it is a dance of beauty, of square-shouldered and gently draped elegance, of Grecian goddesses emerging from the bath. But it is beauty subverted or held immanent, turned away from itself in soft, feminine draping of blond beauty stretched, splayed, rolled, and dunked—languid, peacefully reclined, and fearfully imprisoned in cold marble.

On Rotie

Rotie acknowledges a debt to the foundations of butoh laid by Hijikata Tatsumi and Ohno Kazuo. At the same time, she says she is not trying to dance butoh, but to find her own dance. Like many performers who have studied butoh, she is trying to interrogate butoh stereotypes and assumptions. What she has retained of butoh, it seems to me, is its metamorphic context and transformative essence. Her work would not be as interesting without butoh, but neither would it communicate so well without Neoexpressionist developments in *Tanztheater* and the abstract minimalist tendencies of postmodern dance techniques. Rotie holds as much in common with Wigman, Laban, and Linke as she does with Hijikata.

In *Flying Chair for Da Vinci* (2002), she sways to begin with, wearing a simple black dress below the knee and black slippers. She just sways back and forth near the dining room chair that provides the set for her dance.

> *Out of the Sway*
> Comes the running
> Force of it. The repetitive surge
> On short pert angles
> Forward and Back.
>
> This nervy woman is pressed
> Pushed back, head thrown back—
> To stop in a backbend with her
> Arms feeling their way
> Up.

She speaks silently after the soft grating sounds cease, drawing her center away from her voice and hunching through the tiny, pinched vocal accompaniment.

> She piles sticks under the chair.
> Will she light a fire?
> Stay hunched over like a squeaky old woman?
> Why does she sit in the spotlight?
> When will the shape shift in which she remains?

Her hands thaw gestures in percussive streams of cramped gestures. Now she squats on the chair, her dress draping her legs and feet, as she holds the chair back, arching her spine and huddling close for comfort. The crouching dancer, or bird, cranes her neck, reaching behind her waist so that just the witching gesture of her spreading fingers appear.

> Her arms throw hard flings
> With a vengeance. The pulsing fingers reach high

Stretching her whole body up.
She leans back and sadly hunches over again, with no emotion,
As the music plucks and strums a cold remote air.

By now, we begin to know her.
But then, she shrinks to walk in a low squat,
Casting large shadows on the backdrop.
Finally she is seen looking through the slats of the chair
As the stage lights fade to black, and her face becomes bright.

The dancer gone, an image of a large feather and candle projects onto the back-drop. We watch the feather burn in the flame of the candle. Its spine remains, charred, and only partly solid, like mine I fear. We watch the burning in silence, and meditate on the delicate feather.

Then return to the chair in the middle of the stage,
As the dancer commences where she left off,
Somewhere in the middle of *Tanztheater.*
But she is only one, this solo dancer, and not in social conflicts
Or gender snares. Nevertheless, she is anxious and

Tense with
The sitting
The waiting
The bleak lonely dance
The black dress, while meant for pearls, not festive
The repetition that intensifies
The constant tapping of feet
The residual uneasiness.

Strings play in the musical distance, a blurring repetitious sound.
The woman in black pitches herself into liminal time,
Below which she cannot feel,
Where there is only the in-between, and this
A gray *ma,*
Even as a smile breaks her face.

The stage is dark, but still we see a dress on a hook descend from the ceiling. No, it is a coat with puffy pouches on the bottom, a flying coat that billows round when the dancer puts it on.

Especially when she whips and turns through space.
The inflated coat, adds levitation.
But she comes down,
Sits again on the chair, and pulls feathers
From the pouches, throwing them up

And over her, as she stands up on the chair.
They float white and go gently down, down over her
Flying invention.

Brutality

Rotie's *Brutality of Fact* (2004), performed in three squares of light, is a trio she choreographed for herself and two other women. The narrow lights show sleek costumes of bluish green and pure lines of movement in multiple shadings. This dance moves past butoh and Expressionist sources in its abstract minimalism. Francis Bacon's 1944 painting *Three Studies of Figures at the Base of a Crucifixion,* motivated *Brutality.* Bacon based his work on the ancient Greek legend of the Furies, revealing oddly proportioned and mutated avenging goddesses in confined figures, their heads perched on long necks with bare and sightless eyes.

In the beginning, Rotie rises alone in spurts and tremors; then slowly, the squares light the other two caught in their boxes, until the three dance in unison for a time. The aesthetic of the dance inheres in the movement—how the dancers shift together or with differences in their confinement, extending their legs into long arabesques with their hands fastened to the floor, rippling and twining their limbs like leafless branches.

I notice that the dancers stay close to the floor and don't explore the airy space around them. I am drawn to their sudden fits and starts, their scrambles that

FIGURE 18. Marie-Gabrielle Rotie in her work *Brutality of Fact* (2004). Photograph by Marian Alonso, © 2007. Used by permission of Marian Alonso.

settle down. The dance also features a falling motif with a cruel side landing, not cushioned but really let go. Unison movement unravels with shoulders connected to the floor, heads askew in yogic shoulder stands and bridges that arch the pelvis off the floor. This lends strength to the feet and power to the pelvis, and the unison confirms that these strange shapes sewn together in time are not improvised. Rigid slabs of body roll over in the dance and land in Graham-like contractions from back-lying, adding furious tension to the dance. But these are not really Martha Graham contractions. They have more give in the lift of the head from the floor, and they end in oozing relief.

As the three dancers sit on the floor, I ask myself if I find butoh in their situation. Then, in time, it comes. What birds are these, their undulating spines thrown forward from the back push of the hips, heads finally reaching up out of the spinal flow? What animal animates the spastic section with eerie background sounds? What constraint finally lends neutrality to the three figures? What images carry their metamorphosis? What holds them immanent? Men could certainly do this dance, but these are women throwing themselves into the fray with full force and delicacy, and their gender makes a difference. The dance does not underscore gender as such, but as in a lot of contemporary work gender politics rub through in forcefully risked feminine performativity.

The dancer in the center grounds the work toward the end, while on either side, dancers walk, one forward and one back, while the light follows them, pulling into tight squares on the diagonal. I witness the Furies on their final slant, sensitive to sound and change, connected in a trio of blue. Falling down heavily, over and over, they land on their sides in the contracted dirge. One light is left at the end to frame a solo dancer's face. She lies on her back, arching her spine away from the ground, and looks upside down at the audience with the top of her head connected to the floor. Blood or paint drips down on her face from above.

The fact of this dance can be found in the movement, I believe, as if all movements weren't conditionally factual. In a sense they are. Movement is real, but some movement signals more forcefully the nature of what it is in fact. Movement that is placed onstage and funneled through an aesthetic vision points toward itself, but it colors this fact as well. The movement of this dance is difficult to perform and highly manipulated, both technically and in its theatrical properties of music, light, and costume. So is this dance brutally factual, technically or theatrically so? Or does Rotie ask the audience to think about this? I respond to her dance in kind:

> She certainly makes me think about the factual nature of my body, not its goals or desires so much as its physical drives and subliminal punishments—how I live my manifest movement, purely isolated and falling down occasionally, or a lot, and sometimes hurtfully—my body, not as an instrument, but as living limitation in pleasure and pain—the brutal honesty I must face.

. . .

Rotie, who doesn't usually talk about her motivations for dance, told me in an email interview that she was drawn to Bacon's bleak painting of the Furies because it produces a vision of the dark feminine from his perspective. Although she is not attracted to his work generally, this triptych painted at the end of World War II fascinated her with its phallic birdlike creatures and reference to the Furies, touching a savage impulse. *Brutality of Fact* and *Flying Chair* are part of Rotie's work arising from investigations into the dark feminine, gravity, and bird imagery. The bird theme has carried through in a number of her dances. She uses it to question images of transcendence and spirituality. In this she says:

> I was profoundly influenced by the essay "Divine Women" by Luce Irigaray in her book *Sexes and Genealogies.* Hence the flying chair comes down, and the legs at the beginning of *Brutality of Fact* are up like a crucifixion but then curl into the earth, into imaginary boxes of confinement. I have not resolved my thinking on this, but it seems we have an ingrained body/mind pattern that *up* is transcendent/aspiration and *down* is the opposite—pure materiality. I wonder about this philosophically, and I think Irigaray addresses it well.

Rotie explains this best in terms of her experience when dancing: "I experience the rise of the torso, of breastbone to light as a desire for something *other,* but also a calm acceptance of emptiness, of nothing, of silence."

10

The Cosmos in Every Corner

Takenouchi Atsushi in Broellin (2003)

> As I see a tiny flower selflessly, I meet a dance filled with joy.
> The seeds of memory inside me come into bud.
> —Takenouchi Atsushi

Takenouchi Atsushi has been working on his own *Jinen Butoh* (Dance with Nature) since 1986. "Everything is already dancing," he told me in an interview in 2003. "I simply find the dance that is already happening." *Jinen* is a Japanese word that points to our cosmic connections, as Takenouchi's work reflects. He studied what he calls "the spirit of the universe" under Ohno Kazuo and Ohno Yoshito. He leads butoh workshops in Europe and Asia and dances outdoors in various environments, both natural and man-made, in every corner of Japan and in Thailand, Europe, and North and South America. He likes to work in collaboration with other dancers around the globe, as we see in his work with African artist Tebby W. T. Ramasike and his TeBogO (TBO) Dance Ensemble. Takenouchi and Ramasike provide examples of how cultural synthesis works today. One of butoh's most prolific nomads, Takenouchi dances with Ramasike in Afrocentric and butoh environments to promote responsive globalism. He presented his solo performance *Stone* in France at Theatre Golvine in Avignon in July 2005 and has since choreographed several butoh processions through the city of Avignon to rekindle human powers of healing and community. Takenouchi performed and taught at the New York Butoh Festival in 2007, presenting his philosophy of *Jinen* with global awareness.

"Dance is devotion to life," says Takenouchi. He has followed Ohno Kazuo's example of performing in locations that have strong karmic atmospheres, holding past suffering or joy. He has danced extensively in places where masses of

FIGURE 19. Takenouchi Atsushi dances to heal the earth in various locations around the world. Here he dances *Requiem in the Killing Field* in Cambodia. Photograph by Hiroko Komiya, © 2000. Used by permission of Globe JINEN.

people have died, dancing on "the killing fields," he says, the fields of war and of nuclear testing.

I have been particularly drawn to Takenouchi's dances to consecrate the dead and his dances in forest clearings. In the following works, I remember his butoh on the grounds of Schloss Broellin in Germany on the night of August 15, 2003. He choreographed a dance under the trees for about twelve dancers, who smeared their naked bodies with mud and danced beneath the moon. The dance was a part of the EXIT festival featuring butoh and postmodern dance in tandem. Takenouchi's dance remained nameless. I call it *Discourse in Mud* and write about the circumstances surrounding its choreography, also including other dances in the performance, as I observed them in the making. My poetry aims toward the inner work of making and performing butoh in community.

Under the Moon, Discourse in Mud

Logs and fallen umbrellas,
Stones approach and ask
The plants about the bodies flocking there.
You against the wall
In Broellin Castle,
Etching the dim stall
With your dreambody,
How common you are,
Fierce and funny human body,
Dwarfed by the bodies of trees.

Droning faces of pain and power,
Surprise and silence me. Absurd faces
Laughing, still and timeless faces,
Give me back my own.

Body of sound, banging and salty,
Dusty body, language of mud and astonishment,
Polish my breath, and set right my mind.
Dart! And gather me up,
Ever-chilly moon dancer.

Already Dancing

Says the tree:
I shade you
Who fall under:
I, the summer night
And the great spreading ones,
Content to watch over you.

Tell Me

Tell me, you don't suppose
That we just stand here gazing,
That we don't dance our way to the sun,
The dark rings of years advancing
The ping of winter's walk over us.

Atsushi's Haiku

Wa Wa,
Wa, wa, wa Waaa!
Now you stay in the forest
Condition, ah so.

Laura's Haiku

Take your dizziness with you
And how you touch each other
Is important.

Kata's Ma

Send the audience quickly
Through the space in between.
They will make room for your dance.

Fran's Haiku

Inside your belly
This circle is fun, and you are soft.
Enjoy this scream from inside.

On Yuko Kawamoto

Laugh collective unconscious,
As you cart the doctor on the rough
Path of pilgrims waving arms.

On Phenomenology

My face hurts just watching you
Grip and hold the moments
Of movement, dancing
From your experience to mine.

In Pedestrian Sight

The children play in the tree house overhead,
And a flock enters the café.
Delta surveys the scene,
Takes a few pictures and speculates on the
Size of the audience.
I come down from my room
And Gregor gives me a kiss.
Atsushi waits, his face quizzical.

My Obsession with Finding Something Universal

Maybe there is something in the nothing
In between. Is there a way
Of finding center in polycentric
Forms? *Ma* leaping in the gaps?

Alex and Mariko

Alex has been a bit depressed and working through it, bit by bit, with
the thought of separation and the place of ego—not losing it that is—but
connecting it to something larger than himself. Somehow, he mentioned
this to me: "We are already in the ego circle, within the circle, within
the circle, and will be connected to the circle, even if we resist or don't
understand it."

As he reminded Mariko

You ask if I have ever danced naked?
Don't you remember?
I think you were in the theater,
Drenched in the light of the chilly moon,
The night I first whispered your name.

Jinen

Gathers me up.
"Everything is already dancing," says Atsushi.
"Lean on me," says the tree.
"Small stepping ones, my spreading aura
Clings to your dance."

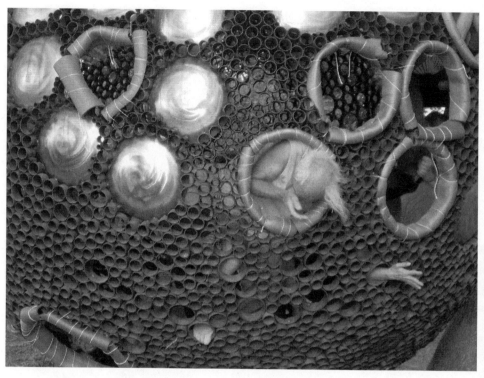

FIGURE 20. Takenouchi Atsushi's choreography in *Broellin* takes place in a clearing under the trees; the muddy and almost-nude dancers crawl into Joachim Manger's large, pockmarked sculpture at the end of the dance, then emerge from the holes of the large ball fully clothed and dancing in fragmented styles to the pounding of drums. Photograph by Sondra Fraleigh, © 2003. Used by permission of Sondra Fraleigh.

11

Risky Plastic

Yoshioka Yumiko at Schloss Broellin (2003)

I love to walk in Broellin
    Early in the morning
The sun rising over
    The castle and the fields.

    To see the dancing pilgrims
        Sail on hope and shaping
    The sun's larger quickness
        Not just the sticky moon's.

        You go over there. OK organize.
            Now you to the middle, try on your
      Long red ballerina skirt,
        And remove your yellow shirt.

        Yael moves Doreena and sends
            Her toward the elbow of the tree.
        Atsushi scurries about, infusing
            The space with catlike power.

"Yoshioka Yumiko is a shaman for our time," says Masayuki Fujikawa, a lighting designer from Tokyo who collaborates with Yoshioka and knows her work well. "She glows with the sparks that scream when sky and earth meet in her empty body. She embodies the present moment, a gift from heaven."

Yoshioka is shown on the cover of this book. She is a dancer, choreographer, and international butoh teacher who was born in Tokyo and has been living in Germany since 1988. She cofounded the art collective TEN PEN CHii in 1995, now residing in Schloss Broellin, a historic castle in Germany about two hours from Berlin. Collaboration is important in her work, and she often choreographs with sculptural installations in her work with Joachim Manger and others. In researching the interactivity between dance and installation art, she breaks from conventional butoh while expanding its shamanic basis and organic alchemy. Her work *Furu-Zoom* (2005) reaches out in still another direction, moving toward *Tanztheater* in collaboration with German Neoexpressionist choreographer Susanne Linke, who is discussed in the ninth essay. Yoshioka has toured her work internationally and along with delta RA'i sponsors EXIT, summer programs in butoh, and contemporary dance at Schloss Broellin, involving well over a hundred choreographers over the years and dancers from around the world.

She belongs to a new generation of dancers who have found a butoh for their own times while moving successfully past cliché. She has a long history with butoh. In the early 1970s and 1980s, she was a member of the first Japanese women's butoh theater, Ariadone. And she performed with Ko Murobushi and Carlotta Ikeda in *Le Dernier Eden* (1987), one of the first butoh performances in Europe. Her dance continues to develop from these roots, but it takes a very individual turn, instantiating typical understandings of nature and then disrupting them. A contemporary shaman, she likes to use technology creatively. We remember that Hijikata Tatsumi was in protest of the ascendancy of technology; now Yoshioka's work engages it. Her problem is how to align technology with butoh's connection to nature. I believe she does this by employing butoh's consistent experimental basis and its morphology. Most conspicuously, her teaching draws upon imagery from nature and the forces of the physical world. She teaches as though there were nothing to learn, just bodily phenomena to be discovered and experienced. There is no right way to do the movement Yoshiko teaches; rather, one learns how to find resonance with the movement by recognizing it in one's own nature.

Yoshioka's butoh is characterized by what she calls "Body Resonance," the dancer's resonance with nature. She explains this in terms of *jibun,* a Japanese word based on two Chinese characters, *ji* (nature) and *bun* (a part). She says these can be read in several ways, as for instance "the self" in terms of "me, mine, and belonging." She used *jibun* to explain human nature during a workshop I took with her in April 2002 in Toronto and again in Chicago in March 2006. We are part of nature, not separate, she emphasized: "Animals, plants, wind, and water live in our body." Nature is a part of "the self"; yet this very self ultimately passes into illusion. The limited world loses its restrictions, and moments of material recognition dissolve toward the universe, moving as through water. Yoshioka urges students to experience their "water bodies" in her classes. She teaches about nature through *jibun* and sees death and illusion as paired with birth. "Everything grows from nature, and we are no exception," she says, talking about taking care of nature, caring for ourselves, and giving back the energy we take from the earth.

I have practiced Body Resonance in several of her dance classes, dropping the weight of my torso down, bending at the hips and knees, and curling my body over:

> Waving my arms in slow motion, I hang my head and squat low, finding pleasure in undulating patterns of nature. Not forcing myself into a shape, I let the motion come easily, hypnotically, as she encourages. Eventually, I am not waving deliberately. Rather I become the wave.

This is "the body that becomes" in butoh, clearing thoughts and emotions, shifting consciousness in the process. The body becoming the wave is not lonely in its journey, even if it is sometimes terrified. The experience is, perhaps, like entering the "unfathomable ocean" that Hijikata said he sensed in front of his body, as he sought to dance. He describes this as "a marvelous spiritual journey"[1] in "Inner Material/Material," a pamphlet he wrote in 1960 for his DANCE EXPERIENCE recital a year after his first butoh experiment, *Kinjiki.* Yoshioka's communal dance work still relates to the material challenges of Hijikata, his poetic articulation from the dancer's point of view of the experiential difference between the dance material, the image or *butoh-fu,* and its final translations in dance.

During her EXIT festivals at Broellin, I marvel at how Yoshioka, Joachim Manger, delta RA'i, and others are able to transform the historic castle, Schloss Broellin, into an imaginative performance space that houses five dance studios. They have, of course, labored for years to realize this and have been fortunate to receive large grants for the transformation of the castle into a space for dance, art installations, and learning. Schloss Broellin is used for workshops and studio performances, but the entire environment is the container and springboard for dance theater and art installations. Every inch of the castle grounds is used, including horse stalls, storage bins, and all manner of sheds and granaries. At night, the grounds are lit so that audiences can see dances under the trees, inside barns and stables, and on winding paths.

Yoshioka invites other artists to teach at Schloss Broellin, so the spaces and performances are shared. She also teaches her Body Resonance work, moving with large circles of students on the wide lawn just outside the dormitory, the dinning hall and café not far away. Yoshioka continues the best of butoh's once bright if sometimes strained ideal of communal living. She updates it at Broellin,

not requiring acolytes to follow her, but providing a welcoming space for experimental work, seminar discussions, and socializing around nightly bonfires.

I have led seminars there, basking in the sun of butoh and contemporary
dance as they resound together in study and performance. Whether in classes
with Yoshioka or watching her communicate her ideas to hundreds of dancers
under the moon at Broellin, I appreciate her flair for theater in community, her
relentless enthusiasm and energy. If men took the first steps in butoh, it seems
more and more that women are carrying through its transformational healing
potentials. Yoshioka stands at the center of an enormous network of goodwill
she is creating, extending from her beginnings in the early days of butoh in Japan to contemporary global alumni, hundreds and hundreds of *butoh-ka* passing
through Broellin. I think it is time to claim the considerable accomplishments
of women in butoh, especially as they have historically been followers and not
leaders, dancers and not choreographers in the development of this art. But not
so any more! Yoshioka is a good case in point. Her shamanic gift is charm, all
the more effective because her ego is out of the way. Most certainly it is absorbed
in her dance. In this she blossoms whole.

i-ki

i-ki: an interactive body dance machine (2003) provides an unexpected example
of Yoshioka's absorptive butoh alchemy. In *i-ki,* she passes through Joachim
Manger's plastic installation, pressing and rolling in the flexible plastic tubes of
his sculptural work for thirty minutes, simulating perhaps the difficult passage
of a body through the cells of a time machine. There is no obvious reference to
nature in this performance; apparently, it will have to be found, even as plastic
finds its elemental formula somewhere in *jibun*.

The atelier during Schloss Broellin's first showing of *i-ki* is packed with dancers and musicians on this hot night of August 13, 2003. Our breathing is quiet,
as though we might all together preserve oxygen for the dancer. A tiny woman,
Yoshioka enters the space of *i-ki* in her baggy white pants with black suspend-
ers and looks over the large, transparent installation with its bed, tubing, and
couch—all made of plastic. She approaches this see-through world tinkling with
soft laughter and tries out the bed. Seeming happy as it inflates around her, she
tumbles akimbo. "Is this bed just right," she seems to be asking?

I enter this place in my body's imagination and sink in sync with her floating
there. I feel how she plants her feet into the pillowed world, using her bones as
spacers. Her butoh creeps up on me from behind; she crawls into the danger of
i-ki, clearing a path through a collapsed bubble, easing past the sticky wrinkles of
it in real time as she conserves her breath. I see her long fingers, the articulation

FIGURE 21. Yoshioka Yumiko in *i-ki: an interactive body dance machine.* She dances inside a plastic installation by Joachim Manger. Photograph by Jens Femerling, © 2003. Used by permission of Jens Femerling.

of her ankles, and how she uses her toes, elbows, and shoulders to sense her way along the closed channel, seeking the final tent of air.

The world she navigates is tunneled and totally fabricated of artificial parts. She moves through its slick, time-lit passages—a slight figure in white with a pocketknife tucked away in case she might suffocate. She lingers here and there in the tubes, feeling her way like a nearsighted person. Of course she cannot speak to us or even gesture outside the dance, but one doesn't wish for more: only the future, when she will emerge. At length, a tenuous freedom expands between us as I sense the dancer's adaptive power in the twisted tubes. I breathe more easily and enjoy the play of emotion crossing her face.

At its heart, the story of *i-ki* is about the sweet tension of order and the cauldron of flow. Yoshioka has to find effective movement in the inflated architecture and make peace with the plastic.

Her final struggle ensues from the shrinking of the tent, and I think how Harry Houdini perfected his theater of escapes. No less does Yoshioka invent herself in the image of plastic escapade. She frees herself from the messy trap, finds a hole, and stands up as a rectangle of plastic inflates around her. Oh, my face hurts just watching her flow though the plastic pores, dancing from her experience to mine. To EXIT means to "go out." So go quickly! Exit the bubble—wet and sweaty as a plastic flower.

12

Fine Bone China

Frances Barbe in London (2004)

Frances Barbe, an Australian dancer living in London, enters the space of her dance *Fine Bone China* (2004) with her white cup lightly clattering in its saucer as she walks. Paintings of colonial women inspire this dance as well as Barbe's own experience of the dualisms of white Australia, she told me in an interview. This dance has obvious historical veneer, but its style is contemporary, notwithstanding the dress and the cup. Constricted clothing and good behavior drive the inner forces of the dancer as she metamorphoses through several states.

Barbe has performed this work in various environments, including the Royal Opera House in London and the Initiation International Festival in Singapore. There she asked for leaves to substitute for the floor of red dirt that was originally the ground for the dance, and they gave her tropical green fanning leaves. I have seen intriguing photographs of this version, with Barbe hiding behind the large leaves as they spread like hands around her slight, white figure—as translucent as the cup she carries. In Brockport, New York, where I saw the dance on May 26, 2007, she again used a floor of leaves, but this time they were light and crackling, strewn in a contained area with an overturned chair placed in the pile.

Though not short on abstraction, this dance might well be a novel. It seems to be a story or character sketch about a woman with a first name. She is familiar, somebody's friend and mother, somebody's wife in the Australian bush perhaps. So I'll call her Frances. She is dressed in Edwardian style, her sand-white, high-neck, long-sleeve blouse is tucked neatly into a long skirt of the same neutral color. The skirt has a bustle and drapes to the ground. Frances moves carefully with her fragile cup, placing it on her head when she enters the floor of leaves, her face sweetly feminine. Stopping, she looks into the cup, stirs the tea with her finger, and sucks it with a pucker. Then she begins to pace lightly and skitter about, halting to find an unlikely balance of the cup on her bustle, turning her back into a table.

What is this woman up to, I ask myself? Why the dress, the cup, and the earth floor? Why not a drawing room? Would a room of any kind be too literal an enclosure for the dance, or the story? Either way, her work is staged for the imaginative mind to wander and ripe for the dramaturge. My mind goes to women in the environment, to women of white Australia, and more widely to women who have been part of colonial settlements wherever they face harsh elements of nature and struggle to forge culture. I think especially of how colonial women import their prior experience in disjunction with new surroundings. In the case of Frances, we see how nature rubs against her fussy dress, porcelain pale skin, and fine china. Tea in all its finery and ritual was imported to Australia, its vast spaces and hot weather more suited in many parts to raising sheep or making wine than to straitlaced polity. Teatime represents culture in the extended empires of the West, their abuses of aboriginal cultures not far behind the ritual.

The drama of Frances is cast into what psychiatry would call "liminal space," named for the somatically resonant space crossing the borders of neurons. The limbic system is the emotional brain, whose affective energy can connect emotional, physical, and spiritual phenomena. The energy of *ma* in Zen is also liminal, realized in the suspended space of meditation when the thinking mind recedes (and hopefully subsides). *Ma* in butoh can be empty and move between things. It could be the space-time gap where one thing passes toward another, even the distance between waking and sleeping, one culture and another, or the interpretive space in the mind between a china cup and dirt, marking not one or the other but the distance itself.

"Have a cup of tea." The dancer offers the audience the cup quietly and in various gestural bodies. The audience responds sometimes, Barbe tells me in our interview, and sometimes not. In any case, the gestures remain a source of improvisation. In one striking episode, Frances stops suddenly in her tracks and falls to her knees in three broken movements, guided perhaps by the image of the cup. Though it never falls and breaks, it could! When she regains herself, Frances runs until a shriek brings her to a halt. Is she crazy—or just frightened?

Her character moves on, voicing, sometimes punctuating a dry, "tsk tsk tsk," the sound of gossiping women, easily turned toward scolding. "Now listen," her body seems to say, "this is what happens when you don't behave." Her sounds of disapproval are contained inside a somewhat inert face. "Tsk, tsk" or "d, d" is articulated percussively from the roof of the mouth and tongue staccato. Frances, like women of this ilk, doesn't want to show the blunt, dark side of her "no, no," politeness. Unable to maintain herself, and glazed over, she suddenly breaks, drops to her knees, and then to her butt; she walks in unpredictable lines, falls again, then finally falls and flips, landing on her back. These surprises come suddenly as scattered movements, dropping among the leaves. The cup lands finally on her belly—still in its saucer.

The dance matures as a wrestling match with the cup and saucer, as I see Frances turn over on her front with the cup pined under her belly. I'm also aware of the piano and the light, improvisational style of the music made for the dance by Keith Johnson, its single tones and clusters interacting with the dance. "Auch, tiss, tiss, tiss"—the dancer sounds her gestures and spreads an occasional twisted smile as part of the lightly woven tale. This carefully painted portrait dismantles Frances the virgin, the bride and crone, even as we might prefer a liberation of the woman beneath the starch. She laughs a little, but not too much, or she might break, of course. Among porcelain products, we have the choice of basic porcelain, china, and bone china. Well-appointed homes stock fine bone china. Indeed, one of the longest-standing customs for a bride and groom is registering for a china pattern.

The cup signals the carrying and balancing of china through dirt, which serves an unlikely fusion for a well-bred lady with shaky circumstances. She finds a surface for her feet and finally stands on the chair, smoothes her dress in brush strokes, and extends a leg to the back in a pedestal ballerina pose, somewhat reluctantly placed, but without a bobble. Bone china is a type of ceramic body— much like that of the ballerina. It was first developed in Britain when English manufacturers wanted to produce porcelain of the quality found in Chinese imports, which had been enjoyed in high society since the sixteenth century when Chinese objects made of jade and semiprecious stones were already in demand among European collectors. By the end of the seventeenth century in Holland and England, collecting centered on Chinese porcelain and ceramics. However, it was the international exhibitions of the later nineteenth century that were to do most to foster a positive understanding of China and Japan alike.[1] Ballet, too, developed in the wealthy courts of Europe during the sixteenth century—and furthers elite traditions still, although we know there are many exceptions to this in its aristocratic history.

The high whiteness, translucency, and strength of china make it a ready comparison with the colonial woman. Calcined ox bone or bone ash is a major ingredient—I found out when I looked up "bone china." And not surprisingly, in alchemy, the thermal process of calcination is one of the vital processes required for the transformation of a substance. And so, too, Frances heats up as she buttons her lip and sews it up firmly. She takes off her blouse, and finally the skirt, by worming out of it, leaving the corset and laces exposed as well as the lift of her breast. When the petticoat comes off and she is left in her bloomers, she laughs in a mad, tinkling way while the music adds layers of electronic sounds. She places her dance back on the floor in another register, now half dressed, morphing from the lady to the woman. She stomps and stamps stubbornly and then falls on her butt, crawling to the cup that she left on the floor, picking it up in her teeth.

The leaves crinkle as Frances ambulates close to the floor in squats. She rises, pointing a finger, and turns in spirals with her finger pointing up. Reclining on her back, she points still, tensely arching her spine up from the floor, her body left not in repose but in a pointing gesture. What is she pointing out, I wonder, what does she want me to look at? Maybe the vast sky of Australia, overarching the tiny taut figure. This straight, soft woman—who with contained strength suffers the weather, the spiders, and boredom—skims and clucks, submerging her bone-clean world in a bed of dry leaves.

FIGURE 22. Frances Barbe in *Fine Bone China* (2004). Here she dances in 2006 at the Initiation International Festival in Singapore, where broad tropical leaves replaced the original red-dirt floor for the dance. Photograph courtesy of Frances Barbe and the Initiation International Festival, © 2006. Used by permission of Frances Barbe.

Frances Barbe is a performer who comes from the tradition of butoh, but she moves past it. The divine neutrality that often serves butoh is subtext for her, lending her work an inner core amid dramatic antics. She makes herself as clear as glass, fine in bone, for this sheer and entertaining dance. She remains staid, even as she stomps. However confined, she draws upon the world of the transformative feminine; quite so, but squatting also, looking out beyond the horizon and diminishing herself against an environment at odds with her. In my mind, I pick her up off the floor and set her upright with the white cup in her hand, growing her a fleshy color from the pit of her arm to the lip of her china.

Shrill Songs for a Visitor

Just step back a few paces, and you can see the whole room, your husband sleeping peacefully under the white-draped, mosquito-netted bed with the mint cover. Look out onto the veranda to your writing table and on across the swimming pool with its false waterfall, out to the true waters of the Pacific at dawn. The sky is a rolling gray this early at Palm Grove in Queensland, Australia, and I've heard the first birds of morning in the dense palms with their overlapping fringes and peeling, ring-marked trunks. The stray sounds sing shrill songs, light and lacey ones repeating, then lose themselves to new songs and sudden squawks. Is this bird in distress or merely expressing its nervous nature? The blats and beeps light up the onomatopoeia of the morning.

In warm climates, I gain perspective—the world at my feet and overhead. Yes, I can hear and see more as my shoulders settle down on my rib cage, these same shoulders that hunch with cold back home in western New York off Lake Ontario. My dreams are affected here. Secret, my cat at home, came to me last night, along with my daughter at a very young age. There was some attempt to catch the cat, as I remember vaguely. It got away, and my daughter and I had to fly after it out into space. This cat could go to high places, and we had no chairs to reach it, so we invented our flying selves for the job. When we got Secret, she had a strangely dead face, somewhere between a fish and spotted trout. She also seemed like a flat, inert cobra. She is a gray-and-black tabby cat, so the head fit the color scheme. The look of her was daunting; the living dynamic had disappeared and shriveled into paper. I said to my daughter Christina, "This cat is a strange flat snake." I don't remember whether I warned her against retrieving the cat or just pointed out what I perceived as being out of whack.

The dream continued with a small boy I had in my charge and was trying to protect or warn against the flat, secret cat. Why this animal came to me in this way—not really disgusting or even very fearful—intrigues me. I settle in to see how:

The morning dove
　　　companions my sitting here.
Its rhythm enters my breath,
　　　The recurring river that moves me now.
How the gray bird flies
　　　to the palm, to the pillar,
As we watch each other, and
The man in the red shirt
　　　sits to untie his shoes
At the pool,
　　　to remove the red,
And swim the day into being.

　　　I heard the curlew cry like a baby last night,
　　　　　and the Green Tree Frog, *bella*,
　　　　　the lizard who clicks and chirps, "tsk tsk, tlot,"
　　　　　keeping the mosquitoes under control,
　　　　　here where the giant Melaleuca trees stand,
　　　　　and watch us sleep.

The mystery of the malingering unknown punctures so much of what I guard-edly call my "self," braving something in its place, someone discovered along the way. In travel I dream, while my heart and domicile roam. In dream I swim to destinations exceeding my vision, while a hazy future connects my imagina-tion to the water, flooding into the "yes" of the unknown. To my left I see what I have been warned about—the dead, they are entombed in silence and floating curiously upright, like people sitting in pews. I am not to swim in that direc-tion, though the scene in itself is quite neutral. Why is the way so fraught with obstacles, I wonder? And will I make it if I swim to the right? I suppose I dream this as the future, my life a watery horizon with no end in sight, something like the world I see at dawn just before opening my eyes.

The world began in dreaming
Through the original people
Lost and found generations linked through song lines
That map Australia's vastness from one geography to the next,
Through spirits that tie them to the land and storytelling,
To art and a difficult colonial history.
In the *Dreamtime*, Aborigines rose from below the earth
Forming bodies of water, the sky, and all of the animals.
In death, the ancestors metamorphosed into nature
In rivers and rock formations, in trees rising from the land.
They remain there still, spiritually alive.

13

Moving MA

Endo Tadashi in London (2005)

> Art impulses are more primitive or more innate than those of morality. The appeal of art goes more directly into human nature. Morality is regulative, art is creative. One is an imposition from without, the other is an irrepressible expression from within. Zen finds its inevitable association with art but not with morality.
>
> —Suzuki Daisetz, *Zen and Japanese Culture*

Suzuki Daisetz in *Zen and Japanese Culture* says that Zen prizes art over the regulations of morality. I don't think this means that Zen is amoral, just that it looks to art for inspiration and not toward ethics. Of Zen's deep connection to art, Suzuki goes further. He says it has been a favorite "trick" of Japanese artists to show beauty in the form of imperfection or ugliness. And when this beauty includes a sense of antiquity or uncouth gestures, "we have then a glimpse of *sabi*, so prized by Japanese connoisseurs."[1] We sometimes see this aesthetic in butoh. At the foundation of his work, Hijikata Tatsumi evoked the antiquated meaning of the Japanese term *butoh*, "ancient dance," and his method included uncouth or socially unacceptable gestures, revealing the beauty of these.

In the case of Endo Tadashi's dance *MA*, we see that antiquity runs through it, as it certainly does in his central use of an earthen urn. The dance also plays with gestures that are antisocial and raw, but this is just part of its story. *MA* is a work of flowing consciousness—and of poverty—prized as *wabi* in Japan. *Wabi* simplicity in the tendency to value the creatively odd and human moment over the norms of institutionalized morality pervades butoh and Zen. I witness these in Endo's *wabi*. His concern for antiquity, Zen sparseness, and austerity link his work to the *wabi-sabi* aesthetic of Japan, in which the meld of *wabi* and *sabi* creates something new in appreciation of age. This aesthetic is recognized, for

FIGURE 23. Endo Tadashi dances MA (2005) in London. Photograph by Sabine Lippert, © 2005. Used by permission of Sabine Lippert.

instance, in worn or chipped objects or the simple beauty of a single wildflower blooming against a weathered barn. It can also be cultivated in dance. Does Endo perhaps make a conscious choice to go in this direction, or is the plainness, once set in motion, second nature to him?

Appearing in a stream of light at the beginning of *MA,* Endo sits unmoved in the middle of the stage for a long time. He is covered with a red drape and sits next to a tall, burnished vessel that looks like an antique ceramic. We watch his face, contained and serene but with a hint of sadness playing at the corners of his eyes. Slowly his face and form begin to move; gradually one bare foot finds the ceramic. In the background, the sound of water washes the scene as Endo's face morphs between states, but not in a dramatic way. Then suddenly his cheeks puff. He begins gestures of listening, and his finger points unexpectedly. The pottery helps ground his movement and is never far from his dance. Endo shows us the art of "presence" in dance; "nothing special, everything special," as presence might be explained the Zen way.

The concentrated light in the center of the stage begins to spread. Without strain, Endo comes to standing and then faces us. As a dancer, he doesn't project anything except breath and waiting. His standing seems more an occurrence than an act of will: He stands up simply, unfolding and glowing, as his arms reach down and extend behind his back with profound tension. His face lifts, and his body suddenly shrinks. Then small steps to the front edge him closer to us. The drape drops away through ensuing gestures as he dances in white, billowy skirt-pants, moving into darkness with momentary fluidity as the lights fade out.

When they come up, we see him standing in a small square of golden light falling from overhead. He lifts the urn high and pours out a steady stream of water. It falls like silken light over the lip of the pot, splashing and pooling on the floor as the simple stream is spiritually cast.

How traditionally Japanese is with this pure focus and single stroke, like the one-pointed awareness cultivated in Zen meditation or the magnifying of a small detail worked into an antique kimono. Endo's dance reminds me of the black one I saw yesterday, its embroidery of a tiny boat engulfed by a cloudy landscape set adrift in a vast sea of fabric. There is something lonely, clear, and strong in the stream as it trickles and splashes in the light, and when the urn is empty, the lights go out.

Presently, the dancer enters the stage from the side, crawling and almost nude, except for the string around his hips and cloth through his crotch. He crawls along a shaft of light, his hands quadrupedal as the fingers curl and paw. He lumbers softly, scratches, and slaps the floor in minimal strokes until he appears reflected in the pool of water on the stage. The water mirrors his golden body as he looks into the pool then spins around in the air, jumping from all fours, landing, flopping into the water, banging and preparing to go again, his skin agleam. The dancer spins until he tires, each airborne turn tinged with metaphysics. Finally he reclines on his side, his back to the audience and floating in *ma,* as sound returns in the guise of the West with the smooth, vocalized pace of cello music by Johann Sebastian Bach, arranged by Bobby McFerrin for Yo-Yo Ma.

The music moves, but there is stillness gathering in the scene as the dancer curls up on his side and his back continues to speak to us. We watch his breath sink through his back to a deep calm as we listen to the quiet music. Drawing us into *ma,* the dancer's back coalesces the length between his body and ours. My eyes look closely, and I blanch when the dancer's spine recedes away from the surface and toward the center of his body. In time the metamorphosis reverses: The long erector muscles, like ropes alongside the vertebrae, expand and curve the back into a rounded sculpture. Some later say they see the dancer become a stone.

In retrospect, I see how Endo moves past physical form, dancing sparely. Molecule by molecule, he travels between the unmanifest object and what can be seen. In the dimension of time, Endo himself remains on the verge of form and lands in *ma,* the Japanese word for the space-time phenomenon in-between things, as this may also include the mysterious spaces of the mind and not just the objects we commonly call "things." In Zen Buddhism, *ma* points toward emptiness—not form but absence, conjuring the meditative gap between forms and happenings as well as people. If movement is the essence of dance, then Endo seeks the opposite. Rather, he empties out and waits; so in the empty field between the dance and the witness, the mind can move.

The lights fade to black, and when they return, Endo comes to the center to bow, creating a spiritual container for his dance.

But it isn't over yet. His bow morphs unpredictably toward the generous unfinished endings of butoh. A smile begins to spread on Endo's face as he dances to a French cabaret song, "Please Don't Leave Me," by Nina Simone. Exaggerating his expressions mischievously to coincide with the overwrought passion of the music, he parodies and pokes fun, relieving the tension of his solo, and we know it's over when the spell of *ma* is broken.

· · ·

MA is Endo's work from 1991, his first butoh after meeting Ohno Kazuo in 1989 and later collaborating with him. I saw Endo perform this work at the Daiwa International Butoh Festival at Jackson's Lane Theatre in London on October 1, 2005. Endo provides an interesting example of the global alchemy of butoh. Although he is Japanese, he was born in Beijing, China, and now lives in Germany. Not moving along a fixed path, he navigates the boundaries between Eastern and Western dance and theater. From 1973 to 1976, he studied with theater director Max Reinhardt. Now he directs his MAMU School in Göttingen, Germany, and is the artistic director of the Butoh Festival MAMU, Butoh & Jazz, which he started in 1992. Butoh and jazz might seem an unlikely combination, but Endo makes it work. Concerning his teaching of butoh in this context, he is not an elitist working only with high-level dancers, but he likes to include people with disabilities in his classes.

Like many others in butoh, Endo globalizes, crossing over cultural lines and blurring performance distinctions and passing between aesthetic genres; indeed, this is part of his *ma*. Through my glimpse into Endo's work and others, it might be clear by now that I think butoh presents a positive form of globalization in its border crossings, whether these be ethnic and aesthetic or based on social norms and gender. Thus we might pause to consider the social and moral arguments against globalization, namely that it lacks a face or encourages greedy scrambles for power, even that the shape of global leadership is changing, leveling the influence of America, Europe, and Japan while moving to include China, India, Brazil, and others. There is also the related question of whether there is too much freedom in the global movement of markets and ideas, including artistic and intellectual property. Who will own anything in the end? Will there be an erosion of markers of identity? More to our subject: Are these concerns for artists and, specifically, for butohists?

Yes, I believe they are. I agree with Suzuki at the beginning of this essay that art isn't bound up in regulations of morality and that creativity is the core value of art, but I would also say that art is the place where ethics and aesthetics meet, that the good and the beautiful are not exclusive, as Plato originally taught. Art-works are original works, not generalizations. They proffer individual faces in unique works that connect humans to their shared humanity. Ethics lies in the attempt to find these faces and to inhabit them, as butohists try to do. Their global quest is to find the transformational face of everyone in their own. I seize the beauty and goodness of butoh in this attempt. The arts can teach us about ethics and morality in a way that other endeavors cannot. They teach from the body and the heart, the visionary eye and hand. And they can turn selfishly inward toward the contracted ego or teach about shared power and interdependence.

14

Weak with Spirit

Gurus in Yokohama, Tokyo, and India (2006)

> Our bodily wounds eventually close and heal, but there are always hidden wounds, those of the heart, and if you know how to accept and endure them, you will discover the pain and joy which is impossible to express with words. You will reach the realm of poetry which only the body can express.
> —Ohno Kazuo

It is July 2, 2006, and my sixty-seventh birthday. I have just returned from Japan where I spent June 14 in Yokohama with legendary father-and-son butoh dancers, Ohno Kazuo-sensei and his son Ohno Yoshito. (In Japan, the surname comes first, and *sensei* means "teacher.") Sensei will be one hundred years old in October, and Yoshito at sixty-eight is one year older than I. So he is my big brother, he says. I had another idea and asked him to marry me. He promised! On the next day, I visited my Japanese mother and mentor, Matsumoto Chiyoe-sensei in Tokyo. These visits sent my thoughts toward the alchemy of friendship, its wider meaning in the world, and my earlier experiences in India.

Thus the following letters flow from the present to the past, threading from Yokohama through Tokyo and back to India, somewhat like my Japanese thread-leaf waterfall maple, its branches changing on the surface while connecting to the past through larger arteries twisting into the trunk, with final fingers flowing richly beneath the ground. This tree connects me to Japan and India and the river of spirit that sustains my relationship to nature; I call it my "butoh tree." I have cultivated it for twenty years—since 1986—the year I discovered butoh.

Letter from Yokohama:
Just Best Friends, Or What Is *Kinjiki*?

June 14 is a hot spring day in Yokohama. I am traveling with my friend and somatics student Arakawa Kayoko, who is a dance therapist in Japan. We are to visit Ohno Kazuo-sensei and his son Yoshito at their home and dance studio in Yokohama. Yoshito meets us at the train station. Together we walk up the familiar hill to his home and studio. He has lived in this comfortable traditional Japanese home with his mother and father, and finally his own family, for sixty-eight years, the first nine of which his father was a soldier in China and in World War II. Yoshito has danced with his father for five decades now, also teaching with him in the modest studio next to their home.

I give Yoshito my two books on butoh (which he already has, I find out). He seems so happy to receive them from me, though. Yoshito, like his father Kazuo, glows with quiet radiance and is eager to talk. He tells us that last December Kazuo was Santa Claus, as he has been for forty-five years for the children at the local elementary school. Yoshito points out the school on our way up the hill as we conjure the picture of a rickety ninety-nine-year-old Santa, loved by the children. Playing Santa, Yoshito says, has been one of the most consistent and important performances of Kazuo's life.

When we arrive at Yoshito's home, I am surprised to find myself a guest and unwary center of attention at a luncheon being prepared by his students. It seems there are at least three students living with the Ohnos and learning butoh: a young woman from Palermo, Italy, a theater student from Stuttgart, Germany, and a local Japanese fellow I have seen there before. During the Italian luncheon prepared by the students, Yoshito brings out photographs of his father—now featuring his chair dances—and some solo shots of his own recent butoh. He gives me two of my favorites.

We discuss butoh, of course: Hijikata Tatsumi and his wife, Motofuji, and the recent memorials for Kazuo, especially the Ohno Kazuo academy and archives in Bologna, Italy. Several sites in Italy will commemorate Ohno Kazuo's amazing life and work. We also discuss World War II. I bring it up in reference to Kazuo, especially the inescapable trauma and separation from home that lent shape to Kazuo's reverence for life and respect for death. We listen to the young student from Stuttgart, who represents yet another generation of Germans trying to shed the burden of national guilt. Or as one of my German students in America puts it, rhetorically, "When will it ever end?"

Yoshito's English is quite good, I find out. Several Japanese students join our party along with another American from Seattle, Washington. At length, I begin to feel comfortable enough to ask Yoshito the question I have wanted to ask for many years: "What was it like to perform in *Kinjiki*?"

Kinjiki was reputedly the first butoh, the famous dance that caused such a stir in the Japanese dance world of 1959. Hijikata choreographed this dance for himself and Yoshito, who was then twenty and a dance novice. And yes, there was one other performer: a chicken. The chicken got killed in some accounts, squashed as Yoshito sat on or otherwise "buggered" it. So I really wanted to unravel this with Yoshito. Who would know better than he what happened to the chicken? ("Why did the chicken cross the road?" I interjected.) Yoshito laughed and answered me:

"Now what is *Kinjiki*? I don't know what *Kinjiki* is. I just danced my instructions from Hijikata, and I was quite young. Hijikata said the dance was about being the very best of friends. I only heard later that some people thought it was about homosexuality."

"And how about the chicken?" I asked.

"Well it laid an egg in the greenroom after the performance!" he said.

We all laughed! But then I asked a question Yoshito wasn't expecting, at least not from me.

"Then you didn't fuck the chicken?" I asked boldly.

"Oh . . . No," he answered with a slight gasp. "Definitely not!"

"Well, you would know," I added with a grin.

Sometimes I ask myself why the taboo of bestiality bothers me so much and why Hijikata wouldn't test this boundary as he had so many others. Well this was not the test, not according to Yoshito, and he was holding the chicken!

Whatever Hijikata had in mind to emulate, or represent, or use for shock or beauty in *Kinjiki,* Yoshito thought the dance was about deep friendship, and that is all he was dancing, he says, even as the stage darkened and the friends chased each other, even as the fluttering white wings glistened in the fading light. How fascinating—this thing called "interpretation." Some observers saw death and bestiality in the dance, sacrifice, and the release of shadowy emotions. The darkened stage left a lot to the imagination as the dancers chased each other and panted. Why wouldn't they pant if they were running? And don't friends sometimes chase and play? In Yoshito's young mind, the dance was about friendship. Hijikata leaves the meaning up to us, or better still, he is just beginning to explore metamorphosis in *Kinjiki* and working through a plot of changing imagery, a style, indeed a genre, that eventually becomes butoh.

As for me, I bask in Yoshito's attention on my pilgrimage return to Yokohama, having been received with such grace and good humor. During the years I have been writing about butoh, appreciating its odd and wonderful dances and doing some myself, I have had no certainty that exponents of butoh, especially the Japanese founders, might appreciate my writing. In fact, artists very often don't like what is written about them, and understandably; the writing may not reflect how they see themselves at all. I have only hoped that Ohno Kazuo-sensei would resonate in spirit with my efforts to catch something of his butoh in writing, as he himself is a poet and writes poems to inspire and prepare his dances.

I write about butoh as truthfully as I can, even as I understand that words and dances are different mediums and I see only the parts I see. Writing is interesting in this respect: I reflect the surface of my vision and experience and hope there are readers (listeners) somewhere out there who will understand me. Somewhere between the reader and me, I feel a third level or invisible ideal listener who will connect me to the real. Yoshito's confirmation of my writing bridged the gap, even as I know his English is sketchy. I notice those around him who read English very well and discuss butoh with him. But he seems to understand me directly, without intermediaries.

Toothless Guru, Enervated with Spirit

During lunch Yoshito told me, much to my surprise, that my books inspire him as a dancer. I don't think I have ever been so pleased to hear that my writing about dance and butoh makes a difference to someone. I had no idea Yoshito knew me through my writing or would remember me from his father's workshops years ago. After lunch, he asked me if I wanted to see Kazuo. Well of course I did, but didn't want to ask, because one never knows how Ohno-sensei will feel.

He was in bed with his teeth out and his eyes closed, but Yoshito assured me he was not asleep and would hear every word I said. "Ohno-sensei," I said, "I have two gurus: Mahatma Gandhi and Ohno Kazuo. Thank you for everything you have taught me and given me for my life." That was it. I cried. And I told Yoshito what my gurus have in common: They have both learned how to make the whole world their friend. Ohno-sensei's eyes fluttered; then I noticed his Christian altar at the foot of the bed.

"Is this Ohno's Christian altar?" I asked.

"Yes," said Yoshito.

"Where is his Buddhist altar?" I wondered.

Yoshito took me to another room to show me. There it was, with Buddhist icons and a lottery ticket on the side: "For good luck," Yoshito said. Then Yoshito pointed to a futon comfortably arranged in the room. "This is your bed," he said. "I thought you might be tired from the trip." How thoughtful. (And I wondered if he would remember me?)

Well, I wasn't tired. So we went to the studio to dance. Kayoko translated and took photographs. Yoshito's students also joined us, and he danced first—an improvisation full of tension continuously released along the way. Then Yoshito and I danced together. He asked me what music I wanted. "You choose," I replied. He chose "Pink Floyd," because I had told him my favorite performance of his was in *Suiren* (Water Lily), in which he dances in a Western suit. He performs this part to Pink Floyd. Yoshito began much as he does in *Suiren,* standing still and seething, then doing a jerky dance in the corner that eventually transforms to a smoother register. I thought I would reconstruct (deconstruct) my memory of Ohno-sensei in the dance. He enters in a gown carrying a parasol. I found a long branch in the studio that I carried over my shoulder like the parasol. And our duet took its course from there.

FIGURE 24. Bank Art Studio's display of Ohno Kazuo's costume
and hat with a wall-size photograph of Ohno in old age. Photograph taken in Yokohama at Bank Art Studio by Daystar/Rosalie
Jones, © 2009. Used by permission of Daystar/Rosalie Jones.

We watched one of Yoshito's students perform in a chemise and his under-
wear. Never leaving the floor, he did a memorable rolling dance. His body was
of ballet, but his dance was butoh. Then Yoshito picked me up from my sitting
position on the floor and opened a parasol for us, as together we performed a
sweet—well, it seemed sweet to me—duet. That's when I asked him to marry me,
and he promised. (Never mind he is already happily married and has children.
Me, too. And it did cross my mind that I should be careful what I wish for.)

Now I remember mostly Ohno-sensei in bed with his teeth out and what Hijikata said about butoh: "Butoh is the weakened body, the weak body you sense
living in your own body." This idea of butoh as the weakened body gets translated into English in various ways. To me, Ohno-sensei's delicate expression and

paper-thin skin, his softly closed eyes, and his sunken mouth without teeth was the personification of butoh—the body enervated (weakened) with spirit. Or to put it another way: Ohno-sensei at one hundred is weak with spirit.

Now I am invited to what Yoshito is arranging as "Ohno Kazuo's Final Performance" in Yokohama in January 2008. I will go to be with Pina Bausch, Carla Fracchi, Carolyn Carlson, and many, many butoh dancers who have loved Ohno-sensei, and there will be hundreds of flowers, his favorite form of life. What a dedicated son Yoshito is, living in his father's shadow so happily and with such an open heart.

As I left the Ohno home and studio, Yoshito covered his heart with both hands and then waved, "Until I see you." Now I reflect on my relationship to butoh and my meeting with Yoshito: I know artists can be skeptical about those who document their work, and they should be. I have not written to flatter butoh, but with a search in mind. Perhaps it is my attraction to butoh and my ongoing search that Yoshito responds to. I am aware mostly of how lightly he touches the world in his dance as in his life. He has danced with Kazuo—to provide the shadowy cantus firmus for his father's light—since he was a young man of twenty. Now with his mother gone, Yoshito cares for his father's every daily need and plans his final performance, even as he breaks out from under the duet to find his solo butoh and new partners.

Flashback to *Kinjiki*

Kazuo merely watched *Kinjiki* and lent his son to Hijikata's inspired craziness. Hijikata always admired Kazuo, as the elder is looked up to in Japan, as a dance partner, and as a mentor with whom he often quarreled. Kazuo is so soft and childlike now, not the great Kazuo whose expressive hands and eyes captured me in *Suiren* and whose lithe body example has sustained many international students in his studio. With his sucked-in, toothless mouth, this almost bedridden centenarian and butoh grandfather faces his Christian altar with its large painting of Mary, a goddess in blue and gold stylized in the medieval. Ohno's picture of Jesus, on the other hand, is as modest and gentle as Kazuo himself, who so loves the world. And I catch a glimpse of what draws me to Kazuo's dancing: It is always simply given; his pleasure in performance is unmistakable.

Letter from Tokyo: Noble Guide

June 15, my second day in Japan, and here I am at Sadachio Ryokan in the Asakusa district in Tokyo, surrounded by all things traditionally Japanese. I'm waiting for Kyoko to get ready and having a coffee after breakfast. We will meet my adopted Japanese mother, Matsumoto-sensei, for lunch in Tokyo at the Four Seasons

Hotel, where she has arranged a private room for our meal in the midst of the leafy-green scene that is part of the hotel's Japanese garden; there is no more picturesque restaurant in Tokyo.

All afternoon the plates of sashimi, seared salmon, and vegetables cooked in front of us arrive in splendid plates. Who could ask for more? I enjoyed mostly the company of Matsumoto-sensei, whom I have come ever more to appreciate for her profound dedication to her work in dance. She has been an incredible force for the development of dance in education in Japan. At eighty-six, Matsumoto-sensei's face is serene. She is gentler every time I see her and always looks so incredibly beautiful. Even now when Japan is no longer rich in economic promise, she maintains an aristocratic bearing, and I mean this in the best sense, not in relation to high social class, though she has this, but as belonging to a world that still remembers the simple elegance of good manners.

From her quiet appearance, you would never suspect the depth of her intellect and knowledge of the world or that she was pioneering creativity in movement and dance in Japan at the same time the legendary Margaret H'Doubler was making history for the same kind of explorations in America. Matsumoto-sensei's discoveries in dance for personal development were coming at a time when Japanese physical education was anything but creative; in fact, it was militaristic and centered on marches and drills. War interrupted her work in dance and education. It is difficult for her to speak about those years, so I don't press her. She returned to teaching as soon as reconstruction of Japan would allow.

Now Matsumoto-sensei could no doubt live a grand lifestyle, and I don't forget that the emperor has decorated her for her contributions to educational research. Never the snob, however, she prefers to continue her study groups on dance education and concentrates on the annual college dance festival that she and other leaders of dance education in Japan present in Kobe every year. I appreciate her as a mentor and model. She knows how to put other people at ease and takes her beauty in stride, directing attention away from herself. Her pearls and tasteful clothes suit her so well, as do her ceremonial kimonos. I'm glad there are still such people in the world who make time circular: those who tend to ritual return. Ceremonies can be humble, they can be friendly, and they can be grand. I'm happy with all of these possibilities and lucky to have experienced them all, again and again, through Matsumoto-sensei, my Japanese mother and friend.

I gave her my new book on butoh: *Hijikata Tatsumi and Ohno Kazuo*. She was happy for me and for the book and spoke about her relationship to butoh. Her husband, now deceased, the famous Kabuki scholar and critic Gungi Masakatsu, wrote a great deal about butoh, and he sponsored butoh performances. I quote his speech on butoh in the second essay. Matsumoto-sensei herself appreciates butoh but was never a big fan. Rather, she saw her mission as that of an educator, bringing dance and creative principles to the consciousness of children and young people. In 1996, I wrote about her wide influence on dance education in Japan.[1] She saw early on that butoh had spiritual concepts behind it, she said, and her concerns for dance were different, more basically directed toward education and creative movement. I remain in her debt for helping me in my quest to find out about butoh when I was living in Japan—even as her own aesthetic differs from mine. As a good educator, she sees the sincere student and guides her.

Letter from India: Wandering into the Yes

I see the tea servant gossiping with his buddies on the adjacent porch and can slip him extra money when the tea comes, although the manager has told me not to tip the servants here at this once grand but now ailing university guest house. I have wandered here and into the abyss of myself, trusting that there is something I don't yet understand that India has to offer. The wanderer never knows what might cross her path; she waits upon lucidity and sometimes stumbles upon it. Ethics comes to her improvisationally. In India, my discussions with others and myself seek a kind of rightness waiting in the din and the dust. M. K. Gandhi, who struggled with ethical questions for a lifetime and wrote about this in his autobiography, was born in the state of Gujarat, where I am spending several months on the verge of this new century in 2000 as a guest teacher at the University of Baroda, or Maharaja's College. In six weeks, I will visit the sanctuary of Gandhi's ashram situated on the bank of the Sabarmati River just outside Ahmadabad, also in Gujarat. Gandhi belonged to a family of prime ministers in several Kathiawar states, but he emphasized that his caste, the Bania, seem to have been grocers. He inherited a penchant for doing the right thing from his mother, who was deeply religious, an avid meditator, and adept at fasting. Near the beginning of his autobiography, *The Story of My Experiments with Truth*, Gandhi recommends a certain human distancing that, like the proscenium stage, lends perspective. His advice moves widely past nationalism and the nation-state he gave his life to bring into existence:

> I am of the opinion that all exclusive intimacies are to be avoided; for man takes in vice far more readily than virtue. And he who would be friends with God must remain alone, or make the whole world his friend.[2]

I understand this advice, and I finally get it now in my sixty-seventh year, even if I still need exclusive intimacy, that of friends and lovers who give me personal validation and warmth. But someday I will surrender everything, as we all will. I prepare for this accidentally, moving into places of aloneness as I'm forced there by circumstances: Sometimes I choose to prepare this place consciously through meditation. None of us thinks that we will lose everything—our friends, our homes, our children, our teeth, and our looks. Will we not wake up to fragrant smells and waterfall maples? Wake up at all? Death is a butoh theme and a theme of existential thought; in both cases it is the teacher and friend we cannot escape. If we deny it, if we can't make friends widely across cultural boundaries and across darkness and light, we will not die well. This is why I travel, as every year it gets more difficult to move into unfamiliar circumstances, and in my dreams I have to find my footing through dangerous terrain that scares me. With difficulty, I remind myself that my Zen name is "Bright Road Friend." I want to make friends with the world, like my mentor Matsumoto-sensei, who traveled out from Japan to Brazil and America as a young woman before World War II, when travel for Japanese women was not the norm, and like my gurus Ohno Kazuo and Mahatma Gandhi, who mellowed through their global travels. They endured great hardships in war and politics and taught, each in his own way, lessons of gentle friendliness to all.

The Crematorium in Baroda

Yesterday, Parul Shah and I completed the sound score for our choreographic project blending *bharatanatyam* and butoh. We have been rehearsing with bits and pieces of poetry and music and can finally put it all together: she reading the poems in three Indian languages and I reading them in English. We have several poems from women poets of India upon which we base the dance cycle and are recording these over music, some traditional and some original. Putting all of this together is a big task. The sound studio is on the outskirts of Baroda next to a crematorium. The air is smoky and the surroundings more quiet than in town—maybe a reason for the studio being here? Somehow, I don't think so. As I ascend the steps to the studio and look over to the crematorium, my heart sinks to my feet. There is the customary tea when we arrive, though, and an old man sleeping on the couch in the receiving room.

I was relieved when we finished our project eight hours later and emerged from the damp, smelly rooms of the otherwise efficient recording studio. I had only lapsed into anxiety and panicked once. I managed not to complain about the smelly, dank studio and retired to sleep for a half hour on a chair next to the old man on the couch. He seemed not to have stirred. My last image of Baroda is of this studio at its outskirts, where sound and death coexist. I welcome the steps that lead me down from the studio, and suddenly I see myself:

> Yes, I'm here in a dusty face with glowing eyes. I see the fish in front of the shack next to the crematorium looking fresh and shiny as they wait near the fire out in the open, ready to cook. Here I grasp the ethics of otherness: I understand that I am not saved alone. I can imagine nothing more fundamental.

And I see the value of welcoming the unknown. We can embrace death and use it as a teacher, as both Gandhi and Ohno taught. Both of them were strongly affected by their mothers and rejected aggressiveness, inviting the vulnerable, invisible space called yin in Asia, feminine darkness and receptivity. Gandhi courted death as a nonviolent revolutionary, and Ohno carried death as a constant companion, through his experience of war, acknowledging those who die for us, and dancing in his mother's memory. "I sit bewildered in the playground of the dead," Ohno says in his "Message to the Universe," a poem for International Dance Day in 1998, when he was ninety-two years old:

> Here I wish to dance and dance and dance and dance, the life of the wild grass.
> I see the wild grass, I am the wild grass, I become one with the universe. That metamorphosis is the cosmology and studying of the soul.
> In the abundance of nature I see the foundation of dance. Is this because my soul wants to physically touch the truth?
> When my mother was dying I caressed her hair all night long without being able to speak one word of comfort. Afterwards, I realized that I was not taking care of her, but that she was taking care of me.
> The palms of my mother's hands are precious wild grass to me.
> I wish to dance the dance of wild grass to the utmost of my heart.[3]

Wandering in Baroda

Guru on Akota Road
How easy in the flesh the horned cows recline,
seven in a cluster in front of the towel stall
next to the chemist on Akota road,
as a jungle of motor vehicles
beep and blare their musical jangles
through the dusty twilight in the Muslim quarters.

Seven small boys in a pack pass by the seven cows,
not giving them room, as I pass shoulders with rickshaws,
saris of green and orange with burnt red,
more green with magenta, and men in white carrying babies,
slim brown men with shirts over their wrap-around cloth skirts,
legions of legs, of trousers, brown and beige,
some muddy, some spotless.

Muslims and Hindus mingle.
And the dust kicked up by the cars and trucks,
scooters, rickshaws and bicycles
covers us all.

The goats,
The mother pig with her seven perfectly snouted little ones—
to the market, and all the way home.
I match my pace with recovering ease to the surrounding flow,
so constant and unassumingly swerving.

They see I am different, but don't mind.
This time, they let me disappear into the stores with hanging scarves,
the shops full of tires and wood,
and flowers being strung in wreaths for the Goddess

Here in Baroda, side stepping the dung
and men pissing against the yellow walls,
I am silent.

One gets the guru one deserves,
as from the haze of yellow air
and exhaust fumes, she a lotus, a woman
just a shadow against the river of bodies, of animals,
vehicles, shapes and gadgets, now comes close.

Her eyes are clear and quiet. They let me be.
Her sari is red with white flowers,
and she carries a basket of clothes on her head.
Without looking, she sees me,
moving past the carts of oranges and grapes,
beans, peas, and black dal, peanuts and chickpeas.

Her walk is neither slow nor fast. It floats on the dust
as her feet touch the ground through the smooth grace of her
leather sandals, her big toe held in a ring.

15

Waking Woman

Lani Weissbach in Chicago (2006)

> In the process of creating an indigenous form of modern
> dance, Japanese butoh founders discovered a universal
> poetry of the body. Rather than transcending the human
> condition, butoh asks us to descend into it—down into
> the turbulence, awkwardness and uncertainty of life—and
> from there, deep in the thick of things, we discover our own
> healing and capacity to love unconditionally.
>
> —Lani Weissbach

> A violent and concentrated action is a kind of lyricism:
> it summons up supernatural images, a bloodstream of
> images, a bleeding spurt of images in the poet's head
> and in the spectator's as well.
>
> —Antonin Artaud, *The Theater and Its Double*

Imagine that your fears are mirrored back to you and ricochet out toward the world or, in the case of theater, toward the audience, and you will grasp the zero point of Lani Weissbach's dance. In *Waking Woman/Messy Beauty,* she wrestles with fear and obsession: This is what comes to me now in the aftermath of her Chicago performance at Links Hall on March 18, 2006. *Messy Beauty* provides a vision of depth psychology in which purity vies with reality in bold imagination. The woman in this dance is a doll, or maybe two kinds of dolls, through which we glimpse a crushing struggle, sometimes draped in satin and at others bound in plastic. Hiding beneath her shiny pink gown, there are four fetish objects that control the performance: knife, doll, jeweled pouch, and shell.

But I am getting ahead of myself. To enter the *ma* of *Messy Beauty,* imagine your need to cut through to something waiting on the other side of a paper house, and think of being perfect at the same time. The interest of this dance exists in the space between its slashing energy and its doll-like character. Lest we forget,

FIGURE 25. Lani Weissbach dances *Waking Woman/Messy Beauty*
(2006) in Chicago. Photograph by Rachel Finan, © 2006. Used by
permission of Rachel Finan.

a doll is not just a pretty girl; it is also a toy to be played with, an object of fascination to be controlled. Dolls don't talk back, and they don't bleed. They are always perfect, or perfectly what they are. They never change, unless they break apart and are reassembled.

Why does Weissbach choose butoh as a way into "the doll"? Think of the little wooden Russian nesting dolls called *matrioshkas*. When you open them, inside there is a smaller doll, and inside this, a still smaller one, and so forth. They remind us of our relationship to things larger and smaller than we are, of replication, and of uncovering secrets. Butoh metamorphosis also bodes secrets, not reaching toward meaning but reaching toward transformation though hidden or mysterious movements. *Butoh-ka* dance in tumultuous places of struggle, not for the sake of struggle, but to trouble fear. Though often unstated, the way of butoh is to dance into fear, to dance until it yields, until finally it is named or bleeds—as in *Waking Woman*.

What is this woman afraid of, I ask myself? From the beginning, her dance is quizzical. Cristal Sabbagh, Weissbach's invisible double, sets the butoh in motion through a striking shadow dance behind a screen. At first we see only the screen and a vague shadow as we listen to a narrative by Daria Fand:

> One night, she dreamt something. Only, this was grander than a dream. When she woke up, she'd have to tell every sky if she were a cloud, every wall if she were a crack, every face if she were human.

The shadow stirs: It was worth an audience this time, but a language for it might not exist. Languages are like her, made up of bits. It's so easy to get swept up among the bits, swept away with the cigarette butts and crumpled things left lying about on the sidewalk.

The shadow agitates: And of course we thought it would, but what we don't expect is the sudden emergence onstage of a glowing doll in a pink satin gown, replete with bouffant skirt. Nor do we expect her too-sweet shiny white mask or how the doll skitters so smoothly in wide swaths as though nothing could smudge or break her. The narrative over, the words echo nevertheless:

> What she heard was unbroken, like the ocean. It was dense as the coal-black water that crushes some but makes a home for others. She heard the waves—the sun rising upon them and the landing of birds. Here, she came up disrobed at the shell's mouth . . . in a glass case, like an exhibit.

In her dress is a secret pocket for the fetish objects, as one by one she finds them and lays them on small pillars at the front edge of the stage. She sets them out, and we see her attachment to them, the symptoms, and perhaps the scars. What is she afraid of? Will she save herself? The mask changes angles and expressions quite blankly through the graceful gestures of the satin dancer. She recedes at length. As a pale doll, she moves into the distance and gives the audience space, but not before setting a contemporary *matrioshka* dressed in black vinyl on its tiny stand. Exchanging one veneer for another, she returns tightly dressed in glossy black vinyl as a large replica of the doll on the stand.

Narrative is not common in butoh, but here the artist throws it out, seemingly as a transformative prop. Now she moves like another kind of doll that little girls adore, not pure and powdered, but not sinful either. There is no feeling in the vinyl dancer as her movement grows violent. Will she shatter? She shows us the doll's jointedness and her teetering on the edges. She leans and rocks, seeks more space, more sound perhaps, but not to get caught in her perfectly black and staggering shape. Life might tell her many things if she could hear, things she might not want to hear. Her dance is sharp and angular and has no curves. It is wild but not free, grabs but cannot grasp. The dancer's hands perform slashing motions against her body, cutting and bouncing back off. "Sometimes it's even harder to wake up than to fall asleep," flashes back from the narration. The liminal mind is heavy, I think: "Wake up." In waking, you may bleed though. Women do bleed.

Images pile up from the objects, as with the knife, the dancer cuts through the paper house, grazes the shell with real breath, and listens through it. Will she recognize herself, the narrator asks brutally? "Would she recognize this genie, nymph, siren, (priss) bitch, 'ho' . . . this tribeswoman, piece of business, piece of property, piece of ass . . . this child, infant, heartbeat, cell?"

The dancer finishes, but she doesn't let us forget the jeweled bag that she drew from her pink satin dress. She sits down, then reclines and opens it. At last, she plunges her hand into (guess what?) a bag of dirt. And I ask myself what Shakespeare would say? ("All that glisters is not gold"?) She observes the dirt and smudges it on herself until she wears a neutral state of messy, playing the day in reverse. And I hear her mind through the dance: "What was I afraid of, fascinated by, or dying for? Do I need to wash my hands? Am I disappointed?"

There is something about facing the truth that is represented by the oracle voice at the beginning and appears again when the dancer comes out in her slip, dressed only as herself. The voice returns as if at points where things must break apart and speaks beside the point at the end while the dancer gathers up the props.

Who is grappling with the issue of control? This woman is not on an analyst's couch. Does her dance set free the victim? Will this woman awake to the asphyxiating fact that her existence is messy? Whatever conflicts haunt the mind, this is the question that wakes her and makes her truly beautiful.

· · ·

The next day, I ask Weissbach if her dance is feminist butoh.

She looks at me curiously and answers, "No."

I realize the distance between minds and interpretations, so I ask the question another way: "Womanist?"

She smiles—a waking woman—"Yes," she says.

Whatever her intent, her morphic mind moves through the violent artifice of her dance. It is also apparent that it moves through the original costumes of Charmaine Koehler-Lodge, a text and mask designed by Daria A. Fand, original music by Joseph Allen Popp, and a set constructed of paper, pipes, and wood by Keegan Boulton and Doug Lodge. These are the several collaborative layers at work in the alchemy of *Waking Woman*.

In addition to choreographing and performing in her own company, Shen & Bones, Weissbach teaches a variety of movement classes to people of all ages and varying needs, extending the butoh community to include meditative and healing dances. She continues to prove through her teaching that the performative values of dance have therapeutic potency that everyone can access, not just those who perform onstage. She herself has chosen the stage as a transformative "seeing place" where she can see herself more clearly, as she is also seen.

By moving instinctively into her emotional life, her lyricism transports the poet's head, the dancer's precarious *ma,* and the spectator's as well.

16

Torn

Robert Bingham in New York (2006)

Torn is a work for Robert Bingham choreographed by Lani Fand Weissbach, whose work we just visited in the previous essay. *Torn* has been performed in several venues in New York, North Carolina, and Pennsylvania. Here we take three perspectives on the dance: that of the choreographer, that of the dancer, and that of the writer as witness.

The Choreographer

Weissbach tells me that her interest in creating this dance is to explore the feeling states of heartbreak and desire. As a butoh choreographer, she finds it fascinating to observe what happens to the body when an image or a feeling inhabits it. The meeting point between two different states or images especially intrigues her—the point of collision where one quality gives way to the other. If we look back into our examinations of butoh morphology and alchemy, we see that Weissbach's interest in finding such points relates to the Japanese concept of *ma*. She also asks the phenomenological question of what happens when the performer experiences a convergence of differences? This is *ma* in another light. Can contrasting images merge in the performer as well as in the performance? Even for a moment? The search for this moment is for Weissbach very unpredictable and exciting. She sees through her choreographic process that both performer and audience may come to realize how seemingly disparate forces are inextricably linked:

FIGURE 26. Robert Bingham dances *Torn* (2006), choreographed by Lani Weissbach. Photograph by Elena Shalaev, © 2006. Used by permission of Elena Shalaev.

As a choreographer, I want to feel that something is genuinely happening for the performer and that his/her physical expression arises from a somatic process. I provide the framework and serve as outside eye and editor, but the essence of the piece—the way the body moves—must ultimately be a manifestation of the performer's own journey. If the piece does not make intuitive sense to the performer, it will most likely come across as pretentious or flat.

Weissbach says that working Bingham was a delight because he was so willing to take ownership of the dance. He sought to find his own truth within her concept and the structures she gave him. Thus, the overall form of the dance emerged as an organic blend of his somatic responses and her choreographic ideas.

The Dancer

I asked Bingham about his experience of performing *Torn*. What he told me is framed through the movement itself, its stillness and rhythm and its directions in space, as these also resonate with his somatic feeling states and cannot be divorced from them. This is how he experiences aspects of the dance:

> The beginning is in stillness, facing upstage. My legs are deliberately placed close together, and my arms are spread wide above the space in front of my head. I begin to turn clockwise as I dissolve towards the floor. The length of time for this process feels infinite. I try to perceive an endlessly receding point, feeling it travel beyond the walls of the space. I'm in nearby streets, towns, and hills. My immediate environment feels less precious, knowing that the landscape outside is infinite. Yet I sense the environment acutely, the sound of near-silence and air moving through nearby pipes.
>
> I rise slowly, feeling my heart—vulnerable, bruised, and hopeful—following that receding point. It can't be reached. I look at the floor; see it pull me back down. That pull becomes power. It surges through my legs, pelvis, trunk, and out through my arms and head. I resist and then yield to it, a circular toss-and-collapse motion. Am I smiling? I can't tell. My breath deepens, and my temperature rises. I feel the intimacy and vulnerability of my relationship to the first row of audience members, a few feet away, watching something happen to my pulse and body's chemistry as I continue tossing and collapsing.
>
> All of a sudden I'm up, spinning, whipping, turning, and using all that I've got to get me back to where I started. Legs close together, arms spreading, upstage corner. I feel the soft cup of my hands as they are drawn further apart, opening up my back. I sustain this moment, the performer who wants to make something happen but resists it. I am patient, my fingertips feeling the molecules of air around them will tell me when it's time.

The Witness

From the audience, I see how Bingham begins in the dimension of time, curling down endlessly into the floor, rolling into it, and treading where? This beginning already holds an ending, unless it morphs considerably. It sends my mind on its way, plying a visceral spiral of psychological perspectives rocking with shudders. The dance is somatically dangerous for me, intimate, and comes in rushes. Luckily, it is also visually distanced. I see the dancer is wearing brown, wrinkled pants and is bare-chested. This gives his dance a rawness that aids affective utterance. His dance does not reach through the air as much as it paws, preferring the comfort of the ground. The dancer enacts descent as a signature, curling his tall, lean frame to go down, sometimes in an instant and other times slowly, consciously folding his joints. He rolls onto his back and spins there, twirling to the side and sitting, repeating the groveling motions in a pattern while tapping and slapping himself. His gaze travels upward a lot, offering tension to the floor of his dilemma.

Electronic music creases the frenzied dance at a crucial point in its performance. Bingham throws his hands into uncontrolled flutters, and the frenzy seems to move internally. He walks back with his arms in a bind and then repeats four far-flung gestures over and over. He begins to run in a backward circle as the music builds repetitious gyrations in ostinato drumbeats and tin metallic sounds. The dancer slaps himself again, bringing about internal shaking. His arms wrap with his body momentum, and his feet vibrate into the colliding rhythms.

As it morphs, this dance releases a liminal state that is compounded as the dancer's back arches up from the floor, his head and butt anchoring the bodily arc. At the end, Bingham stands still in the flat light, turning once, twisting his torso away from us while keeping his feet connected to the ground.

Torn is a physical tempest, and it is also a sign language of spiritual gestures. Does it express desire and heartbreak at once? Well, if I didn't know the choreographer's intent, I'm not sure I would say so. The impression is not so clear. But then the impressions of dance never are, unless they proceed from narrative that is purely plotted. I gain power from the dancer's plunge into uncertainty, his courage and soul, from his flying hands and fallen limbs, from the mental alchemy trembling through his dance. And I understand how the choreographer's intention is also cast in alchemy and hope. The end is not in the beginning and not the same way twice.

17

Butoh Ritual Mexicano

Diego Piñón in Mexico and Chicago (2006)

Diego Piñón was born in Mexico City in 1957. He comes from the Purepecha culture, now identified with the Tarascan Indians, and was exposed as a child to their primal dances. The Purepecha resisted Spanish culture, even retaining their own language. When I interviewed him in March 2006 in Chicago, Piñón told me that he doesn't remember a time when he did not dance. He began his formal study of dance and somatic modalities in 1975 with Mexican teachers of a form called Energetic Movement. In 1979, he completed studies in the social sciences and began dancing at the Centro Superior de Coreografía in Mexico City. He continued learning through the study of body therapies and modern dance forms originating in the United States. Since 1987, he has trained in butoh with many of the progenitors of this form. Piñón eventually developed a unique voice for butoh through his Butoh Ritual Mexicano, pouring his unique inheritance through intercultural alchemy.

Ito

> Life is provocation for releasing our sacred selves,
> and butoh opens up this irritation to my most intimate self.
> —Diego Piñón

In shamanistic style, Piñón's solo dance *Ito* is performed to enchant the hot Mexican desert. His dance fosters a warm and dry desert psychology, like that

FIGURE 27. Diego Piñón dances *Ekua Itsi II* (Behind the Mirror) in 2006 in Chicago. Photograph by Florence Poulain, © 2008. Used by permission of Florence Poulain.

of other famous shamans in Mexico, mystical psychologists who have been influential in the West, especially Don Miguel Ruiz of the Toltec and ethnologist Carlos Castaneda. Ruiz teaches in his *Four Agreements* (1997)[1] an impeccability of word and spirit similar to that of Piñón's butoh, and in several volumes beginning in 1968, Castaneda teaches somatic psychology through the trickster wisdom of his Yaqui shaman tutor Don Juan Matus, daring readers to mysterious adventures of the soul and nonordinary reality in the Sonoran Desert. The question of whether Castaneda's books are fictional or serve as anthropological data remains unresolved, though certainly not unchallenged.[2] In any case, they filled a need in their time for those who sought truths beyond the proofs of modern science and still apply to those who transmogrify, if only in their dreams and dances. I read all of Castaneda's works, enthralled, and only tired of their repetition toward the end. I loved his stories and advice and wondered that he might be playing two roles at once: that of himself as student and that of Don Juan as teacher and Mesoamerican shaman. I learned from his stories most about the blurry line between fiction and reality, how to be resilient, the importance of expanding my horizons by losing personal history, and that it might be desirable to disappear sometimes. When I see Piñón dance, I feel the presence of Ruiz and Castaneda and the deep wisdom teachings of Mexico.

Piñón's dance is stainless: True to the desert, his untiring presence is honed of butoh alchemy, changing slowly with the sunset, the soft sounds of chanting, and the shifting sand. Piñón shuffles, slowly walking on the smooth sand, a flowing figure with a long, white cloth wrapped around his middle, feathers stuck to his body, and ritual painting covering his head, arms, and chest like lines of beads. Without heroism, his dance faces the day as it fades into shadows. Piñón dances into dusk, a recovered fragment of Hijikata Tatsumi struggling to stand upright. He returns for the night and the darkness, listening for what? His hand presses his head as we hear a waltz in the distance, a Mexican folk tune played on the guitar. The dance creates a dream state, a lost world we can enter through the dancer's search for a more innocent state. His body glows pink in the night against the dark blue of the receding desert. "For me," Piñón says, "life is provocation for releasing our sacred selves, and butoh opens up this irritation to my most intimate self."

Piñón credits Ohno Kazuo-sensei with deepening the spirit of his dance: "Ohno guided me through a pure connection to my mother." Piñón told me that when he first met Ohno and prepared to dance for him, he said (as in a mysterious time warp): "I've already seen you dance." What he gathered from Ohno in his three months of study with him was "part of his aura," while Ohno's son Yoshito provided the patient practice Piñón needed and a perspective on butoh.[3] Ohno-sensei gave Piñón a single instruction: "Dance with this post; it is your mother," then left him alone to struggle with it for weeks. Ohno led him toward the feminine yielding archetype in a somewhat Zen way. We see how this served his creativity in related works that he created for his father and Ohno-sensei, *Ekua Itsi I* and *Ekua Itsi II*. I examine the latter for Ohno-sensei next and speak of the first one for his father toward the end of the essay.

Ekua Itsi II (Behind the Mirror)

> Strange dear, but true dear, when I'm next to you dear. . . .
> I'm yours till I die. So in love with you am I.

So the Cole Porter song goes as Piñón dances in the interstices (the *ma*) between the lover and the loved, attached to romance in a curious way. He minces like a shy woman in his black pants, carrying a Japanese fan, wobbling a bit in white high-heeled shoes in the manner of a Japanese schoolgirl with her toes turned in demurely. *Ekua Itsi* also plays with American nostalgia in its use of an old familiar song. But this is veneer; the source of the dance is Mexican. Yet it does not hail solely from Mexico, and even though some of the outward signs are Japanese, it isn't really that either. To further confuse the issue, the dancer has a red cloth flower in his mouth, not a rose for a tango, but a stuck-on red pout that creates a half mask of his face. Piñón's shaven white head is covered with a woman's black satin hat, such a beautiful hat as Ohno Kazuo might have worn.

Why this parade of the feminine in pastiche, I ask? Piñón performs this section of his dance as "Homage to Kazuo Ohno" for his hundredth birthday in 2006. Ever since Ohno Kazuo and Hijikata Tatsumi danced aspects of femininity in their highly original dances at the root of butoh, the masculine way into the feminine has been a part of its transformative alchemy. *Butoh-ka* move from masculine to feminine, not so much as a drag queen might, but more within Japanese aesthetic convictions of the male finding (or constructing) his feminine side onstage, like the Kabuki *onnagata,* for instance. The butoh way of transforming gender strikes me as a masquerade, not a parody or comedy. When I see men find their way into feminine wiles, even if these have long since been updated in masks of equality, I am conscious of their style. The butoh style has never struck me as funny or offensive; rather, I usually go with it, and I'm amazed at how seriously I see into my own feminine masks through the butoh masquerade.

What is a masquerade? Is it deception? Facade? Affectation? Charade? Pretense? Or is it, as in theater, an imagined presence transformed through disguise, revealing more than it hides? Just as we know women no longer need to be imprisoned by engendered weakness and simpering, we can also see how men might expose soft enigmatic qualities—how they might look behind the mirror that looks back at them every day.

Piñón explores his feminine underbelly in two ways: by looking behind the mirror to explore the feminine other in a masquerade of undying romance and by remaining nevertheless visible as a man underneath the facade. "So in love," haunts the dance, and "Till I die." Thus do we see how Piñón's dance is not trying to fool us into believing he is a woman. That would be the way of the transvestite. The butoh way seems quite in tune with human metamorphosis. To enter into changing states, moods, and genders in the dance is enlightening. To embody the minds of others is revealing. We learn that we are not as solidly present as we think, and perhaps we have more than one body. Metamorphic dance teaches us this as our several bodies coalesce, separate, and reintegrate.

Piñón shows us his several bodies and how they relate in the fullness of his dance. His morphing through several incarnations also crosses musical palettes, beginning with breath and trembling as his mouth opens like a hungry bird. Another body appears through ritual use of bone and a king's crown. Piñón gathers fierce strength with this body, snaring the crown as he dances with the bone. In another embodiment, he carries a crocked stick and moves alongside death. In play with his own history, he pulls a dance from Spain to Mexico that could be compared to the slow, simmering *Chaconne,* albeit Piñón's slow dance involves a crumpled country hat and, except for the crown, no heavy court finery, as did the grand baroque of Mexican modern dancer José Limón, a predecessor of Piñón. The butoh elements behind the mirror morph in surreal juxtaposition through a unique ritual style—the chacun à son goût—the expression of the individual "taste" of the dance.

Piñón uses the language of the Purepecha to name this dance. The ancient Purepecha culture, still alive in the volcano area of Michoacán where Piñón choreographs and teaches his international students, is full of traditions of music, song, and dance. Piñón says this language and the energy of the region inspire him. He uses symbolic words from various ancient languages of Mexico to name his dances. He says the exact meaning of *Ekua Itsi* is "the woman who opens." His first dance on this theme, *Ekua Itsi I: Requiem for My Father,* was a dance for his father after his death. At the end of this dance, Piñón says: "I move my feeling into the feminine universe to open the path for my father to reach his liberation." *Ekua Itsi II: Behind the Mirror* came at some point from the same place as the first, he says, but is also his homage to Ohno Kazuo on his hundredth birthday. In this work, as in many of Ohno's, the archetype of the feminine provides the alchemy for several transformations, the most spiritual of which is Piñón's vision of death as his dance becomes more naked and he doubles himself behind the mirror. With his clean-shaven head and white visage, he is classically butoh. But the heart of his work is Mexican. We see how the alchemy of butoh provides a space for this and how the difference between Mexico, Japan, and America creates the *ma* of Piñón's butoh.

18

Mourning the Earth

Eiko and Koma with Leng Tan in New York (2007)

Foreshortened in perspective, two dancers lie on a leaf-strewn stage, feet facing to the back and heads facing us. Their legs and hips are covered with black fur, and their bare chests and faces are powdered white. Fragrant branches lie on the floor in front of the stage, and the stage itself is covered with leaves and dark earth. In the audience, we wait: lights to half—to dark—silence. The pianist, Margaret Leng Tan, is barely visible in the darkness as she begins to pluck the strings, playing prepared piano with impediments placed on the strings, as John Cage might have but with a difference. Her music is governed not by chance but by her profound keyboard technique.

Lights stream from above, molding the dancers as they start a meticulously slow turn onto their sides. A giant tree trunk is revealed in the background rising from the soft floor of leaves; its rugged bark looks back at us.

This soft and rolling dance remains undefined in shape, continually inching into radial dimensions. It proceeds without inflection for the most part with just an occasional leg thrust or body bump settling in half measure. What are these strange, belly-squiggling animals, I wonder? They are male and female, I see, but they seem incomplete. Their rooting and undulating shapes move low to the ground, worming in, prolonged and softly rustling in the leaves.

In real life, they are Eiko and Koma, the incomparable pair who have been performing their slow-morphing dances since 1976 at home in New York and around the world. Their teachers were Ohno Kazuo and Hijikata Tatsumi in Japan

FIGURE 28. Eiko and Koma in *Offering,* performed after the September 11, 2001, terrorist attacks on New York City, in July 2002. *Mourning,* as described in this essay, is similar in costume and its connection to the earth. Photograph by Varga Mátyás, © 2004. Used by permission of Varga Mátyás.

and Manja Chmiel in Germany. They began performing with Hijikata's company in Tokyo and later worked with Ohno in the early 1970s. Eiko and Koma are no strangers to dances in and about nature. Much of their work has been about this. They have performed their butoh-inspired dances in gardens, public plazas, lakes, and rivers. The visionary musician Margaret Leng Tan, a major figure in the American avant-garde, performs with them in *Mourning,* both on toy and grand piano.

Mourning

I
Eschewing drama for physical memory,
Two dancer animals make their way gently
Rising and falling, morphing
With breath and undulation
In slow motion pictures barely animate,
One image into another through faultless transitions.

Initially disconnected, presently in nearby collision
One dancer finds the other, the man the woman.

He nose-nuzzles her butt,
Then falls over her in one heft of body,
As the pling and rumble of the piano
Thickens the dance.

She bear walks back, jutting elbows
In sluggish agon, not counting,
But through sound and weight,
Moving fur as she goes—
Muddy amoeba—
Oozing visual art at a crawl.

In time the performers peek out at us
From under their bodies,
Smeared with black dust, and gold with light.
From under the leaves, they slog,
Pillaging gold-black silence.

He backs up into her open legs,
Asexually and without emotion. She throws herself
On him twice, and he grunts, throwing himself
Over her again, as she starts to bite him.
He moves away without desire, rolling low.

II
Tan removes the implements fettering strings;
Not through wasted melody, her playing blisters the ear.
As the dancer bends forward and reaches from sitting—her
Hand and fingers outstretched, she picks up a
Handful of dirt, and brings it to her mouth,
Squats and eats it, then lies down,
Her legs spread carelessly.

She curls up with her head lifted. He rolls off-stage
In front of us. We hear single strands of color, firmness
In the pure monotone of improvised music,
As he creeps on his belly
Back up onstage.

In time, the dancers find each other.
Or rather, he finds her lying there,
Limpid. His inching along the floor so soft
In creature likeness. Now in the air—
A simple repetitive tune on a toy piano.

He lifts his legs, plowing his head into the ground
Beneath her; reaches around himself

And strangles her. She lets go a guttural
Sound and collapses.

What has he done?
Gently sloping her into his neutral arms,
He doesn't know.
Carrying his innocent prize, dragging himself and her
Along his way, he inches ahead, nuzzling,
Scooting her close to the audience.

The murderer shows her,
Rummages under the leaves, uncovers a
Cloth, and stuffs it into his mouth,
Plummeting, gagging,
Over the edge of the stage.

The piano trembles soon, as the dead she-animal begins to stir.
He comes back to her on the green-covered stage,
Bearing a stack of leafy branches
To cover her with canopy,
And engulf her body with his.

III
Tree limbs and bodies twine,
Separate then, as through mitosis.
The dancers' faces find each other
In one elegant moment,
And he bites her neck, tenderly.
Digging in, they awake to the tree and each other,
Their injured arms branch out.

Bearing each other with some difficulty, they stand.
Butting, falling and finding how, they walk.
Holding and pushing, partnering for support,
He presses her against the tree, falling down along her body.

Disadvantaged, forced and etched
His bundle of leaves,
A gift to her on exit, a hope
For matched pairs and doubles,
And that the soil regain its intelligence.

Intimates, they
Slide down the tree together,
Shuddering,
Sleep into the tree,
Die into the height and bark, the pure beauty of rest.

Solid within
The tree upon which they hang, the post that supports
Their spines and natures. Mixing with the rough
Covering, their fur rubbing together.
Going deeper through contact,
But wounded still—their contact with man.

I read this dance as a history of sexuality: the discovery of one's lost half in the animal struggle to connect and the leafy gift of natural wholeness at repose on the forest floor. The simple, dirty elegance of the dance is wrought with pain amid man's (our) mistreatment of the environment that is trying to support us, as trees might if we let them. When we damage nature, the dance reminds us, we damage ourselves; our ability to reproduce, connect, and communicate is damaged. Through the hidden messages in *Mourning*, we seize our relationship to nature, directly through bodily experience, not didactically through useless advice.

19

Quick Silver

Murobushi Ko in New York (2007)

Murobushi Ko trained and performed with butoh's creator Hijikata Tatsumi and was a founding member of the long-running Dairakudakan butoh company. Now Murobushi leads the Edge Company from his base in Japan and tours internationally. He performed the U.S. premiere of his solo *Quick Silver* at the Theater for the New City in New York on November 9, 2007.

The theatrical acuity of this work is rare, a kind of butoh rendition of theater of the absurd. In *Quick Silver,* Murobushi gives expression to the anguish and isolation of the individual with a consciousness that can only be described as existential. Like the search for human essence in Samuel Beckett's *Endgame,* and with the same purity and minimalism, he defies a standard plot. In the beginning, he moves like an actor, but when he moves out into the space, it is with rare athletic grace and mercurial surprise. He leaps and darts as a dancer, folds and twists from spot to spot, falling up through the air and landing backward onto the stage, only to spring back up again with frantic intensity. His repetitive movement radiates in waves, rolls like quicksilver, and is equally difficult to grasp. It seems the earth might collapse under him. In his business suit, Murobushi reminds me of one of the dancer-actors in Pina Bausch's *Tanztheater,* but when he morphs to boundless energy wearing only his silver-painted skin and a loincloth, I know I'm in the presence of butoh, and surely in view of physical theater.

In a lecture at the New York Butoh Festival of 2007, Murobushi described the global process of butoh as organic, "bringing in seeds from all over the world to create a new flower."

FIGURE 29. Murobushi Ko in *Quick Silver* at the CAVE New York Butoh Festival 2007. Photograph by Dola Baroni, © 2007. Used by permission of CAVE.

His own butoh gathers seeds from European physical theater techniques as well as historical butoh, and it is not exactly like a flower, more human and troubled, as I distill in verse below. The word he uses to describe his own work is *uncertainty.*

The man in dim light

Hiding behind a dark suit with a stocking on his head,
Why does he snap his fingers?
Is he the man taking tickets on the train,
Or the ghost inside your head?

Eerie ennui and arid sound, rumbling head shakes
And voice blurs, the perfect fitting of eel shapes:
Right in wordings of death on its way,
Ghoulish capers, sacks of cloth around his head,
What will we see in the half-light?
The black out?

Four lights glare across the floor from the left, and he is on the floor
Struggling through the horizontal streams of dim light,
With his breath suffering and his body silver.
"Who are you," he asks softly.
"I am a stranger."

His back to the audience, his bronzed body expulsed,
Except for the string between his ass and crotch-pouch loincloth,
He knee-drops into alchemy, eyes blinking, as mine are strapped.

Stranger, connected to the floor and facing the audience,
Organically morphing from head, neck, and back
To one whole piece, as arising awake with everything moving,
Who are you?

He falls on his back
Thud! One leg held up off the floor, his other leg what?
His hand lifts,
Sidling up and down in folds holds and stops,
Engulfing a crossed-leg sitting.

My body is curious, and wanders a bit,
Falling back a little. Cloven hoofs arrive
On the menu and a shoulder stand.

One light from the side remains in the blank silence,
While he, tiling across the stage,
Streaks and chokes into another shoulder stand.

We see a curious headless yogi,
Bending under his shoulder and speaking:
"I was sleeping. . . . I don't want to sleep too much. Why is she here?"

"She drowned in this water in Japan. I will find her."
He doubles over, animal walking, with his knuckles down.
Looks down into a dark spot on the stage,
A magic fountain, a black hole,
A pool, he kneels over it.

No, it's sand
And he throws it up in the air.

Sand snakes mercury and memory.
Music electric covers the hush darkness in a howl.
Howl.
Hands and feet condense the feline lines, as they go up.
He falls down—rolling between lights from both sides of the stage, and
　　　lands
In the middle light.

Why Clov's first speech in Beckett's *Endgame*?
(With fixed gaze and delivered tonelessly):
"Finished, it's finished, nearly finished. . . ."
No it's just barely started.

Become splitting sound, and high,
Too loud, the full screech over and over.
Murobushi falls back on his back,
Hard, over and over.
But why?

And Clov goes on: "Grain upon grain, one by one, and one day, suddenly, there's a heap, a little heap, the impossible heap. (Pause.) I can't be punished any more."

20

Daemon of the Riverbank

Kei Takei in Tokyo (2008)

Kei Takei lived in New York and performed throughout America for many years. Now she lives in Tokyo and continues to perform internationally. In this essay, I use her familiar stage name, first name first, and depart from the common reverse order, family name first, used in Japan.

It is September 21, 2008, and the premiere of *Dancing Fairy of Five Leaves—Metamorphosis of Okuni* at the International Performing Arts venue. In this historic concert, six women perform different styles of dance in honor of Izumo no Okuni, female founder of the original Kabuki. We wait for it to begin at Theater X (Cai) in Sumida-ku, Tokyo. Kai Takei's dance—*Onigawara* (Daemon of the Riverbank)—is first on the program and sets the tone for everything to follow. The music for her dance, *From Light 23,* is by Takehisa Kosugi.

With her feet planted wide and dark hair tumbling, Takei draws a portrait of the bewitching Okuni, who was born toward the end of the sixteenth century. Her decision to move as a shaman attempts to conjure Okuni and to dance her ambivalent situation. In her youth, Okuni was an attendant of the Izumo shrine; throughout her life, she experienced the strict isolation of the sexes demanded by Buddhist ethics in her day. Eventually, she became an original secularizing force, a symbol of the common people and the freedom of women.

Other dancers on the same program explore Okuni's grace, her elegance and beauty, playfulness and strength. But Takei moves beneath these and toward the soul of Okuni, the dancer and transformer. She enters the stage by lifting the paper backdrop that will become a canvas for spray-paint calligraphy in sub-

FIGURE 30. Kei Takei dances *Daemon of the Riverbank* in Tokyo on September 21, 2008, at the premier of the International Performing Arts concert *Dancing Fairy of Five Leaves — Metamorphosis of Okuni,* celebrating Izumo no Okuni, female founder of the original Kabuki. Photographs by Kosuga Desuga (left), © 2008, and Kusano (right), © 2008. Used by permission of Kei Takei.

sequent dances. Crawling from underneath the large canvas, she slowly comes to her feet wearing a large red silk wrap with a bright blue outer apron. More important, she wears her dance as a second skin. One is not aware of the technique behind it or that it takes considerable discipline and skill to move slowly in low, sustained squatting and to rise out of low positions without effort. I see Kabuki in Takei's flair and largesse, not Kabuki's modern refinements nearly so much as its enduring boldness.

Kabuki is the art of dance and song, the legacy of the famous Okuni. Originally through her it was called both *Okuni Kabuki* and *Onna Kabuki* (Women's Kabuki). We know that Kabuki was eventually taken over by men, who played all of the roles, including those of the females. *Onnagata,* the transformation of the male into the female, provides a central aesthetic in modern Kabuki, as we have noted in other contexts. In a way, we could say that *Onnagata* is part of the aesthetic alchemy of Kabuki (and of butoh).

I provide a brief history of Okuni and the female roots of Kabuki at the end of this essay, but first I imagine in poetry Takei's shamanist link to the struggles of Okuni, who birthed a new form of art in the dry riverbeds of Kyoto so very long ago, her grace and beauty influenced to greater abandon by Sanzaburo, a composer who had been sent by his family in Nagoya to be trained for the priesthood in the famous Kennin Temple in Kyoto. But as it turned out, Sanzaburo was more interested in songs than the priesthood. Through him, Okuni learned to dance to popular songs of the day, even as she retained something of her spiritual legacy.

A few of Okuni's *Kugara* (Shinto dances) survive today in the form of poetic songs. *Tenshi Wago Mae* (Dance of Heaven and Earth Affinity) blends Buddhist suppression of emotion with nature myths from Shinto. Thus spiritual sublimation rests side by side with carnal interpretations, the latter most apparent in old Japan, where under Buddhist influence love was passing passion and ultimately an illusion.

Kai Takei's dance, *Daemon of the Riverbank,* opens a path to Okuni that is neither carnal nor exclusively spiritual. She conjures Okuni as a shaman would, not as a beauty of the river, but as a daemon with metamorphic powers. Takei's dance inspires my poetry toward Okuni's endeavors in her dance of heaven and earth:

With Great Endeavor

I
Okuni's arms sweep
Extending from the heart.
Hanging free, her black hair hovers over her face.
Will the work she has finished
Fail to mark as worthy?

The god of power, she sings
Lives within my being:
I dance between this world and another.
My breath is a shrine, buried between my shoulders.

Ringing with sounds of music, I splash the water
Clear and sparkling, as I watch my reflection,
And untie my blue apron.
Pouring, pouring, the river water
Smoothly over my shoulders, pouring.

II
Kei Takei dances a river eternal, holding her torso still
Against the mutated stirring of her arms,
Then floats as in a dream.

Suddenly she folds over and builds strength,
Dropping and hanging from the creative thrust.
Her red drape drops slightly,

White silk wraps her hips
Had there been none,
She would be naked.

Like to the falling,
Her face is but a mask.
Her legs are bare,
And newly created.

Life is only dew,
And a breath that drieth up.
If dew-drops falling in the river had
Hardened to vanity and illusion,
What would there be to love?

III
The dancer daemon breaks her pace.
Now in a white tunic tied at the waist,
Her arms flail wildly as she sends signs
And signals into the earth.

Electronic music fills the audience for the dance
Dense sounds, now rumbling, become light and soft.
Gone are the worries.
The back canvas lifts and
All is forgotten;
As for the first time the river daemon looks up.
Then crawls back under the painter's paper canvas.

IV
The next dance is already in progress
With a spray gun painting from behind
Its massive calligraphy.

Paint drips down the thin paper
In lighted streams,
While in the daemon's place,
Her ugliness and thunder, flows relief
And great joy.

About Okuni

During the period of the Ashikaga shogunate (1338–1573), Kyoto was the center
of luxury and culture among the wealthy. The first half of this era, known as the
Muromachi period, was characterized by an increase of education, gentility, and
leisure in *Cha-no-yu* (tea ceremony), *Ikebana* (flower arrangement), and *Ko-*

awase (incense judging). *Noh* theater also exercised a civilizing social influence. While the upper classes amused themselves openly in cultured ways and secretly with practices of an exclusively male society, the common people were entertaining themselves upon the dry riverbeds or in vacant lots of Kyoto with popular sports of rude promiscuity, where men of rank also found entertainment.

Okuni of Izumo entered in this popular arena somewhere about the end of the sixteenth century, when England's William Shakespeare was in his prime, She was the daughter of an ironworker and in the service of the Shinto shrine at Izumo. Her dancing met with such welcome in Kyoto that she remained to create a new dance drama rising from the midst of the common people. Okuni reached the pinnacle of her popularity by 1604 and established stages in various parts of Kyoto. Soon she was invited to perform before nobility, and the number of Kabuki playhouses multiplied. Even so, Kabuki developed as an entertainment of the common people in protest against the prevailing social system as well as dramatic conventions.

Eventually, unbridled licentiousness made Kabuki a social danger, and as early as 1608 it was confined by official order to the outskirts of the cities. In 1629, *Onna Kabuki* was prohibited because of its immoral influence and because of its reputation as a source of dangerous thought and popular freedom. To this day, Okuni is a female hero, a symbol of protest, and a spear of freedom in the face of conformity.

Significantly, women are once again entering into performances of Kabuki. And in butoh, which is less restricted by custom, they are becoming increasingly prominent as performers, choreographers, teachers, and producers of butoh concerts and festivals. If men originally invented butoh, women and the feminine archetype nevertheless inspired them, as we have explored. Now butoh is a globally responsive art that promotes gender exploration and the creative voice of women, as in Okuni's example.

Part Three

Ursprung Unfinished

21

Ursprung

Hijikata Tatsumi, Ohno Kazuo, and Ohno Yoshito

> This language which evokes in the mind images of an intense natural (or spiritual) poetry provides a good idea of what a poetry in space independent of spoken language could mean in theater.
>
> —Antonin Artaud, *The Theater and Its Double*

Ursprung is German, that favorite word of Martin Heidegger's metaphysics. It means "origin" in the sense of a leap, an auspicious beginning that springs up as from a foot or from a spring of water. An *ursprung* is not just any beginning; it is a genuine beginning, a first cause, just as we know that first causes and origins are the subjects of metaphysics. We also know that origin signifies belonging as well as beginning: Your origin is the place you come from, your tribal identity, and your roots. As we approach completion here in part 3, we loop toward beginnings in the *ursprung* of butoh, which, it has been my purpose to show, is both avant-garde and primal, a root still morphing and unfinished.

Hijikata Tatsumi and Ohno Kazuo found themselves smack into the middle of an *ursprung* by about 1968, nine years after Hijikata's first odd dance, *Kinjiki,* performed for the conservative All Japan Dance Association and named after Mishima Yukio's homoerotic, tragic novel *Kinjiki,* meaning "Forbidden Color." The dance had three famous performers: Hijikata; Ohno Kazuo's twenty-year-old son, Yoshito; and a chicken. On a darkened stage, Hijikata chased Yoshito in circles. Audience members recall panting sounds and saw beautiful, slow, sustained movement. At the end, Yoshito held the chicken with its white wings fluttering stunningly in the fading light, and perhaps he sat on the chicken. At least this was the impression, as some interpretations and gossip about the dance would have it.

Dance critic Goda Nario, who became one of butoh's heroes, wrote that it caused a darkness and shudder to run through his body in which he felt finally a psychological relief. Motofuji Akiko, who would later become Hijikata's wife, was also in the audience. She said of Hijikata's dance that she felt electricity run through her body. This was 1959, just on the cusp of the postmodern dance movement in America, which had its *ursprung* in about 1962, the year I graduated from college. At that time, butoh was not yet a glimmer in my mind. I discovered it twenty-three years later in 1985 when I saw Nakajima Natsu, a student of Hijikata and Ohno, dance *Niwa* (The Garden) in Montreal. Through her, I became a student of butoh.

What happened to the chicken at the *ursprung* of butoh? We'll never really know. Art is like that; it gets you thinking and wondering. Is it a chicken or a chair or a piece of cheese hanging in the air? What happens in a dance, and what it means, is certainly a part of the dance, but it is also in the eye of the beholder. Some in the audience for *Kinjiki* were outraged.

Yoshito told me he thought *Kinjiki* was about being best friends. But if it was about friendship for Yoshito as he danced the work, what was in Hijikata's mind as he conceived the work? Homosexuality and suicide as in Mishima's novel? Hunger? Ritual sacrifice? Curiosity? Surrender? We seldom have direct access to the mind of the choreographer, and this is how it should be. The dance then stands on its own; the embodied intentions of the choreographer as understood and danced by the performer are what we read, and readings will vary. Butoh dancers (*butoh-ka*) might say their dances don't "mean" anything; they exist to be experienced in the changing moment. Having watched a great deal of butoh, however, I would say that butoh dances do have themes, and the witness can go past the changing moment of direct experience to carry away something of the essence of the dance, its meta-messages (its meaning) and metaphysics. Butoh to me is not one thing; it is a genre with different styles and approaches, but at the same time, there are identifying factors at the core of anything we call "butoh." What makes butoh butoh, we have asked? This book has attempted to answer this in several ways. Here I propose a further glance by looking at butoh's *ursprung* through Hijikata Tatsumi and Ohno Kazuo, and then in *Kuu*, the last chapter, by describing a current dance of Ohno Yoshito. (In order to distinguish between the two Ohnos, I sometimes use first names.)

Just beyond the shamanist basis of their dances, I read Hijikata's as political and Kazuo's as spiritual. Hijikata wanted to rescue the Japanese body from effacement after World War II, as we have seen. He encouraged a radical approach to dance in which arms and legs would "sprout" from their hiding places within the body, being born again and again. He wanted his dance to be a "purposeless nonproduct" and his dancers to be "dreaming murder weapons." Thus he cultivated an imperfect body that can show weakness and disease, and he called this "the emaciated body." This was his surrealist language for combating the rise of capitalist production and the spread of technology during the rebuilding of Japan in respect to American occupation after the war. We remember that Hijikata's dance arose amid the turmoil of postapocalyptic Japan. Never before had such unilateral destructive power been unleashed on a single country in such a short space of time. Butoh rose from the ashes of Japan. This is basic to its alchemy, whatever new forms might emerge. There is light and surrender in ash and, as in butoh, an antiwar message blowing in the wind.

Kazuo's dance was also responsive to the war but from another perspective. We have seen that he was a soldier for nine years beginning in 1938, first in China then in New Guinea, spending the last two years as a prisoner. Kazuo's response to war was not political but personal and spiritual. He hasn't spoken much about his war experiences, but Yoshito believes he carries them, nevertheless, in his body and in his dance. Indeed, dancing has offered a means toward transforming them. If Kazuo doesn't speak directly of horrifying experiences, it is because he is never literal. What he did say bears repeating, "When I dance, I carry all the dead with me." I believe this declaration is one of his poetic *butoh-fu*, a motivating image for his dance and not removed from daily life. Concerning the latter, he spoke to his students of their debt to the dead and admonished them: "You are not the be-all and end-all of life."

We have also seen that Hijikata's dance was based in profuse imagery or *butoh-fu* that he shaped from his own imagination and intercultural sources. Waguri Yukio has categorized these in relation to seven worlds, arising cosmologically from wet and heavy qualities to light and dry, as we took up in chapter 1. Thus Hijikata developed his dance to reflect material sources, as Waguri emphasizes. Ohno, on the other hand, believed that form follows spirit when the movement goes beneath objective reality. Together these artists produced dialectics of form and spirit resounding in two schools of butoh—one closer to choreography through *butoh-fu,* and the other deriving more from improvisation. They both fulfill Antonin Artaud's call for a theater of the senses, Hijikata perhaps more directly because he was strongly affected by Artaud, Jean Genet, and European surrealism. But Ohno Kazuo also incorporated surrealist tactics in his dances; even as he retained a lyric thread from the time he was a young modern dancer before the war.

Both of these artists hone strong theatrical elements. Their work developed in the direction of physical theater with dance at the center. Artaud saw that his dream of a theater without words had more precedent in Asia than in Western theater with its narrative traditions. In the differing personalities and approaches of Hijikata and Ohno Kazuo, the hope of Artaud found fertile ground. Despite butoh's Western sources, Japanese elements played a larger role in butoh's *ursprung*—namely in Hijikata's desire to create a modern Kabuki that would be true to premodern sources in Japan and in Ohno's emptiness and self-surrender, as well as his blurring of the lines between life and death in the Buddhist image of *konpaku:* that place "nowhere out there," as he taught his students, where the living and the dead mingle together peacefully.

Hijikata's political *ursprung* is represented in his language. In naming his dance, he used the word *butoh* in its older meaning, "ancient dance," as Takenouchi Atsushi, a contemporary *butoh-ka* who experienced Hijikata's choreography first-hand, told me at the New York Butoh Festival. Butoh also means "imported dance, like Western social dance," says Takenouchi, "but Hijikata sought the ancient usage to represent his dance and distinguish it from extant forms." (Takenouchi is represented in the essays.) Dance and theater—like all art—is motivated by language, images, and ideas, and we can ultimately read the beliefs of the artist in the work. The work then frames possibilities for our intuitional and cognitive reception. We discern the intentions of the artist through the lens of our reading. So our readings themselves become part of the politics. Hijikata left much to the imagination and reading of the audience, according to butoh critic Goda Nario. That is what Goda appreciated so much about Hijikata, he told me in an interview in 1990: the unfinished, nontotalizing style that trusted the audience to enter into the dance experience. Experience is key in butoh, as I have tried to demonstrate in this work. Hijikata stated this clearly in the title of his first recital: *Hijikata Tatsumi DANCE EXPERIENCE no Kai,* produced in 1960. Ohno Kazuo played a vital role in this recital, dancing *Diviinu sho* (Divine) based on Jean Genet's writing and choreographed by Hijikata.

Together, Hijikata and Ohno placed the direct experience of dance in the spotlight, as though to affirm the direct bodily exchange between the audience and the dancer. Their way of doing this contained something that we in the West might associate with stream of consciousness in writing, an element of surrealist art. However, the butoh way has its own unmistakable morphology—a bodily state of "becoming"—as Hijikata himself defined it. Butoh holds high theatricality alongside meditative elements, morphing from image to image unpredictably as in a meditation, and it can float or lull or startle with sharp edges. It does not deny ugliness or suffering, and in activating the energy of the body's root chakra emanating down from the pelvis, it sinks into the legs and into the earth, connecting the human animal to other animals. Because Hijikata and Ohno founded butoh in such an elemental, shamanist *ursprung,* the butoh we now see still probes root imagery, even inching endlessly along the ground, as in *Mourning,* Eiko and Koma's performance of 2007 that I write about in the essays. After half a century of butoh, many artists like Eiko and Koma still extend the influence of its *ursprung,* if not its label.

In examining my own mind through the essays of part 2, I see how butoh carries forth a shamanist and healing form of dance with morphology as its sustaining tone and transformative aesthetic. Other witnesses might see different qualities or experience them differently from their own perspective. There is no one single truth in butoh. Concerning butoh themes of nature and metamorphosis, great butoh performers like Ohno Kazuo have become containers whereby audiences can experience their own transformative possibilities. Ohno, well past one hundred years old, stands for life in transition, making his aging process central to his dance. Aging is the ongoing metamorphosis that we all undergo. Ohno gives us a *wabi sabi* distillation of this in his very person. *Wabi sabi* is the traditional Japanese appreciation of beauty in weathering age.

In the twenty-first century, Ohno Yoshito carries forward the living legacy of his father, as well as his memories of Hijikata, having danced with him and in many works directed by him during the last four decades of the twentieth century. In the next chapter, I describe the premier performance of Yoshito's work *Kuu* in New York City and fragments of his workshop words at the CAVE New York Butoh Festival in 2007. In the spirit of "not finishing" and "not starting," Yoshito waits at the *ursprung.*

22

Kuu (Emptiness)

Ohno Yoshito and the Patience of Not Starting

> Keep on eating of yourself, copiously.
> —Ohno Yoshito

It is October 27, 2007, and Ohno Kazuo's birthday. He is 101. Ohno Yoshito, his son, stands like a statue with his head bowed and his back to the audience as we enter and take our seats for the premier of his work *Kuu* (Emptiness) at the CAVE New York Butoh Festival.[1] Ohno is framed by a creamy white stage, and his suit is the same color, his shaved head lightly powdered to complete the white-on-white stage painting. As the house lights dim to half, Johann Sebastian Bach's organ piece *Toccata and Fugue in D Minor,* suddenly floods the house with monumental sound. We become quiet and listen while Ohno, off-center and upstage left, continues to stand in unblinking stillness.

His containment against the grand Western strains of Bach draws the audience to him, and I ask myself if this isn't one of the techniques of butoh. When the performer goes so deeply inward, he projects the inside out without overtly expressing anything. Ohno goes inside so clearly that he evokes the space of *ma,* connecting himself to the audience and to his father in absentia. Ohno's *ma* is an intensification of the spatial and psychological connections that exist between humans and connect us to nature as well. In this case, Bach underlines the condition for *ma* and waiting, while Ohno practices what he preaches, "the patience of not starting," often a workshop theme of his.

The dancer's shoulders lean slightly forward as part of the downward slope of his neck and head. The house lights remain at half for the entire twelve minutes of organ music and Ohno's patient stillness. This means that the dancer has been standing without moving for at least twenty-two minutes. As the music stops, his

FIGURE 31. Ohno Yoshito waits in place as the audience assembles for *Kuu* (Emptiness) at the Japan Society performance during the CAVE New York Butoh Festival in New York City in 2007. Photograph by Ann Rodiger, © 2007. Used by permission of Ann Rodiger.

back unfolds; his head rises, and he gradually turns around. I have seen Ohno perform several times, but this time I notice that, characteristically, his chin is held down creating a stern expression, a posture he often employs.

Ohno moves slowly in silence for a while and then to the sounds of wind. When he finally frees himself from the single spot onstage, his chin releases as well, and he becomes light, performing graceful curves in space and caressing the stage floor like Isadora Duncan, but with soft dance shoes that might do for jazz, the tango, or postmodern plain dance. He falls down to the floor on his hands, recovers, and then once more takes his beginning position of waiting. This time his hands begin to claw, reminiscent of his riveting solo at the opening of *Suiren* (Water Lilies), his duet with his father in 1987. As also in *Suiren*, he takes a walk on the diagonal, tossing one leg out in a blunt kick, crossing it low over the other leg, and then repeating the kick again. This is a reference to the blocky-man opening section in *Suiren*, Yoshito's contrast to the more flowery dance of Kazuo. It is obvious that *Kuu* is an original but that it quotes Ohno's already established repertory with his father, using a postmodern strategy of appropriation, or of self-appropriation in this case. Yoshito's butoh is "eating of itself copiously," as he teaches in his workshops. I'm not sure he is talking about self-copying here, but there is definitely an element of this in his advice and in the word *copious*. Be yourself, would be closer to his meaning, I think, and do this with the same pleasure you take in eating a wonderful meal. How can you be more of who you really are? This would be the dancer's quest.

Ohno also seems to say that "new is not necessarily better." I welcome the return of familiar butoh elements in a new context and am reminded that every artist repeats himself to a certain extent, either consciously or without noticing. Ohno's repetitions are intentional and clear; they evoke his father and his connections to him through dance. In *Kuu,* Ohno Yoshito develops his familiar language of movement, crossing his clawed hands and wrists over each other with tremendous tension. In one of the most dynamic movements, he flings himself out of this tension, landing in a squat with his right arm twining around his leg and grabbing it. This first episode of the dance finishes with Ohno's catlike, slow scratching of the air as he turns offstage into the wings, leaving it empty for a time and the audience waiting for his return.

He enters from the other side, upstage right in back, having changed his costume to billowy white sailor pants with a high waist and buttons placed diagonally down the sides of the slanting pockets. His chest is bare, and his body is lean like his father's. The upright ease of his movement, the masterful stylizing of costumes that I so admire in Japan strike my eye. This integrates with the white, shaved head and line of white powder etching Ohno's spine. He travels the stage in a slow shimmy, his head balanced gracefully and bobbing childlike

FIGURE 32. Ohno Yoshito dances *Kuu* (Emptiness) at the CAVE New York Butoh Festival in 2007. Photograph courtesy of the Ohno Kazuo Archives.

on his neck, then finishes by descending into the ground to the light strumming of guitar. Once again he leaves the empty space to our imagination, elongating his back in elegant waves as he leaves.

The dancer returns, moving in silence and wearing a cutaway short kimono jacket to match his off-white pants, one sleeve painted elaborately in salmon and turquoise and moving like a wing. Soon we hear the sound of tinkling bells mingling with Japanese flute. His hand holds an imaginary oar and his fists vibrate as he metamorphoses surreally from image to image. I let go of any desire for narrative and go with him. He looks up, kneels, and returns to the paddle, pushing away his own shaken steps. He holds the object again and then releases it, his wings reaching back to nowhere. The music of bells and flute develop electronic threads winding through the movement. Ohno pulls himself inward toward his center as the acoustics float the ascending sounds repetitiously across the audience; he remains still against the rising weave of the electronic music. I see color and an image of a peacock and pink shells sliding from his arm as the music adds sounds of wind, and the dance trembles.

The dancer's hands manage to find his face, framing it in tremolo from the front and back. His few facial expressions open up a hole for his mouth, and his whole body catches the vibrations of his hands. I understand Ohno's world as a struggle to shake beauty free. What does he see overhead? A bird escapes him, perhaps? He collects himself, regenerating his stillness, his place, and then executes a few tiny skips backward. He finds a way out upstage right at the back, also extending his right arm overhead as he goes, opposing this reach with a downward gaze and texturing his exit.

Reflecting Mortality

We wait again. This is our part in the emerging pattern of the dance, a most valuable one. As Tibetan Buddhist teacher Pema Chodron says, "It is a transformative experience to simply pause instead of immediately filling up a space. By waiting we begin to connect with fundamental restlessness as well as fundamental spaciousness."[2] Ohno comes back after the silence wearing a ruffled collar instead of the jacket, a bit of lace on his bare chest, as his father might have worn. He breaks character and speaks to someone offstage, asking for something. A stagehand enters and brings him a box of tissues. Ohno takes one out of the box, folding and shaping it into a gauzy origami bird. He takes his time, and when the bird is finished he carries it tenderly in two hands, replicating nature in miniature. The lightness of the tissue flutters with him when he dances and when his hands shake even slightly. He drops the bird lightly. Ballet enters into his steps as he does a butohlike double-time bourrée, skittering along with a downward gaze. Then he surprises us by falling out of the momentum and onto both knees at once, not an easy feat for a sixty-nine-year-old. We can easily forget how old Yoshito is. Will he be remembered as forever young because he is his father's son?

How tender are the steps of Yoshito and Kazuo, both of them. In Yoshito's dance, I feel the presence of Kazuo, his luster and kindness—one person conquering himself more valuable than the conquering of thousands by aggressive means. As I take a broad view, I'm aware that in the seething movements and shaking of Kazuo and Yoshito, there is no trace of anger, just the tension of the dance coming and going in bodies of primal vibration. The notion that butoh expiates anger and aggression is a mistaken analysis. The fierce expressions of butoh are seldom angry; rather, they excavate the torture that humans inflict on themselves and others. Not pushing this down, they acknowledge it for the same reasons that artists of conscience have perennially exposed pain and injustice, foreshadowing transformative action.

Ohno's dance reminds me that art can indeed provide the impetus for action in its challenges. Relating to a good dance, like reading a good book, can help one grow and question. But unlike a book, a dance is nonverbal, existing in the middle space between the dancer and the witness. The artist and the witness meet through the work, each through their own experience. At some point, a reflective and maybe analytical process begins to operate for the witness as she comes to terms with the truth of the work for her. Good works stimulate feeling and cognition, the heart and the head. Transformative action comes from there. (In Socratic views, true knowledge contains action.)

> One of the truths of butoh for me has been the growing understanding that I don't have to give up dancing as I grow older. I have the example of Kazuo and Yoshito to thank for this. I can continue to "eat of myself copiously." I also grasp their messages of beauty and hope, of patience and emptiness, the sheer value of surrender. How then, I ask myself, can I carry these messages into my own teaching?

The younger Ohno finds the tissue bird he has dropped, smoothes the earth, and resurrects the bird. Or is it a flower he has lost and found? As he dances with the white, small flutter of tissue, it seems to become a dove. Then he skips like a child, this man on the verge of seventy. Yoshito leaves the stage and then returns in his last incarnation with pictures of his father Kazuo projected on the white background of the stage. Kazuo, loved by so many through his world tours well into old age, escaped the designations of modern dance, moved past postmodern forms and eventually butoh itself. Kazuo is like Isadora Duncan or Vaslav Nijinsky, independently great but unlike them; he teaches dancers how to incorporate age into their art and not to deny it. On the background screen of the stage, we see photographs of Kazuo as a centenarian, in bed smiling peacefully with his eyes closed and his teeth out. We see Kazuo's great large hands lined with spiny veins; Pina Bausch kissing Kazuo on his toothless mouth; Kazuo teaching students from around the world in his Yokohama studio; Yoshito continuing the teaching in his father's stead; Kazuo tumbling over happily; a tree, symbolizing Kazuo's great bond with nature.

Presently, the light begins to capture Yoshito's hand holding a tiny finger puppet. As the puppet becomes focused on the background, we see that it has the generous face of Kazuo and his large expressive hands. The puppet's tiny black dress falls over Yoshito's hand, and we see Yoshito's face also dancing. (The ingenious puppet, I learn later, is a present to Yoshito from a Mexican student.) The photographs on the background continue to overlap the puppet dance, and we see Kazuo, not in an elder home, but in his own home in Yokohama with Yoshito and his family taking care of him. There is a brief showing of a photograph of La Argentina, the beautiful flamenco dancer who inspired Kazuo to dance when he saw her as a young man. He carried the memory of her for fifty years, before dancing his homage to La Argentina.

How fitting for Ohno Yoshito's dance of nonattachment and freedom to frame his father on the night of his birthday. One hundred and one years after the birth of Ohno Kazuo in the port city of Hakodate, Japan, his son Yoshito holds a finger puppet of him against a stage screen in New York City. Kazuo's likeness, made in Mexico, dances through the fingers of his son to the strains of Elvis Presley's "I Can't Help Falling in Love with You," Kazuo's favorite.

Kazuo continues to dance in Yoshito's *Kuu*, a global multimedia work cast in the light of Buddhist nonattachment. *Kuu* morphs across imagery and continents as the pure focus of the dancer captures the global charm of butoh. In contradistinction to the dance of Hijikata, this is not muddy butoh, even as its alchemy derives from the muddy origins of butoh that Yoshito experienced first-hand with Hijikata during the turbulent period that linked Japan to America and Europe on the verge of the 1960s. This was a time when no element of life was unaffected by social upheaval and political protest. Yoshito was just twenty years old when he danced with Hijikata in *Kinjiki* (Forbidden Color, 1959), the first inkling of butoh. Now he carries his own seasoned butoh out to the world, dancing in the memory of his father with a finger puppet. In his short program note for *Kuu* (Emptiness), Ohno says:

> I decided on *Kuu* to express my belief that I have been given my life by many people, or rather, by everyone around me. *Kuu* is the body itself. The idea of emptiness resonates with the themes I explore in my butoh work—non-attachment and freedom.

In the patient emptiness of *Kuu,* the invisible becomes visible; the use of paradox uncovers the truth of contradictions and differences. In *Kuu,* we cross over the boundaries of difference as they dissolve in the shared material of the human body, not racially marked or attached but in transition.

Ohno Yoshito's Workshop Words: On Flowers, Snow, and Paper

By now, it should be clear that butoh thrives on morphing imagery. Lifelike, it has a changing, unfinished essence. In Ohno Yoshito's workshops, there is always a focus on nature as a source for butoh and attention to the morphology of transformative process. He also foregrounds his references to nature through ukiyo-e, demonstrating a tie to his own past dances with his father. This would not be nature in the raw; it would be stylized, not necessarily refined and manicured, but in states of change. Ohno Kazuo and Ohno Yoshito danced *Suiren* in response to Claude Monet's water lily canvases, as we explored briefly in chapter 1. We also examined the influence of the Japanese ukiyo-e wood-block prints on Monet and other Impressionists in Europe to understand the cycle of global alchemy. Flowers have been a major theme of butoh with Ohno Kazuo and Ohno Yoshito as well as with Hijikata.

When Yoshito teaches, he emphasizes, as his father did, that the eyes and head don't need to be lifted high. Rather, when the head is slightly lowered, the audience will want to come toward the dance. This erases the proud gaze that is often inculcated in dance techniques.

Yoshito finds material sources to inspire flower consciousness, sometimes showing calligraphy of "snow, moon, and flower," as he did in New York at the 2007 Butoh Festival. "The Sakura flower that comes in the spring is only around for a very short time; it is like the snow, which falls and then melts."[3] Like his father, he uses his workshop words to inspire the dancers. It is not enough to say, "Be a flower." What kind of flower, we want to know? And what is happening to the flower? Yoshito speaks of an old Japanese idea, that flowers blowing around have fallen from heaven, and he frames improvisations on this. Everyone finds his or her own way into this experience:

> When I dance butoh on the theme of flowers, I feel tenderness and introversion, a soft central point as Yoshito explains it. I become less important than the flower; I want to find the flower in me, and I feel my eyes soften.

In material contrast, Yoshito demonstrates with paper how to CUT through the space in an instant, as when you very quickly cut through or tear paper. We have said that butoh has material or objective sources, especially through the material processes of Hijikata. Likewise, Yoshito has people tear the paper and then immediately cut through the space themselves. In this way, the paper is the object to spur the dance and the somatic feeling of ripping. "Start with the paper," he says. If the start is good, the dancing cut through the space is good. "Each rip is one moment. This moment is important—the moment of shining."[4]

Yoshito sometimes uses the music of Frédéric Chopin for this cutting through space. His teaching emphasizes somatic process and sense perception, moving and morphing with music through various images of flowers, remembering his father's favorite form of life in the lightness of snow and ripping paper. Our learning lies in the art of not starting:

> Lacking art, we wait,
> as shaken flowers, as snow,
> we lose ourselves so.

Biographies of Dancers

Frances Barbe (born 1971), a performer and choreographer living in London, is one of the major non-Japanese exponents of butoh and butoh-influenced dance. She has trained in butoh since 1992, originally in Australia, then in Japan, and most recently in Germany with Endo Tadashi, with whom she has performed since 1997. She tours internationally, performing and teaching. She was awarded a prestigious fellowship in 2001 from the Arts and Humanities Research Council (AHRC) and the Daiwa Anglo-Japanese Foundation to develop her research, which uses Japanese performance, both butoh and the Actor Training Method of Tadashi Suzuki, as inspiration for rethinking training, methodology, and aesthetics in contemporary European dance and theater. Her unique perspective is informed by her application of butoh in a variety of contexts, from actor training to dance and from opera to youth projects. She has been instrumental in inviting a number of Japanese butoh artists to the United Kingdom to perform and teach. She was artistic director of the Daiwa International Butoh Festival in London in 2005.

Robert Bingham (born 1970) is visiting artist in residence in dance at Alfred University. He received his MFA in dance from SUNY Brockport, where he was a Pylyshenko-Strasser Award recipient. Prior to attending graduate school, Bingham danced with several New York–based companies and artists, including De Facto Dance, Ishmael Houston-Jones, and Jennifer Monson. His work has been included in programs at various venues, including PS 122 and the Painted Bride in Philadelphia. Recently he has danced in works by Kelly Donovan, dance scholar Sondra Fraleigh, and butoh-based choreographer Lani Fand Weissbach, and he regularly collaborates with Alfred University colleague D. Chase Angier, with whom he has performed frequently throughout the East Coast and in Mexico as Angier/Bingham Dance. Bingham is a featured dancer in the dance on film *Broken Images,* which has been shown nationally. He has had extensive training in somatic modalities, including certification to teach yoga (Integral Yoga Institute, 1996) and graduation from Eastwest Institute for Dance and Somatic Studies (2003). His dance and yoga studies take him regularly to India, where he has also taught, choreographed, and performed. In summer 2007, he traveled there to study *kalaripayettu,* a South Indian martial art that he has since incorporated into dance-technique classes and choreography.

Eiko (born 1952) and *Koma* (born 1948) studied with both Ohno Kazuo and Hijikata Tatsumi, performing early on with Hijikata in Tokyo and later with Ohno in the 1970s. They also studied in the tradition of German modern dance with Manja Chmiel in Germany. As seasoned performers, they were named MacArthur Fellows in the United States in 1996 and have received two Bessie Awards for outstanding choreography. Their work has been widely recognized, also receiving the 2004 Samuel H. Scripps American Dance Festival Award and the 2006 Dance Magazine Award. They live and work in New York City and travel widely, performing their metamorphic dances for audiences worldwide.

Endo Tadashi (born 1947) began his life as a Japanese national living in Beijing, China. From 1973 to 1976, he studied at the Max Reinhardt Seminary in Vienna, Austria, and in 1989 he met Kazuo Ohno, who profoundly influenced his development and choreography. Endo developed his own special dance style, however, which explores the *ma* between Eastern and Western culture and between theater performance and dance. He calls his work "Butoh-MA," explaining at the London Butoh Festival in 2005 that in Zen Buddhism, *ma* means emptiness as well as spaces between things. Endo visualizes these spaces in their very fine changes. The moments when one figure changes to the next or one image changes to the next with nearly invisible movements and a very strong tension are more important to him than the representation of a figure or image. This tension, which he radiates with utmost concentration, transforms his dance continuously. Endo is head of the Butoh Center MAMU in Göttingen, Germany, and artistic director of the MAMU Festivals in Göttingen and Tokyo, through his MAMU Dance Theater. He has produced performances with jazz musicians Toshinori Kondo, Aki Takase, Kozutoki Umezu, Steve Lacey, Conrad Bauer, Peter Kowald, Günter Sommer, and Ulrich Gumpert. His work has been shown in Europe at festivals in Munich, Leipzig, Salzburg, Athens, Naples, Palermo, and St. Petersburg. He often cites his friendship with his mentor, Ohno Kazuo, as the springboard for his creativity.

Denise Fujiwara began her career in childhood as a gymnast and competed internationally on the Canadian rhythmic gymnastics team. Upon completing an honors BFA in dance at York University (1974–79), she cofounded Toronto Independent Dance Enterprise (TIDE), a company that danced across Canada for ten years. She subsequently created and commissioned six solo concerts that have moved audiences at festivals and theaters from coast to coast in Canada and internationally. *Sumida River,* a butoh work created especially for her by acclaimed choreographer Nakajima Natsu has been featured in dance festivals in New York, Seattle, Washington, DC, Vancouver, Calgary, Copenhagen, Krakow, Colombia, Costa Rica, Ecuador, and India. It continues to tour along with her other repertoire, *Komachi,* by Waguri Yukio, one of Hijikata Tatsumi's most noted students, and with her own works *Water, No Exit,* and *Conference of the Birds.* She has pursued dance as a path to insight. Her most influential mentors include Tokyo butoh master Nakajima Natsu, Montreal master dance pedagogue Elizabeth Langley, the late Judy Jarvis, and members of the now disbanded Mangrove Dance Collective of San Francisco. Fujiwara leads workshops and master classes across Canada and abroad. Her teaching integrates butoh with postmodern American improvisation principles, an approach she has developed over thirty years of intensive practice.

Furukawa Anzu (1952–2001) was born in Tokyo and died in Berlin, Germany. She studied from 1972 to 1975 under Professor Yoshiro Irino in the Toho-gakuen College of Music. She worked from 1973 as a choreographer, performer, and scenarist in various groups in Japan and Europe on many international festivals. She also worked in 1979 as a solo dancer in the Dairakudakan butoh group. She was an accomplished ballet dancer, modern dancer, studio pianist for ballet companies, and a student of modern composition of music in addition to being both a teacher and a performer. She worked with Carlotta Ikeda, Murobushi Ko, and Ushio Amagatsu's Sankai Juku. She cofounded the butoh company Dance Love Machine with Tetsuro Tamura. In her lifetime, she created fifty-three original theater pieces and toured in Europe, America, Japan, and Africa.

David Grenke (born 1962) founded ThingsezIsee'm Dance/Theater in 1994 as a multimedia vehicle for his artistic vision. He was a principal dancer for the Paul Taylor Dance Company from 1989 to 1996. He has also danced for Dennis Wayne's Dancers, the Joffrey Concert Dancers, and was a founding member of the Armitage Ballet. His choreography has been presented in New York at City Center, the Joyce Theater, Carnegie Hall, the Clark Studio at Lincoln Center, the Guggenheim Museum's Works and Process Series, and Riverside Church. Outside New York, his works have been performed at Jacob's Pillow Dance Festival, the American Dance Festival (ADF), the Cannes International Dance Festival, Open Look International Festival, as well as tours of Russia, Poland, Denmark, Taiwan, and Argentina. Support for these tours has come from the U.S. State Department, the Trust for Mutual Understanding, the Lower Manhattan Cultural Council, and the Harkness Foundation. Grenke is a recipient of the ADF's 1998 Doris Duke Award for new work, the 1997 Scripps/ADF Humphrey-Weidman-Limón Fellow for Choreography, and the Nora Kaye Award for dance. He participated in the

ADF's 1997 International Choreographers Commissioning Program, where he was in residence creating a new work for ADF dancers. He is on the faculty at the Taylor School. Grenke now resides part-time in California, where he is professor of dance and chair of the Department of Theatre and Dance at the University of California, Davis, and has received an outstanding student advisor award.

Hijikata Tatsumi (1928–86) is a central figure in twentieth-century dance and theater. He developed a style of performance now known internationally as butoh, the dance of darkness. His early work was influenced by the writings of Jean Genet and Antonin Artaud and flourished in the underground arts of Tokyo of the 1960s. By the late 1960s, he began to develop his own unique style of tightly choreographed dance with stylized gestures drawn from his childhood memories of his northern Japan home in Akita. The "weak body" philosophy of dance that he developed has profoundly affected the direction of environmental and theatrical dance globally. In the early 1970s, Hijikata worked intensively with a few female dancers, most notably Ashikawa Yoko, further developing his famous collage style, as he encouraged dancers to improvise through hundreds of images, transforming endlessly. In final workshops, he urged dancers to disappear into nothingness.

Joan Laage (born 1948) first encountered butoh in 1982 when she saw *Dairakudakan* in Tokyo. She studied under Ohno Kazuo and Ashikawa Yoko in Japan and performed in Ashikawa's group *Gnome* in 1988–89. Laage moved to Seattle, Washington, in 1990, where she founded Dappin' Butoh. In November 2008, she resettled in Seattle after two years each in Krakow, Poland, and South Korea. Since 2005, Laage has performed under the name "kogut" ("rooster" in Polish). She has appeared in butoh festivals in Paris, New York, Seattle, Portland, and San Francisco. Laage has taught at the Portland International Performance Institute and has been an artist-in-residence at Ohio State University and other universities. She has received several grants in support of her work and appeared on Seattle's KCTS Channel 9 Current Artist Series. Laage is featured in Sondra Fraleigh's *Dancing into Darkness: Butoh, Zen, and Japan.* Her doctoral dissertation from Texas Woman's University is entitled *Embodying the Spirit: The Significance of the Body in the Contemporary Japanese Dance Movement of Butoh.* Her background includes modern dance, improvisation, tai chi, yoga, and the classical dance forms of India, Indonesia, Japan, and Korea. In 2005, she launched Operation/Anatomical Theater Project, which led to productions in London; Uppsala, Sweden; Gdańsk, Poland; and Seattle (supported by a city grant). While living in Europe, Laage created and performed *Drumming Up Oskar,* inspired by her paternal grandfather. A certified Laban Movement analyst, she is intrigued by the relationship between early German modern dance and butoh and has used her exploration of her German roots as another entrance into the butoh world.

Ledoh is an internationally renowned multimedia performance artist. He trained in Japan under his butoh mentor Katsura Kan, a member of the radical 1970s butoh collective Byakko-Sha. He has since performed for audiences around the globe for more than fifteen years with his solo and ensemble performances. Born into the Ka-Ren hill tribe, Ledoh came to America at age eleven to escape the oppression of his people by the brutal dictatorship holding power in Burma. As artistic director of Salt Farm, Ledoh choreographs with a raw movement vocabulary and directs the production of sets, video art, and musical scores to create a vital, visceral brand of live theater and site-specific installations that can soothe and shock within the span of a moment.

Susanne Linke (born 1944), a German dancer and choreographer, was born in Lüneburg, Germany. She studied at the Mary Wigman Studio in Berlin from 1964 to 1967 and at the Folkwang School in Essen from 1967 to 1970, later dancing with Folkwang Dance Studio and collaborating with Pina Bausch and others. She then became choreographer with the Folkwang Dance Studio (1975–85), creating works such as *Satie* and *Ballet of Woman*. Linke eventually developed a contemporary expressionist style with political and autobiographical concerns. Since 1985, she has created works for her own group as well as for other companies, such as the Netherlands Dance Theatre. In 1994, she was appointed codirector with Urs Dietrich of the Bremer Tanztheater, for which she has choreographed *Hamletszenen* and other works, and in 1996 she was also appointed artistic director of the Choreographic Centre in Essen. Her work hails from the same expressionist roots as butoh, but butoh diverged significantly from these. Linke's new expressionist dances relate to a direct line of German dance through her work with Mary Wigman and Pina Bausch. Significantly, Linke's work relates to butoh through a collaboration with Yoshioka Yumiko, *SU-i* (2006).

Murobushi Ko (born 1947) trained and performed with butoh's creator Hijikata Tatsumi in 1968 and was a founding member of the long-running Dairakudakan butoh company. Now Murobushi leads the Edge Company from his base in Japan and tours internationally throughout Europe and North and South America. He performed the U.S. premiere of his solo *Quick Silver* at the Theater for the New City in New York on November 9, 2007. Murobushi is one of the best-known butoh dancers of our time. Born in Tokyo, he was a little boy when butoh was created in 1959 by Hijikata Tatsumi, but in 1968 he was already studying and performing with Hijikata in Japan. After this first contact with butoh, Murobushi left the stage in 1970 to practice ascetic life and shamanism for two years as a *yamabushi* in the Japanese mountains. Later he moved to Paris, where he choreographed for the all-female butoh company Ariadone as well as for Carlotta Ikeda, Endo Tadashi, and others. His improvisational performances led to cooperation with Wim Mertens and the Glenn Branca Orchestra in Tokyo in 1986. After 1988, he focused on duo productions with Urara Kusanagi, and his very successful solo production *En* brought him to Mexico and South America. Recently, Murobushi created *Edge 1* and *Edge 02-Bach Sketch.* In 2002, he was invited to India to the Cross Cultural Exchange between Japan and India, where he created *East Wind III—no boat in sight.* In 2003 and 2004, he worked in Portugal, New York, Paris, London, and Germany; later he led research projects, workshops, and performances in Brazil, Mexico, India, Malaysia, and the Philippines.

Ohno Kazuo (born 1906) is one of the principal founders of butoh. He premiered his solo directed by Hijikata Tatsumi, *La Argentina Sho,* in 1977 and won the Dance Critic's Circle Award for it. Ohno has toured throughout Europe, North and South America, Australia, and Asia and starred in the films *The Portrait of Mr. O* (1969), *Mandala of Mr. O* (1971), and *Mr. O's Book of the Dead* (1973), directed by Chiaki Nagano. He also appears in *The Scene of the Soul* (1991), by Katsumi Hirano, and *Kazuo Ohno* (1995), directed by Daniel Schmid. Ohno has earned the love and respect of audiences worldwide and continues well past his hundredth birthday to inspire students in all arenas of dance. His style is informed by butoh but surpasses designations. Ohno represents the entire spectrum of dance in the twentieth century, having studied Western Expressionist dance in the early 1900s, performing through the modern/postmodern period of the late-twentieth century and into the twenty-first. His dance themes have been drawn widely from around the world.

Ohno Yoshito (born 1938), son of Ohno Kazuo, was born in Tokyo. In 1959, he danced the role of a young boy in *Kinjiki* (Forbidden Colors), directed and choreographed by Hijikata Tatsumi. This dance, a duet for Hijikata and Ohno Yoshito, is considered the first creation of butoh. Subsequently, Ohno Yoshito participated in concerts of the work *House of Artaud* and Hijikata's group Ankoku Butoh-ha. His dance studies included classical ballet and pantomime with Hironobu Oikawa. He performed his first solo recital in 1969 and then suspended stage appearances. Ohno Yoshito returned to performance in *The Dead Sea* with Ohno Kazuo in 1985. Since then, he has directed all of his father's performances. In 1998, he performed a solo recital, *The Last Picture of Dorian Gray,* based on the manuscripts left unpublished by Gunji Masakatsu. Gunji was a famous critic and scholar of Kabuki as well as a butoh scholar, and he was the husband of Matsumoto Chiyoe-sensei, the dance educator included in part of essay fourteen. Ohno Yoshito was the featured performer at the New York Butoh Festival in 2007 with his work *Kuu* (Emptiness). He continues to teach at the studio next to his home established by himself and his father in Yokohama, Japan, inspiring dancers from around the world.

Diego Piñón (born 1957) completed studies in the social sciences in 1979 and began dancing at the Centro Superior de Coreografía in Mexico. He continued learning through the study of body therapies originating in the United States, including bioenergetics, core energetics, and Gestalt therapy. In Mexico, he studied contemporary dance in the Martha Graham, José Limón, and Lester Horton methods, and he studied theater techniques, especially ritual theater, training with teachers of theater companies such as the Odin Theater, the Roy Hart Theater, and Teatro Tascabile. He also learned the contemporary movement and therapy techniques of Release, Alexander, and Klein. Since 1987, Diego has trained in master techniques of butoh. Among his teachers are the renowned butoh masters Nakajima Natsu, Ohno Kazuo, Ohno Yoshito, Min Tanaka, Hisako Horikawa, and Mitsuyo Uesugui. In 1993, Piñón was invited to participate with the Japanese butoh dance group Byakko-Sha in the dance *Hibari to Nejaka*. In 1994, he was invited to an artistic encounter in Japan with the butoh dance group Maijuku, directed by Min Tanaka, dancing in the piece *The Ancient Woman*. He also presented his first butoh ritual dance piece, *Zacuala,* in Kyoto. Supported by the Japan Foundation, Piñón returned to Japan in 2000 to develop a dance work with the guidance of Ohno Kazuo and Ohno Yoshito. Currently, he performs and teaches butoh throughout Mexico, Europe, and North America.

Marie-Gabrielle Rotie (born 1967) was born in Wales. She studied at Wimbledon School of Art and encountered butoh in 1992, studying with teachers in Japan and Europe, notably Murobushi Ko, Carlotta Ikeda, and Tetsuro Fukuhara. She was awarded a Lisa Ullman travel scholarship and an Arts Council grant to research butoh in Tokyo in 1999. In Tokyo, she was a student at Asbestos Memorial Studios and with Kim Itoh and Ohno Kazuo. In 1997, she established Butoh UK (http://www.butohuk.com) and has organized more than seventy workshops and four butoh festivals. She has performed duets with Murobushi Ko, Katsura Kan, and Takenouchi Atsushi. Since 1994, she has created more than twenty funded company productions, which have toured internationally, including the Royal Opera House, Laban, the Place Theatre, and numerous European festivals, and she performed in Tokyo at Die Pratze in 2006.

SU-EN (born 1966) lived in Tokyo from 1986 to 1994. She was an apprentice with the Tomoe Shizune and Hakutobo group from 1988 to 1994, when the legendary Ashikawa Yoko was choreographing. Su-En also holds a *nattori* license, under the name Kei Izumo, in the traditional Japanese dance form *Jiuta-mai* (Yoh Izumo school). Since 2006, she has been the curator of Friktioner International Performance Festival in Uppsala, Sweden. SU-EN Butoh Company was formally started in Tokyo in 1992. It is currently based in Haglund Skola, Sweden. The company tours domestically and overseas in proscenium and site-specific performances, workshops, film production, projects, and lectures. Major productions include *Kaze no Cho* (1992), *Shadows in Bloom* (1996), *Scrap Bodies* (1998), the film *Universal Body* (1999, collaboration with Gunilla Leander), *Atomic* (1999), *Headless* (2000), *Slice* (2003), *Fragrant* (2005), *Cracks* (2008), and wide-ranging events such as *Scrap the Truck* (1998), *The Scrap Project* (2000), *Atomic Event* (2000–2001), *The Fish Series* (2000–2002), and *The Chicken Project* (2003). SU-EN Butoh Company has performed in Europe, Japan, North America, and South America.

Tamano Hiroko (born 1952) brought the Harupin-Ha Butoh Dance Theater to Berkeley, California, with her husband Tamano Koichi in 1987 when they relocated from Tokyo. Koichi remains the leader and artistic director, though it is often Hiroko who teaches classes or offers the images to guide a dancer's movements during training. She performs with Harupin-ha internationally and also dances solo works. Hiroko was born in Fukuoka, Japan. Her butoh debut was in *Gibasa,* by Hijikata Tatsumi, in 1972 in Kyoto. This dance was a precursor to Hijikata's *Summer Storm* (1973), a work described in the first essay of this book that contains a section called "Gibasa." Tamano Hiroko joined Harupin-Ha in 1973 in Tokyo. Her first performance in the United States was for the Isamu Noguchi exhibition at San Francisco Museum of Modern Art in 1979. Her husband, Tamano Koichi, was born in Shimada, Shizuoka, Japan, in 1946. His first butoh performance was in *Barairo Dansu* (Rose-Colored Dance), by Hijikata Tatsumi, in 1965 in Tokyo. *Nagasu-Kujira* (Finback Whale) is considered the first Harupin-Ha performance and was choreographed by Hijikata Tatsumi in 1972 in Tokyo. The Tamanos are well known to international audiences, performing with the esteemed Japanese musician Kitaro on his world tour in 2000. Tamano Hiroko is a noted butoh teacher who has influenced a generation of dancers, musicians, and creative artists. The Tamanos are strongly influenced by Hijikata's style of butoh.

Kei Takei (born 1946) enrolled as a young woman in the Sakaki Bara Dance School, where she was drilled in folk dances, ballet, and the subtleties of *buyo,* or Japanese classical dance. She was aware of Japan's "merciless search for self-expression" after World War II and, eventually, its self-discovery through butoh, she says. Her studies were eventually influenced by this new kind of experimental dance emerging from Japan. When she came to the United States in 1967, choreographer Anna Sokolow recommended her for a Fulbright Scholarship to study in New York. Within two months of starting her studies at the Juilliard School, Takei made her solo debut in the New Choreographers Series at the Clark Center for the Performing Arts. She also studied at the schools of Martha Graham, Merce Cunningham, Alwin Nikolais, and the American Ballet Theatre School. As she puts it, she had become "a Japanese seed growing in American soil." Since those early days, Takei has received choreography grants from the National Endowment for the Arts, the New York State Council on the Arts, and two Guggenheim Fellowships. So far her career has embraced seventy cities in the United States and seventeen countries abroad. Now she lives in Tokyo and is the director of the Moving Earth Company. Eschewing labels, she doesn't necessarily identify with butoh, yet many see its influence in her dance.

Takenouchi Atsushi (born 1962) is a third-generation butoh dancer who appreciates the work of Hijikata Tatsumi but has taken his own unique direction. He danced from age eighteen to twenty-four in Hopo Buto Ha, the company of

Bishop Yamada, or Yamada Ippei. Hijikata choreographed *Takazashiki* (1984) for Yamada's company—Takenouchi's last performance with them. He has been working on his own *Jinen Butoh* since 1986 and created solos *Tanagokoro* (The Palm) and *Itteki* (One Drop) as universal expressions of nature, earth, and ancient times. He toured Japan between 1996 and 1999 and says he studied "the universe as spirit under Ohno Kazuo and his son Yoshito." He toured *Sun & Moon* in 1999 and led butoh workshops in Europe and Asia for six months. Since then, his tours have included natural materials musician Hiroko Komiya. In 2002, he was based in Europe for a fellowship funded by the Japanese government. Takenouchi danced *Stone* (2005), a solo performance, at the Avignon Festival in France and choreographed a butoh procession through the city of Avignon during the festival. Now in his forties, Takenouchi has danced in many countries and in every corner of Japan, exploring the earth's terrain through environmental and theatrical works. He stages butoh rituals in social and natural environments. Takenouchi's butoh respects Japanese animism, he says: "The very wide meaning of *Jinen* is that everything exists inside a living God." Takenouchi says that Ohno Kazuo and Ohno Yoshito made a deep impression on his *Jinen Butoh*.

Lani Fand Weissbach (born 1970) has been a dancer, teacher, and choreographer of Western contemporary modern dance and butoh for more than fifteen years. As founder of her own company, Shen & Bones Performance Group, she has created and performed work in Hawaii, Washington, DC, Chicago, New York, and throughout northwestern Pennsylvania, where she now lives. She was born in the island atmosphere of Hawaii and from 1990 to 1993 was a principal dancer in Honolulu's first butoh company, Iona Pear Dance Theater. Since then, she has studied butoh with several artists, including SU-EN from Sweden, Diego Piñón from Mexico, and Yoshioka Yumiko, Waguri Yukio, Yoshimoto Daisuke, Kasai Akira, and Katsura Kan from Japan. Weissbach initiated the instruction of butoh at several colleges and universities and was invited to teach master classes in butoh at the American College Dance Festival in 2000 and 2003 as well as for the Eastwest Institute for Dance and Somatic Studies.

Yoshioka Yumiko (born 1953) was raised in Tokyo and has lived in Germany since 1988. In the early 1970s and 1980s, she was a member of the first Japanese women's butoh dance company, Ariadone. In 1978, she performed with Murobushi Ko and Carlotta Ikeda in *Le Dernier Eden* in Paris, the first butoh performance outside of Japan. From 1988 to 1994, she was an active member of the German-Japanese dance theater company Tatoeba—Theatre Danse Grotesque with Minako Seki and delta RA'i. In 1995, Yoshioka founded the art formation group TEN PEN CHii with visual artist Joachim Manger from Germany and music composer Zam Johnson from the United States. TEN PEN CHii resides at Schloss Broellin, an old castle and international art research location in the northeastern part of the former East Germany. Yoshioka researches the interactivity between dance and visual art, moving away from conventional butoh dance to explore new zones in body works and performing arts in her collaborations with Joachim Manger and other artists. TEN PEN CHii has created a number of works, such as *N. YOiN* (1996), *DA-PPi* (1998), *i-ki: an interactive body dance machine* (1999), *Test Labor* (2000), *Minus Alpha* (2002), *Furu-Zoom* (2005), a collaboration with Susanne Linke, *SU-i* (2006), *Waku Déjà Vu* (2007), and *KET-SUI* (2008). Her collaborations with other companies and artists include *The Song of Iris,* premiered in Athens and directed by Rena Konstantaki (2008), and *Three Sorts of a Kind,* produced by Teatro Rebis in Italy (2008). Yoshioka has toured her works throughout Asia, Europe, Oceania, and North and South America. With delta RA'i, she has been an art director of the butoh and contemporary dance project EXIT since 1995. Nearly a hundred choreographers and dancers from all over the world join their yearly summer programs.

Notes

INTRODUCTION

1. Hijikata Tatsumi as quoted by Ohno Yoshito in *Kazuo Ohno's World from Within and Without,* trans. John Barrett (Middletown, CT: Wesleyan University Press, 2004), 137.

2. Sondra Fraleigh and Tamah Nakamura, *Hijikata Tatsumi and Ohno Kazuo* (London: Routledge, 2006).

3. For Jungian explanations of alchemy, see Lyndy Abraham, *A Dictionary of Alchemical Imagery* (Cambridge: Cambridge University Press, 1998), 71.

4. John Nathan, *Japan Unbound: A Volatile Nation's Quest for Pride and Purpose* (New York: Houghton Mifflin, 2004).

CHAPTER 1: BUTOH ALCHEMY

1. These various meanings were discussed at the "Symposium on the Origins and Legacy of Butoh" at the New York Butoh Festival, November 12, 2007. Waguri Yukio, who was one of the original students of Hijikata, and Takenouchi Atsushi, a later student of Hijikata, participated in the discussion of the various translations and meanings.

2. Ishii Tatsuro, "Symposium on the Origins and Legacy of Butoh," CAVE New York Butoh Festival, November 12, 2007.

3. See the chapter called "My Mother's Face," in Sondra Fraleigh, *Dancing into Darkness: Butoh, Zen, and Japan* (Pittsburgh: University of Pittsburgh Press, 1999), 87–103.

4. The Meiji Restoration was a political revolution in Japan that overthrew the Tokugawa shogunate (military government) in January 1868 and replaced it with the Meiji emperor, who reigned from 1867 to 1912. This restoration, or revolution, marks a tide of modernization and youthful reformers. Japan opened its borders to the outside at this time after more than two hundred years of self-imposed isolation.

5. Siegfried Wichmann, *Japonisme: The Japanese Influence on Western Art in the 19th and 20th Centuries,* trans. Mary Whittall, James Ramsay, Helen Watanabe, Cornelius Cardew, and Susan Bruni (New York: Harmony Books, 1981).

6. Ibid., 6.

7. Ibid., 46.

8. Fraleigh and Nakamura, *Hijikata Tatsumi and Ohno Kazuo,* chapter 3.

9. Wichmann, *Japonisme,* 51.

10. China had already shown its artistic strength at the Great Exhibition in London in 1851. China and Japan were both represented at the international exhibitions of the following decades. Japan's art became influential through the international exhibitions held in London in 1862 and in Paris in 1876, 1878, and 1889. An important early work in the study of Japonisme is Sir Rutherford Alcock's *Art and Art Industries in Japan,* published in London in 1878. Alcock was president of the Royal Geographical Society and possessed a wealth of ethnological experience. For more on this subject, see the introduction of Wichmann, *Japonisme.*

11. In 1633, shogun Iemitsu forbade travel abroad and almost completely isolated Japan in 1639 by reducing contact to the outside world to very limited trade relations. In addition, all foreign books were banned. During the Edo period and especially during the Genroku era (1688–1703), popular culture flourished. New art forms like Kabuki and ukiyo-e became very popular, especially among the common people. Butoh grew in part through Hijikata's desire to rescue elements of Japanese culture close to the folk, if not literally, at least in feeling. In his turning back, Hijikata sought to create what he called Tohoku Kabuki.

12. Wichmann, *Japonisme,* 6.

13. Ibid.

14. For a full description of of the dance *Ishi-No Hana* (Flower of Stone), see Fraleigh, *Dancing into Darkness,* 97–103.

15. Hijikata Tatsumi, "Program Notes," *Kinjiki,* 1959.

16. *Hijikata Tatsumi DANCE EXPERIENCE no kai* (Hijikata Tatsumi's Dance Experience Meeting) was the title for Hijikata's first dance recital in July 1960. It was written in capital letters in English with the Japanese ending presenting a cross-cultural collage title.

17. Hijikata Tatsumi, "To Prison," ed. Kurihara Nanako, trans. Jacqueline S. Ruyak and Kurihara Nanako, *The Drama Review* 44, no. 1 (Spring 2000): 47.

18. For a full description and analysis of this dance, see chapter 3 of Fraleigh and Nakamura, *Hijikata Tatsumi and Ohno Kazuo.*

19. Mary-Jean Cowell, "East and West in the Work of Michio Ito," with Satoru Shimazaki, *Dance Research Journal* 26, no. 2 (Fall 1994): 11.

20. Fraleigh, *Dancing into Darkness,* 32.

21. For further discussion of the global influences of ukiyo-e on modern dance and the specific influence of Michio Ito in the cultural exchanges of modern dance, see Jonette Lancos, "The Movement Style and Technique of Charles Weidman" (master's thesis, State University of New York College at Brockport, 1991).

22. Ernst Scheyer writes that in Dresden in the mid-1920s, Wigman's interest in the East was through her contacts with the Dresden Ethnological Museum and with Felix Tikotin, who exhibited his collection of Oriental art in the Gallery Arnold in 1923. However, he believes that Greek art in its classical and archaic phases formed the bedrock of her taste; Ernst Scheyer, "The Shapes of Space: The Art of Mary Wigman and Oskar Schlemmer," *Dance Perspectives* 41 (1970): 20–23.

23. I digress a moment in order to explain this: Unfortunately, what has become known generally as "jazz" in dance has lost the improvisational flair of African music and dance and the reciprocity of "call-and-response" in the relationship between African music and dance that is the hallmark of tap dance when it is performed within the jazz vernacular. Vernacular tap dance with its improvisational elements may be the only authentic jazz dance we have left. Bill Evans, for instance, continues to hone a call-and-response style in relation to live jazz music, tap dancing well into his seventies. Contemporary jazz dance to squared rhythms settles instead on cute, pseudosexy routines that are replicated in commercial studios throughout America. It is difficult to call such dance "jazz," given the vitality of jazz music; maybe we should just call it "commercial dance," as the seasoned jazz dance teacher and Hollywood choreographer Jack Cole suggested.

24. I discovered Hijikata's importance to theater in attending and speaking at theater conferences in America, London, and Poland. Poland has a strong tradition of physical theater, and, therefore, a special affinity to butoh. My keynote speeches were "Butoh Morphology," for the Human Body, an International Sign, International Conference on Physical Theater and the Body, Krakow, Poland, 2003; and "Butoh Alchemy, Bridging Histories," for the London Grounded in Europe Conference: From German Expressionism to Tanztheater, sponsored by the Center for Performance Research in 2001.

25. Sondra Fraleigh, *Dancing Identity: Metaphysics in Motion* (Pittsburgh: University of Pittsburgh Press, 2004), 109–11.

26. I learned how to create situations for such realizations and transformations in team-teaching with Harada Nobuo in Fukuoka, Japan. I think of these as butoh templates, or forms for dance experiences.

27. Tebby W. T. Ramasike, "A Passage through Time-Space and the Traditional Body" (Artist's unpublished statement on his work, 2007).

28. Katherine Mezur, "Butoh California Style and High Orientalism" (conference paper, Congress on Research in Dance 40th Anniversary Conference, Barnard College, New York City, November 8–10, 2007).

29. Megan Nicely, "Butoh as Migratory Practice" (conference paper, Congress on Research in Dance 40th Anniversary Conference, Barnard College, New York City, November 10, 2007).

30. Waguri Yukio, "Symposium on the Origins and Legacy of Butoh" (symposium with speakers Ishii Tatsuro, Waguri Yukio, and Sondra Fraleigh, New York Butoh Festival, November 12, 2007).

31. "Butoh-ka: The Last Samurais" is a short article written for the Butoh and Break-Dance Festival in Chicago in 2006, commissioned by Nicole Le Gette.

32. Lafcadio Hearn, *Lafcadio Hearn's Japan,* ed. Donald Richie (Rutland, VT: Charles E. Tuttle, 1997), 142.

CHAPTER 2: THE MORPHOLOGY OF BUTOH

1. Eric Hansen, *Rocks and Plants: A Pocket Field Guide to the Geology and Botany of the St. George Basin* (Central, UT: Shop Chicken Publications, 1997), 73.

2. See Fraleigh and Nakamura, *Hijikata Tatsumi and Ohno Kazuo.* In chapter 4, Ohno Yoshito explains his father's exploration of "Be a stone" and his experience of dancing pain in the stones of Auschwitz.

3. Takenouchi Atsushi, email communication with Sondra Fraleigh on his *Yin Yang Butoh* procession, December 27, 2008.

4. Kasai Akira, interview in Fraleigh, *Dancing into Darkness*, 236–37.

5. Immanuel Kant, *Critique of Judgment,* trans. Werner S. Pluhar (Indianapolis: Hackett, 1987).

6. Pema Chodron, *When Things Fall Apart: Heart Advice for Difficult Times* (Boston: Shambala, 2000).

7. Waguri Yukio, *Butoh Kaden,* CD-ROM and booklet (Tokushima, Japan: Just System, 1998). For a fuller explanation of Waguri's *Butoh Kaden,* see Fraleigh and Nakamura, *Hijikata Tatsumi and Ohno Kazuo.*

8. Ohno Kazuo, *Hyakka Ryouran, Homage to Kazuo Ohno at 100* (gala performance and booklet to celebrate Ohno's hundredth birthday, Kangawa, Japan, Arts Fusion, 2006).

9. Jacob Needleman, "Is America Necessary?" *Parabola* 32, no. 4 (Winter 2007): 70.

10. Hijikata Tatsumi, "Hijikata Tatsumi: Plucking off the Darkness of the Flesh," interview with Shibusawa Tatsuhiko, trans. Jacqueline Ruyak and Kurihara Nanako, *The Drama Review* 44, no. 1 (Spring 2000): 49–55.

11. Hijikata speaks of the children tied to posts while their parents work in the rice fields and babies kept all day in *izume* (rice baskets), their "gluttonous cries" reaching toward the skies; Hijikata Tatsumi, "Wind Daruma" (*Kaze daruma*), ed. Kurihara Nanako, trans. Jacqueline S. Ruyak and Kurihara Nanako, *The Drama Review* 44, no. 1 (Spring 2000): 74–78.

12. Mikami Kayo, "Deconstruction of the Human Body" (unpublished paper, 2002), 1.

13. Fraleigh and Nakamura, *Hijikata Tatsumi and Ohno Kazuo,* chapter 1.

14. I examine Wigman's work extensively in light of Brooks's views in Fraleigh, *Dancing Identity,* 39–44.

15. "Kaze Daruma" ("Wind Daruma") was Hijikata's speech for the Tokyo Butoh Festival of 1985, one year before his death. A *daruma* is a doll weighted so it can't be knocked over, symbolizing persistence.

16. Quoted from Raymond Moriyama's presentation in the keynote panel on architecture at the Annual Conference of the American Society for Aesthetics in Banff, Alberta, November 1980.

17. Richard Tarnas, *The Passion of the Western Mind* (New York: Ballantine, 1991).

18. Ashley Meeder, "Exploring Affinities in Japanese Butoh Dance and Somatic Theory" (unpublished paper, 2006).

19. Jean Viala and Nourit Masson Sekine, *Butoh: Shades of Darkness* (Tokyo: Shufunotomo, 1988), 94.

20. I describe a workshop with Kasai Akira in Fraleigh, *Dancing into Darkness*, 248–49.

21. Ishii Tatsuro, "Symposium on the Origins and Legacy of Butoh," CAVE New York Butoh Festival, November 12, 2007. Ishii Tatsuro explores the shamanistic tendencies of butoh at the New York Butoh Festival and how butoh moves out internationally because of this. Shamanism is deeply embedded in Asian sensibility, as he shows on film.

22. Rotie Productions, email communication with Sondra Fraleigh, February 9, 2008.

23. Linda Hartley, *Wisdom of the Body Moving: An Introduction to Body-Mind Centering* (Berkeley, CA: North Atlantic Books, 1995), 222.

24. This description is written with the assistance of workshop notes of Ohno Yoshito's longtime student Robert Lyness; Robert Lyness, "Notes from Ohno Yoshito's Workshop," CAVE New York Butoh Festival, November 29, 2007.

25. For Kasai Akira's commentary on discarding the ego, see Fraleigh's interview with him in Fraleigh, *Dancing into Darkness,* 238.

26. Abraham, *A Dictionary of Alchemical Imagery,* 12.

27. Chokei, in Lucien Stryk and Takashi Ikemoto, trans. and comps., *Zen Poems of China and Japan: The Crane's Bill* (New York: Grove Press, 1973), 6.

CHAPTER 3: IS BUTOH A PHILOSOPHY?

1. Ishii Tatsuro quoted this statement by Hijikata at the opening of his speech at the New York Butoh Festival in 2007.

2. For one of the first dance celebrations, see chapter 1 of Barbara Sparti, *Women's Work: Making Dance in Europe before 1800,* ed. Lynn Matluck Brooks (Madison: University of Wisconsin Press, 2007).

3. Hijikata Tatsumi, letter to Nakajima Natsu, 1984.

4. Chikako Ozawa-De Silva devotes a very illuminating paper to the ethnocentric view of social constructivists; Chikako Ozawa-De Silva, "Beyond the Body/Mind? Japanese Contemporary Thinkers on Alternative Sociologies of the Body," *Body and Society* 8, no. 2 (2002): 21–38.

5. Hijikata Tatsumi, "Inner Material/Material" (*Naka no sozai/sozai*), ed. Kurihara Nanako, trans. Jacqueline S. Ruyak and Kurihara Nanako, *The Drama Review* 44, no. 1 (Spring 2000): 36.

6. Hijikata, "To Prison," 48.

7. For a full account of Hijikata's rebellion against Western materialism, see the exposition of this through his words and dances in Fraleigh and Nakamura, *Hijikata Tatsumi and Ohno Kazuo.*

8. Nagatomo Shigenori examines this in *Attunement through the Body* (New York: Sate University of New York Press, 1992), xvii–xviii. Nagatomo further states that in going beyond this limitation, Ichikawa develops the idea of "the body as structure," the body subject as related to the objective body.

9. Sondra Fraleigh, *Dance and the Lived Body* (Pittsburgh: University of Pittsburgh Press, 1987), 14–15.

10. Ichikawa quoted by Ozawa-De Silva, "Beyond the Body/Mind?" 27.

11. Mikami Kayo, "Deconstruction of the Human Body" (unpublished paper, 2002), 1.

12. Friedrich Nietzsche, *Thus Spoke Zarathustra,* trans. Walter Kaufman (New York: Viking, 1966), 15.

13. See Ephia Gburek and Jeff Gburek, "Dictum," *Djalma Primordial Science,* 2007, http://www.djalma.com/dictum.html, accessed October 23, 2009.

14. Hijikata, "Wind Daruma," 73–74.

15. Carl Jung studied the East extensively and wrote the preface for the Wilhelm Banes translation of the *I Ching.* He used the Taoist yin and yang symbolism to explain the interpenetrating characteristics of male and female, active and receptive principles in human life and in his psychology.

16. See C. G. Jung, *Symbols of Transformation,* trans. R. F. C. Hull (New York: Bollingen, 1956).

17. Ibid.

18. Ibid. Jung presents this work as an extended commentary on the prodromal stages of schizophrenia, paralleling the meaning of the archetypal context.

19. Hijikata Tatsumi, "Fragments of Glass: A Conversation between Hijikata Tatsumi and Suzuki Tadashi," ed. Kurihara Nanako, trans. Jacqueline S. Ruyak and Kurihara Nanako, *The Drama Review* 44, no. 1 (Spring 2000): 68–69.

20. Ohno Yoshito quotes his father Kazuo on "delicateness" in his workshop at the New York Butoh Festival; see Lyness, "Notes from Ohno Yoshito's Workshop."

21. Kasai speaks of butoh as fully committed dancing in the San Francisco Butoh Festival, Butoh Symposium, August 1997.

22. "Are We Carrying Our Bodies into the World of the Dead?" is the title of his improvised solo dance of 1997, performed at the San Francisco Butoh Festival.

23. Tamah Nakamura, email communication with Sondra Fraleigh, June 2001.

24. See "Existential Context of Modern Dance," in Fraleigh, *Dance and the Lived Body,* xxxii–xxxviii.

25. Hijikata, "Fragments of Glass," 68–69.

26. Antonin Artaud, *The Theater and Its Double,* trans. Mary C. Richard (New York: Grove Press, 1958), 99.

27. Mikami Kayo, *Utsuwa to shite no shintai* (Body as Vessel) (Tokyo: Namishobō, 1993).

28. Maureen Fleming, lecture demonstration and performance on butoh, Hobart William and Smith College, Geneva, NY, 2005.

ESSAY 1: ONE THOUSAND DAYS OF SUNSHINE AND PEACE

1. For research into this topic, see Noguchi Hiroyuki, "The Idea of the Body in Japanese Culture and Its Dismantlement," *International Journal of Sport and Health Science* 2 (2004): 8–24.

2. Hijikata Tatsumi, "From Being Jealous of a Dog's Vein," ed. Kurihara Nanako, trans. Jacqueline S. Ruyak and Kurihara Nanako, *The Drama Review* 44, no. 1 (Spring 2000): 56–59. Article originally published as *"Inu no jomyakuni shitto suru koto kara"* in *Bijutsu Techo* (May 1969), 57.

ESSAY 2: WHOLE WORLD FRIEND

1. Interview with Gunji Masakatsu by Laurence R. Kominz, JADE Conference, Tokyo, 1993.

2. Ian Buruma and Avishai Margalit, *Occidentalism: A Short History of Anti-Westernism* (London: Atlantic Books, 2004), 144.

3. Ibid., 148.

4. See English translations of Ohno's poetry in chapters 2 and 3 in Fraleigh and Nakamura, *Hijikata Tatsumi and Ohno Kazuo.*

5. For a further description of this dance, see chapter 3 of Fraleigh and Nakamura, *Hijikata Tatsumi and Ohno Kazuo.*

6. Interview with Gunji, JADE Conference.

7. Ohno Kazuo, *Keiko no Kotoba* (Comments on Training), trans. Inada Takushi (Tokyo: Film Art, 1998).

8. James, *The Varieties of Religious Experience*, 272–74.

ESSAY 3: HISTORY LESSONS

1. André Breton as quoted in Martin Esslin, *The Theater of the Absurd* (Garden City, NY: Anchor Books, 1961), 274.

2. Ibid.

3. Peter Eckersall, "The Body and Gekidan Kataisha," in *Japanese Theater and the International Stage,* ed. Stanca Scholz-Cionca and Samuel L. Leiter (Boston: Brill, 2000), 317.

4. Ibid., 319.

5. A part of this dance can be seen in Alegra Snyder and Annette Macdonald's film on Wigman's work, *When the Fire Dances between the Two Poles,* 1983.

6. Isa Partsch-Bergsohn, *Modern Dance in Germany and the United States: Crosscurrents and Influences* (Chur, Switzerland: Harwood Academic, 1994), 112.

7. Susan Manning, *Ecstasy and the Demon: Feminism and Nationalism in the Dances of Mary Wigman* (Berkeley and Los Angeles: University of California Press, 1993). This work presents Wigman's dilemma in keeping her work alive during the Nazi regime and speculates about whether she promoted or resisted fascism. Manning determines her points of view primarily through a reading of Wigman's dances that she sees as becoming more soft and "feminine" during the rise of the Nazis, in keeping with a domesticated view of woman. Was this just Wigman's feminine side being expressed, or was she catering to the dominant view of Fascism?

ESSAY 4: CROCODILE TIME

1. Ephia Gburek, email communication with Sondra Fraleigh, January 2008.

2. For the full interview, see Fraleigh, *Dancing into Darkness,* 231–38.

3. Esslin, *The Theater of the Absurd,* 294.

4. Ibid., 315.

ESSAY 5: GOYA LA QUINTO DEL SORDO

1. The foregoing aspects of Goya's life are explained and illustrated with color photographs of his paintings in José Gudiol, *Goya* (New York: Library of Great Painters, Harry N. Abrams, n.d.).

2. For more on Heidegger's early relationship to Nazi ideology, see Fred Dallmayr, *The Other Heidegger* (Ithaca, NY: Cornell University Press, 1993); Victor Farias, *Heidegger and Nazism* (Philadelphia: Temple University Press, 1987).

3. Furukawa Chikashi, "Anzu Furukawa" (letter to the editor), *Contact Quarterly: Biannual Journal of Dance and Improvisation* 27, no. 2 (Summer/Fall 2002): 5.

ESSAY 6: THE SOUNDING BELL

1. Professor Frank Hoff of the University of Toronto provides information on urban planning in Tokyo and the *Noh* play *Sumidagawa* in the program of Fujiwara's dance.

ESSAY 7: ANCIENT DANCE AND HEADLESS

1. Martin Heidegger, *Being and Time,* trans. John Macquarrie and Edward Robinson (New York: Harper and Row, 1962), 401–3.

2. Martin Heidegger calls *Wesen* (Nature) "the inmost sway" as setting the groundwork for his *Contributions to Philosophy (From Enowning)* and uses *enowning* to mean "enabling." This work was written in 1936–38 and not translated into English until 1999. Heidegger's ends and beginnings are not final but infinite: If nature (to be, to exist) is in sway, in "fullness" and "gifting" lie hidden "the most sheltered essential sway of the not, as not-yet and no-longer"; Martin Heidegger, *Contributions to Philosophy (From Enowning),* trans. Parvis Emad and Kenneth Maly (Bloomington: Indiana University Press, 1999), 288.

3. Juliette Crump, "'One Who Hears Their Cries': The Buddhist Ethic of Compassion in Japanese Butoh," *Dance Research Journal* 38, nos. 1 and 2 (Summer/Winter 2006): 62–63.

4. Email communication with SU-EN by Sondra Fraleigh, October 17, 2008.

ESSAY 9: DA VINCI

1. Simone de Beauvoir, *The Second Sex,* trans. H. M. Parshley (New York: Bantam Books, 1961), xxix, 33.

2. Camille Paglia, *Sexual Personae: Art and Decadence from Nefertiti to Emily Dickinson* (New York: Random House, Vintage Books, 1991), xiii, 3.

3. For a complete analysis of the development from existentialism to structuralism and culminating in deconstruction, a line of thinking developed principally through French literature and philosophy, see Norman F. Cantor, *Twentieth-Century Culture: Modernism to Deconstruction* (New York: Peter Lang, 1988).

4. "We dance to answer the question, Who am I?" Mary Wigman often said; classes at the Wigman School in Berlin, Germany, 1965.

5. Jean-Paul Sartre, *Existentialism,* trans. Bernard Frechtman (New York: Philosophical Library, 1949), 27–51.

6. De Beauvoir, *The Second Sex,* xxviii.

7. A description of Linke's *Affecte* appeared first in Fraleigh, *Dancing into Darkness,* where I related butoh to German Expressionism. Here I develop Linke's work more fully, including its ties to existential thought and feminism, and for the first time I describe *Dolor,* the center section of *Affecte.*

8. Interview with Susanne Linke by Sondra Fraleigh, Montreal, Quebec, 1985; Susanne Linke, *Program of the Festival International de Nouvelle Dance* (Montreal: Editions Parachute, 1985), 14.

9. Friedrich Nietzsche, "The Madman," section 125, in *Joyful Wisdom,* trans. Walter Kaufman (New York: Viking, 1966). Nietzsche influenced early modern dance in both Germany and America. Mary Wigman often quoted Nietzsche in classes, and Louis Horst admired him as well. Nietzsche's *Birth of Tragedy* formed the basis for Doris Humphrey's technique of fall and recovery.

10. Nietzsche, "What Our Cheerfulness Signifies," section 343, in *Joyful Wisdom.*

11. Nietzsche, "The Madman," section 125, in *Joyful Wisdom.*

ESSAY 11: RISKY PLASTIC

1. Hijikata, "Inner Material/Material," 41.

ESSAY 12: FINE BONE CHINA

1. Wichmann, *Japonisme,* 6.

ESSAY 13: MOVING MA

1. Suzuki Daisetz T., *Zen and Japanese Culture* (Tokyo: Charles E. Tuttle, 1959), 24.

ESSAY 14: WEAK WITH SPIRIT

1. Sondra Fraleigh, "Chiyoe Matsumoto: Mother of Dance Education in Japan," *Dance Teacher Now* (October 1996): 88–95.

2. M. K. Gandhi, *An Autobiography, or The Story of My Experiments with Truth,* trans. Mahadev Desai (Ahmadabad, India: Nanajivan, 1998), 16–17.

3. Maura Nguyen Donohue, "Still Dancing the Dance of Wild Grass, Ohno Turns 96," *Dance Insider,* August 19, 2006, http://www.danceinsider.com/f2002/f1028_1.html, accessed November 2, 2009.

ESSAY 17: BUTOH RITUAL MEXICANO

1. Don Miguel Ruiz, *The Four Agreements* (San Rafael, CA: Amber-Allen, 1997).

2. For more on Castaneda, see Daniel Noel, *Seeing Castaneda: Reactions to the Don Juan Writings of Carlos Castaneda* (New York: Putnam's Sons, 1976). Castaneda claims that his best-selling books on his adventures with Don Juan are not fictional. Many disagree, especially academics, who challenge his books by pointing out their inconsistencies and that no one but Castaneda ever met Don Juan.

3. Interview with Diego Piñón by Sondra Fraleigh, Chicago, March 2006.

ESSAY 22: *KUU*

1. The CAVE New York Butoh Festival commissioned a portion of this chapter in 2007.

2. Chodron, *When Things Fall Apart,* 32.

3. Lyness, "Notes from Ohno Yoshito's Workshop."

4. Ibid.

Bibliography

Abraham, Lyndy. *A Dictionary of Alchemical Imagery.* Cambridge: Cambridge University Press, 1998.

Artaud, Antonin. *The Theater and Its Double.* Translated by Mary C. Richard. New York: Grove Press, 1958.

Beauvoir, Simone de. *The Second Sex.* Translated by H. M. Parshley. New York: Bantam Books, 1961.

Buruma, Ian, and Avishai Margalit. *Occidentalism: A Short History of Anti-Westernism.* London: Atlantic Books, 2004.

Cantor, Norman F. *Twentieth-Century Culture: Modernism to Deconstruction.* New York: Peter Lang, 1988.

Chodron, Pema. *When Things Fall Apart: Heart Advice for Difficult Times.* Boston: Shambala, 2000.

Ciane, Fernandez. *Pina Bausch and the Wuppertal Dance Theater: The Aesthetics of Repetition and Transformation.* New York: Peter Lang, 2001.

Cowell, Mary-Jean. "East and West in the Work of Michio Ito." With Satoru Shimazaki. *Dance Research Journal* 26, no. 2 (Fall 1994): 11–22.

Crump, Juliette. "'One Who Hears Their Cries': The Buddhist Ethic of Compassion in Japanese Butoh." *Dance Research Journal* 38, nos. 1 and 2 (Summer/Winter 2006): 61–73.

Dallmayr, Fred. *The Other Heidegger.* Ithaca, NY: Cornell University Press, 1993.

Eckersall, Peter. "The Body and Gekidan Kataisha." In *Japanese Theater and the International Stage.* Edited by Stanca Scholz-Cionca and Samuel L. Leiter. Boston: Brill, 2000.

Esslin, Martin. *The Theater of the Absurd.* Garden City, NY: Anchor Books, 1961.

Farias, Victor. *Heidegger and Nazism.* Philadelphia: Temple University Press, 1987.

Fleming, Maureen. Lecture demonstration and performance, Hobart William and Smith College, Geneva, NY, 2005.

Fraleigh, Sondra. "Chiyoe Matsumoto: Mother of Dance Education in Japan." *Dance Teacher Now* (October 1996): 88–95.

———. *Dance and the Lived Body.* Pittsburgh: University of Pittsburgh Press, 1987.

———. *Dancing Identity: Metaphysics in Motion.* Pittsburgh: University of Pittsburgh Press, 2004.

———. *Dancing into Darkness: Butoh, Zen, and Japan.* Pittsburgh: University of Pittsburgh Press, 1999.

———. "Spacetime and Mud in Butoh." In *Performing Nature: Explorations in Ecology and the Arts,* edited by Gabriella Giannachi and Nigel Stewart, 327–44. Oxford: Peter Lang, 2005.

Fraleigh, Sondra, and Tamah Nakamura. *Hijikata Tatsumi and Ohno Kazuo.* London: Routledge, 2006.

Furukawa, Chikashi. "Anzu Furukawa," letter to the editor. *Contact Quarterly: Biannual Journal of Dance and Improvisation* 27, no. 2 (Summer/Fall 2002): 5.

Gandhi, M. K. *An Autobiography, or The Story of My Experiments with Truth.* Translated by Mahadev Desai. Ahmadabad, India: Nanajivan, 1998.

Gburek, Ephia. Email communication with Sondra Fraleigh, January 2008.

Gburek, Ephia, and Jeff Gburek. "Dictum." *Djalma Primordial Science,* 2007. http://www.djalma.com/dictum.html, accessed October 23, 2009.

Greene, Brian. *The Fabric of the Cosmos.* New York: Alfred A. Knopf, 2004.

Gudiol, Jose. *Goya.* New York: Library of Great Painters, Harry N. Abrams, n.d.

Hansen, Eric. *Rocks and Plants: A Pocket Field Guide to the Geology and Botany of the St. George Basin.* Central, UT: Shop Chicken Publications, 1997.

Hartley, Linda. *Wisdom of the Body Moving: An Introduction to Body-Mind Centering.* Berkeley, CA: North Atlantic Books, 1995.

Hearn, Lafcadio. *Lafcadio Hearn's Japan.* Edited by Donald Richie. Rutland, VT: Charles E. Tuttle, 1997.

Heidegger, Martin. *Being and Time.* Translated by John Macquarrie and Edward Robinson. New York: Harper and Row, 1962.

———. *Contributions to Philosophy (From Enowning).* Translated by Parvis Emad and Kenneth Maly. Bloomington: Indiana University Press, 1999.

Hijikata, Tatsumi. "Fragments of Glass: A Conversation between Hijikata Tatsumi and Suzuki Tadashi." Edited by Kurihara Nanako. Translated by Jacqueline S. Ruyak and Kurihara Nanako. *The Drama Review* 44, no. 1 (Spring 2000): 62–70. Article originally published as *"Ketsujo to shite no gengo-Shintai no kasetsu"* (Language as Lack and Temporary Construction of the Body) in *Gendaishi Techo* (April 1977).

———. "From Being Jealous of a Dog's Vein." Edited by Kurihara Nanako. Translated by Jacqueline S. Ruyak and Kurihara Nanako. *The Drama Review* 44, no. 1 (Spring 2000): 56–59. Article originally published as *"Inu no jomyakuni shitto suru koto kara"* in *Bijutsu Techo* (May 1969).

———. "Hijikata Tatsumi: Plucking off the Darkness of the Flesh." Interview with Shibusawa Tatsuhiko. Translated by Jacqueline Ruyak and Kurihara Nanako. *The Drama Review* 44, no. 1 (Spring 2000): 49–55.

———. "Inner Material/Material" (*Naka no sozai/sozai*). Edited by Kurihara Nanako. Translated by Jacqueline S. Ruyak and Kurihara Nanako. *The Drama Review* 44, no. 1 (Spring 2000): 36–42. Article originally published in July 1960 as *"Naka no sozai/sozai,"* a pamphlet for *Hijikata DANCE EXPERIENCE no kai* (recital).

———. Letter to Nakajima Natsu. Copy in the butoh collection of Sondra Fraleigh, 1984.

———. "Program Notes." *Kinjiki. Zen'nihon buyo kyokai shinjin koen* (All Japan Dance Association New Face Performance), 1959.

———. "To Prison" (*Keimusho e*). Edited by Kurihara Nanako. Translated by Jacqueline S. Ruyak and Kurihara Nanako. *The Drama Review* 44, no. 1 (Spring 2000): 43–48. Article originally published in January 1961 as "*Keimusho e*" in *Mita Bungaku* (The Mita Literature): 45–49.

———. "Wind Daruma" (*Kaze Daruma*). Edited by Kurihara Nanako. Translated by Jacqueline S. Ruyak and Kurihara Nanako. *The Drama Review* 44, no. 1 (Spring 2000): 71–79. Article originally published as "Kaze daruma" in *Gendaishi techo* (May 1985).

Horst, Louis, and Carroll Russell. *Modern Dance Forms*. San Francisco: Impulse, 1961.

Ishii, Tatsuro. "Symposium on the Origins and Legacy of Butoh." CAVE New York Butoh Festival, November 12, 2007.

James, William. *The Varieties of Religious Experience*. New York: Viking Penguin, 1982.

Jung, C. G. *Symbols of Transformation*. Translated by R. F. C. Hull. New York: Bollingen, 1956.

Kant, Immanuel. *Critique of Judgment*. Translated by Werner S. Pluhar. Indianapolis: Hackett, 1987.

Lancos, Jonette. "The Movement Style and Technique of Charles Weidman." Master's thesis, State University of New York College at Brockport, 1991.

Linke, Susanne. *Program of the Festival International de Nouvelle Dance*. Montreal: Editions Parachute, 1985.

Lyness, Robert. "Notes from Ohno Yoshito's Workshop." CAVE New York Butoh Festival, November 29, 2007.

Manning, Susan. *Ecstasy and the Demon: Feminism and Nationalism in the Dances of Mary Wigman*. Berkeley and Los Angeles: University of California Press, 1993.

Meeder, Ashley. "Exploring Affinities in Japanese Butoh Dance and Somatic Theory." Unpublished paper.

Mezur, Katherine. "Butoh California Style and High Orientalism." Conference paper, Congress on Research in Dance 40th Anniversary Conference, Barnard College, New York City, November 8–10, 2007.

Mikami, Kayo. "Deconstruction of the Human Body." Unpublished paper, 2002.

———. *Utsuwa to shite no shintai* (Body as Vessel). Tokyo: Namishobō, 1993.

Nagatomo, Shigenori. *Attunement through the Body*. New York: Sate University of New York Press, 1992.

Nakamura, Tamah. Email communication with Sondra Fraleigh, June 2001.

Nathan, John. *Japan Unbound: A Volatile Nation's Quest for Pride and Purpose*. New York: Houghton Mifflin, 2004.

Needleman, Jacob. "Is America Necessary?" *Parabola* 32, no. 4 (Winter 2007): 68–73.

Nguyen Donohue, Maura. "Still Dancing the Dance of Wild Grass, Ohno Turns 96." *Dance Insider*, August 19, 2006, http://www.danceinsider.com/f2002/f1028_1.html, accessed November 2, 2009.

Nicely, Megan. "Butoh as Migratory Practice." Conference paper, Congress on Research in Dance 40th Anniversary Conference, Barnard College, New York City, November 10, 2007.

Nietzsche, Friedrich. *Joyful Wisdom*. In *A Casebook on Existentialism,* edited by William Spanos, 256–60. New York: Thomas Y. Crowell, 1966.

———. *Thus Spoke Zarathustra*. Translated by Walter Kaufman. New York: Viking, 1966.

Noel, Daniel. *Seeing Castaneda: Reactions to the Don Juan Writings of Carlos Castaneda*. New York: Putnam's Sons, 1976.

Noguchi, Hiroyuki. "The Idea of the Body in Japanese Culture and Its Dismantlement." *International Journal of Sport and Health Science* 2 (2004): 8–24.

Ohno, Kazuo. *Hyakka Ryouran, Homage to Kazuo Ohno at 100*. Gala performance and booklet to celebrate Ohno's 100th Birthday, Kangawa, Japan, Arts Fusion, 2006.

———. *Keiko no Kotoba* (Comments on Training). Translated by Inada Takushi. Tokyo: Film Art, 1998.

Ohno, Kazuo, and Ohno Yoshito. *Kazuo Ohno's World from Within and Without*. Translated by John Barrett. Middletown, CT: Wesleyan University Press, 2004.

Ozawa-De Silva, Chikako. "Beyond the Body/Mind? Japanese Contemporary Thinkers on Alternative Sociologies of the Body," *Body and Society* 8, no. 2 (2002): 21–38.

Paglia, Camille. *Sexual Personae: Art and Decadence from Nefertiti to Emily Dickenson*. New York: Random House, Vintage Books, 1991.

Partsch-Bergsohn, Isa. *Modern Dance in Germany and the United States: Crosscurrents and Influences*. Chur, Switzerland: Harwood Academic, 1994.

Ramasike, Tebby W. T. "A Passage through Time-Space and the Traditional Body." Artist's unpublished statement on his work, 2007.

Ruiz, Don Miguel. *The Four Agreements*. San Rafael, CA: Amber-Allen, 1997.

Sartre, Jean-Paul. *Existentialism*. Translated by Bernard Frechtman. New York: Philosophical Library, 1949.

Scheyer, Ernst. "The Shapes of Space: The Art of Mary Wigman and Oskar Schlemmer." *Dance Perspectives* 41 (1970): 20–23.

Sparti, Barbara. "Isabella and the Dancing Este Brides, 1473–1514." In *Women's Work: Making Dance in Europe before 1800,* edited by Lynn Matluck Brooks, 19–48. Madison: University of Wisconsin Press, 2007.

Stryk, Lucien, and Takashi Ikemoto, trans. and comps. *Zen Poems of China and Japan: The Crane's Bill*. New York: Gove Press, 1973.

SU-EN. Email communication with Sondra Fraleigh, October 17, 2008.

Suzuki, Daisetz T. *Zen and Japanese Culture*. Tokyo: Charles E. Tuttle, 1959.

Takenouchi, Atsushi. Email communication with Sondra Fraleigh on his *Yin Yang Butoh Procession,* December 27, 2008.

———. "Interview with Sondra Fraleigh." EXIT Butoh Festival, Broellin Castle, Broellin Germany, August 15, 2003.

Takushi, Inada. *Dancers in Shades of Darkness: Photographs by Inada Takushi*. Translated by Hiraishi Izumi. Tokyo: Takushi Inada, 1998.

Tarnas, Richard. *The Passion of the Western Mind*. New York: Ballantine, 1991.

Thoreau, Henry David. *A Week on the Concord and Merrimack Rivers*. New York: Penguin Classics, 1998.

Toland, John. *The Rising Sun: The Decline and Fall of the Japanese Empire 1936–1945*. New York: Penguin Books, 1970.

Viala, Jean, and Nourit Masson Sekine. *Butoh: Shades of Darkness.* Tokyo: Shufunotomo, 1988.

Waguri, Yukio. *Butoh Kaden.* CD-ROM and booklet. Tokushima, Japan: Just System, 1998.

———. "Symposium on the Origins and Legacy of Butoh." Symposium with speakers Ishii Tatsuro, Waguri Yukio, and Sondra Fraleigh, New York Butoh Festival, November 12, 2007.

Wichmann, Siegfried. *Japonisme: The Japanese Influence on Western Art in the 19th and 20th Centuries.* Translated by Mary Whittall, James Ramsay, Helen Watanabe, Cornelius Cardew, and Susan Bruni. New York: Harmony Books, 1981.

Yuasa, Yasuo. *The Body: Toward an Eastern Mind-Body Theory.* New York: State University of New York Press, 1987.

Index

absurdity, in butoh, 112–14, 116, 201
active imagination, in Jung, 70–71
Affecte (Linke), 142, 244n7
Afghanistan, 104
Africa, 6, 24–25, 131, 149, 229, 239n23; butoh migrations to, 34; ceremonies of, 28
African artists, 28, 34
African dance, 77, 149; polyrhythm, 25
age, in butoh, 11, 222; butoh alchemy of aging, 44; example of Ohno in aging, 3, 44, 92, 217
Akita, Japan, 230
alchemy: the albedo stage, 54, 61; bodily kind and *ma* in, 36, 76; bodily type and healing, 41; definitions of, 1; *A Dictionary of Alchemical Imagery* (Abraham), 237n3; in feminine archetype, 195; in friendship, 172; global in butoh, 16, 62; in Hijikata's frustration with the West, 19; in history of butoh, 17, 239n24; human experience of, 116; Jungian explanations of, 3; in *Kuu*, 223; in *MA,*170; in motion, 41–44; in Ohno and Ohno, 17, 100, 222; in *Onnagata* and Kabuki, 206; in Piñón, 191, 193, 194, 195; in *Quick Silver*, 203; in shamanism, 13, 156; somatic in butoh, 49; in *Summer Storm,* 83–84; thermal process of calcination, 163; in

Torn, 190; in Weissbach, 186; in Yoshioka, 156, 158. *See also* ash, metamorphosis, shamanism, transformation
al-Qaeda, 93
American modern dance, 11, 16, 21; in Japan, 6, 18
Ando, Mitsuko, choreographs for Hijikata and Ohno in German style, 6, 46; Hijikata studies with, 22
Ankoku Butoh (Hijikata's darkness dance), 22–23, 45–46, 55, 70–71, 82–83, 133; *Ankoku butoh-ha,* Hijikata's company, 232; "ecstasy without obstacles," 67; new genre, 3; revolutionary means of, 94
Antonia, Merce, 96
aragoto, 60, 103
Arai, Misao, 74, 81–83, 89, 90
Ariadone, 90, 117, 156, 231, 235
Armitage, Karole, 27, 229
Artaud, Antonin, 22–23, 27, 73, 103–4, 116, 230; his "bleeding spurt of images," 183; poetry in space, 213; theater of the senses, 215
Art Nouveau, 19
ash, 45, 49; alchemy of in butoh, 61–62; ashen butoh bodies, 6, 17, 54; butoh rising from ashes of Japan, 215

Ashikawa, Yoko, 33, 38, 44, 48, 70, 81; influential woman in the beginning of butoh, 16, 51; Laage studied with, 105, 107; principle protégé of Hijikata, 32, 38, 105, 230; SU-EN studied with, 132

assimilation in butoh, 1–3, 18, 25–28

Attunement through the Body (Nagatomo), 66

audience, 6, 14, 23, 33, 61, 224; dancer's relation to, 49, 132; empathy, 50; experience of, 34–35, 136–38, 187, 217; Fleming dances inside of, 77; healing of, 50; Hijikata jolts, 66; Hijikata transforms and touches, 82; in *ma*, 131; Ohno lets in, 92, 96–97, 99, 101; perception of, 41–42; response, 133, 162; truth for, 73; as witness, 43–44, 189–90, 216

Aum Shinrikyo Cult, 4

Auschwitz, 39, 105, 239n2

Australia, 6, 33, 161–66, 227, 232

avant-garde, 20–22, 27, 30, 93, 115, 213; Leng Tan in, 197; testing strategy of, 104

Bach, Johann Sebastian, 95, 169, 218

ballet, 11, 35, 51, 61, 93, 112; blends and fusions of, 25; bodily sublimation in, 3; classical proportion and context of, 63–64, 72; defies gravity, 48; developed in wealthy courts of Europe, 163; in Furukawa, 122; Hijikata's struggles with, 85; idealized body of, 65, 68, 75; oriental imitations in, 24; ornamental, 16; postmodern, 27; proud bearing of, 28; upward and outward, 4, 61; use of floor in, 52

Ballets Russes, 24

Barbe, Frances, 33, 77, 161–66; biography, 227

Baroda, India, 179–81

Bath Tubbing (Linke), 143

Bausch, Pina: absurdity and grotesque in, 116, dancer-actors in, 201; first feminist responses to, 104; kissing Ohno Kazuo in *Kuu*, 223; neoexpressionist, 140; *Tanztheater* of, 29, 31–32, 47, 74, 98, 142

"Be a stone," Ohno's instruction, 13, 38, 169, 239n2

Beauvoir, Simone de, 139–42, 244n1, 244n6

Beckett, Samuel, 114, 201, 204

Before the Dawn (Yoshioka), 15

Being and Time (Heidegger), 131, 244n1

Berlin, Germany, 5, 27, 110, 116, 141, 156, 229; Wigman Studio in, 231

bharatanatyam, and butoh, 180

Bingham, Robert, 187–90; biography, 227

Black Widow, (Laage), 106

body: in community, 41, 52, 156; global, 41; Hijikata's rescue of the Japanese body, 4, 30, 83, 129, 214; incomplete in butoh, 54, 75; *mi* and *ki* (expansive spiritual energy) in, 69; nonrepresentational butoh body, 48; unconscious body, 27, 60, 64, 67, 70, 73. *See also* "the body that becomes"

Body Resonance, technique of Yoshioka, 156–57

The Body: Toward an Eastern Mind-Body Theory (Yuasa), 65

Body Weather company (Tanaka Min), 17

Brazil, 6, 31, 34, 77, 170, 180, 232

Breton, Andre, 103, 243n1

The Bride Stripped Bare of Her Bachelors, Even (Duchamp), 115

Broellin, Germany, 149, 151, 154–58, 235

Brooks, Peter, 46, 240n14

Brutality of Fact (Rotie), 146–48

Buddhism: compassion in, 2; as detachment and ethic in SU-EN, 134; as emptiness and nonattachment in Ohno Yoshito, 223; healing potentials of, 114; in Hijikata's death, 1; in Hijikata's themes, 30; in *Kuu*, 218–23; in life of Ohno Kazuo, 101, 128; as nothingness in butoh 1, 46, 114; patient mind of, 2; as psychology of nonviolence, 15; as redemptive suffering in butoh, 74; in *Summer Storm*, 87; in unconscious mind of butoh, 114. *See also* Zen

Burma, 6, 135, 231

Buruma, Ian, 93–94, 242n2
Butch Cassidy's Cabin (Fraleigh), 39–40
Butoh: alchemical morphology of, 5,
    11–17, 191–94; alchemy in motion,
    41–44; ancient dance meaning of, 3, 12,
    32, 167, 216; anti-utopian, 73–76, 104;
    assimilates the West, 21, 215; awkward-
    ness in, 116; backgrounds of, 17–23;
    basic walk of, 48, 88–89; *Butoh Kaden*,
    43; disappearing in, 47; distances from
    German Expressionism, 46, 102; East-
    ern ethos of, 74; expressionist foun-
    dations of, 5–6; founders of, 2–6, 10,
    29, 41, 102, 123, 144; fusions of, 25–29;
    global sensitivity and mixtures of,
    30–34, 223; metamorphic context of, 2;
    as mixture of East and West 11, 16–19;
    my connection to, 5; newer amalga-
    mations of, 33; nondualistic, 47–48;
    as a philosophy, 63–78; pre-Western
    Japanese roots of, 19–21, 215–16; sev-
    eral words for dance, 4; shamanist
    basis of, 11, 216; space and time in, 128,
    130–31, 137; spiritual, 6, 115, 134, 138,
    179, 192; surrealism in, 6, 103; syner-
    getic global art, 34; as transcultural,
    34; two schools of, 215; unique form
    and vision of, 6, 33; weakness and vul-
    nerability of, 16, 176–77; Zen in, 128,
    167–71. See also *Ankoku Butoh* (dark-
    ness dance)
butoh-fu: "Ash Pillar," 61; collage records
    of Hijikata and his followers, 14, 21, 27,
    32, 45, 51; of Ohno, 95, 215; scrapbooks,
    43; worlds, 43
butohist, 21, 34, 38, 90, 100, 105; ethics of,
    170–71
butoh-ka: and ancestors, 13; the last samu-
    rai, 34–36; metamorphic signature of,
    16. *See also* shape shifters
Bye-Bye: The New Primitive, (Shimizu),
    73, 104, 138

calligraphy, 60, 106, 205, 208, 224
Casals, Pablo, 142

chakra, 39, 57, 85, 216
Chicago Butoh Festival, 34, 156, 183–84,
    191–92
Chicken Project (SU-EN), 14, 133–34, 233
China, 6, 19, 33, 104, 161–65, 170, 173; ar-
    tistic strength of, 238n10; Ohno soldier
    in, 215
Chodron, Pema, 42, 221, 240n6
Chopin, Frederic, 95, 97, 106–8, 225
Chopin Dances (Laage), 106–8
Christianity, 2, 87, 101
collage. See *butoh-fu*
colonization: of the Japanese body, 4, 30
consciousness: existential in Murobushi,
    201; of performer, 41–42, 46–47, 49–51,
    57, 60; science of, 100, 131; shamanistic,
    13–14, 46; stream of, 216; weak body
    in, 64
Contributions to Philosophy (Heidegger),
    131
cosmology, 45, 181
costume, 20, 23, 43, 56–59; eclectic and
    global, 27, 30, 36
Crematorium in Baroda, 180–81
The Crocodile Time (Furukawa), 112–15;
    Figure 13, 113
Crow (1954), Ando's modern dance for
    Hijikata and Ohno, 6, 23, 46
Cunningham, Merce, 29, 115, 130, 142, 234

Dadaism, 103, 114
Daily Bread (Ohno), 97
Dairakuda-kan, 82, 117
Daiwa International Butoh Festival (Lon-
    don), 15, 170, 227
Dalai Lama, 104
Dalcroze Technique, 21, 24
Dance and the Lived Body (Fraleigh), 65,
    67, 241n9
DANCE EXPERIENCE, approach of Hi-
    jikata, 82, 157
Dance for Blessing the Elderly (Ohno),
    91–93
*Dancing Fairy of Five Leaves—Metamor-
    phosis of Okuni* (Tokyo), 205–9

Dancing Identity, (Fraleigh), 27, 67, 239n25, 240n14
Damasio, Antonio, 100
Dappin' Butoh company, 230
darkness, 36, 94, 110, 116, 214; in alchemy, 54, 70; in Hijikata and Jung, 69–70; major trope of butoh, 3; sign in butoh, 1; in soul work, 74; spiritual, 76; as *Yin* in butoh, 40, 181
darkness dance. See *Ankoku Butoh*
The Dead Sea (Ohno), Figure 1, 10
death, in butoh, 13, 44, 55, 69, 180–81; as companion for Ohno, 68–69, 95, 97–98; Hijikata's focus on, 67; in Linke, 141–42; in Piñón, 195
Debussy, Claude, 18, 23
Degas, Edgar, 18
Degenerate/Art (Grenke), 109–11
Delsarte, Francois, 24
delta RA'i, 156
democracy, 54, 85, 117; Hijikata's view of, 11, 67, 94
Denishawn School, 23–24
Die Bruke (The Bridge), 19
Different Trains (Reich), 118–19
Diviinu sho, Hijikata's dance for Ohno, 22, 216
Dixon Gottschild, Brenda, 25
Djalma Primordial Science, 30, 68, 241n13
Dolor, Linke's dance for Hoyer, 141–42, 244n7
Dreh Monotonie (turning monotony), 141
Duchamp, Marcel, 21, 115
Duncan, Isadora, 71, 142, 219, 222
Dunham, Katherine, 25

Earth Mouth Open (Laage), on suffering of "Comfort Women," 105
Eguchi, Takaya, Ohno's modern dance teacher, 5–6, 22–23, 25–26, 46, 97
Eiko and Koma, 30, 77, 196–200, 228
Ekua Itsi I: Requiem for My Father (Piñón), 195
Ekua Itsi II: Behind the Mirror, (Piñón), 193–95

Elegie (Faure), 143
El Greco, 87–88
empathy: in butoh, 15–16, 48–49
Endgame (Beckett), 201, 204
Endo, Tadashi, 6, 167–70, 231; biography, 228
Esslin, Martin, 103, 114, 243n1
ethnology, 85
existentialism, 46, 114, 140, 143, 244n3, not knowing in, 64; the void of, 46
EXIT Festivals, 151, 156–57, 160, 236
experience: butoh as experiential, 48, 132–33, 136, 214, 216. See also DANCE EXPERIENCE
Expressionism, 3, 103; butoh traced to, 19, 21–22, 26, 46, 60, 110; existentialist, 64; many faces of, 31, 47; unconscious in, 70. See also German Expressionism

Falling Souls, (Laage), 105
Fand, Daria, 184, 186
fascism, 74, 119, 243n7
feminism, 104, 139, 141, 186, 243n7, 244n7
Fine Bone China (Barbe), 33, 161–66
Fleming, Maureen, 6, 76–78, 242n28
Flood (Linke), 143
flowers, Ohno's love of, 71, 224
Flying Chair for Da Vinci (Rotie), 144–46
Fokine, Michel, 24
Fraleigh, Sondra, 30–40, 154, 227
France, 6, 18, 19, 30, 67, 103; existentialism in, 140; Laage in, 106; Takenouchi in, 149, 235
freedom, 100, 104, 130–31, 137, 140, 159; in global movement, 170; in Ichikawa's theories, 67–68; in *Kuu,* 223; in modern dance, 72; sexual, 139; Western-style, 4; of women in Okuni, 205, 209
From Being Jealous of a Dog's Vein (Hijikata), 75, 85, 242n2
From Heliogabalus, or The Anarchic Crowned (Artaud), 23
From Light 23 (Takehisa Kosugi), 205
Fujiwara, Denise, 48, 55–56, 123–28, 228–29

Furukawa, Anzu, 21, 48, 61, 74; *Crocodile*, 112–15; *Goya*, 116–22, 229
Furu-Zoom (Yoshioka and Linke), 156

Garner, Erroll, 25
Gauguin, Paul, 18, 19
Gburek, Ephia, 112, 117, 121, 241n13, 243n1
Gekidan Kaitaisha (Theater of Deconstruction) company, 73, 103
Genbaku to Hesoo (Atomic Explosion and the Navel, Hosoe), 117
gender, 5, 10, 54, 78, 104, 139; globalization and, 170, 209; in Kabuki, 20, 194; in metamorphic butoh, 140; Ohno, gender-transformation artist, 17, 92, 97–98, 100; in Rotie, 147
Genet, Jean, 22, 27, 103, 215–16, 230
German Expressionism, 4, 93, 98; butoh antecedent, 60, 102, 110, 114, 116; my connections to, 5–6, 108; renewed in Linke, 140–42; revitalized by Grenke, 110; studied by Ohno and Hijikata, 22, 102
German modern dance, 21–22, 46; in creative ferment of butoh, 46, 110; Hijikata and Ohno learned, 93–95; Hijikata studies, 85. See also *Neue Tanz*
Germany, 6, 18, 21, 23, 31, 67; fascism in, 119; in Laage, 103; origins of modern dance in, 85, 102, 110
globalism, 28, 149
globalization: of butoh, 2–4, 12, 17, 31, 33–34, 72; butoh resists utopia in, 61; *ma* connective in, 6; positive form of, 170; social and moral arguments against, 170
Goda, Nario, 214, 216
Goddess, 38, 115, 143, 146, 177, 182
Gods, 25–26, 45
Goya La Quinto del Sordo (Furukawa), 116–22
Graham, Martha, 21, 24–25, 64, 102, 138, 147
Grenke, David, 109–11; biography, 229–30
grotesqueness, 22, 26, 71, 116, 235; "enough

grotesqueness," Ohno, 71; in Hijikata, 29; in *Neue Tanz,* 46
Gunji, Masakatsu, 93, 98, 232, 242n1
guru, 172, 180, 181–82; Ohno as spiritual guru, 2; Ohno as toothless guru, 175–77
Gymnopedies (Satie), 143

Hanagami, Naoto, 81
hanging body prototype, 75, 105, 136
Harupin-Ha Butoh company (Tamano Koichi and Hiroko), 129, 234
H'Doubler, Margaret, 178
healing dances, 3, 5, 12–15, 17, 39, 41–42; alchemy of, 54; butoh promotes, 64; of Fleming, 78; morphology of, 216; pain in, 50; spirituality of, 57, 114; of Takenouchi, 149; of women, 158, 183, 186
Heidegger, Martin, 47, 74, 119, 243n2, 244n1; ecstasy of time in, 131; *Ursprung* in, 213
Hijikata, Tatsumi: admires Ohno, 177; as alchemist, 3, 17, 44, 61, 70, 83–84; animal motifs of, 137; antiwar themes of, 2, 30, 86, 215; Artaud's influence on, 23, 73; attitude toward the West, 29, 67, 93–94; biography, 230; butoh philosophy of, 63; choreographs for Ohno, 22, 97; dances femininity, 194; dark soul of, 60, 81; defines butoh as "ancient dance," 12; East/West amalgamations of, 45; *Emotion in Metaphysics*, 74; experiments with pain, 73; as fallen Western dancer, 93; flower themes of, 224; *global* genealogy of, 17; inspired by Jean Genet, 22, 103; inspired by pre-Western Japan, 19–21; inspires personal ethnologies, 28; Japanese identity of, 4, 75; lineage of German Expressionism, 22, 46; model for metamorphic method, 27, 30; objective material of, 32; otherness and *ma* in, 50; questions social mores, 22; *Rebellion of the Body*, 23; rejects dualism, 47; rejects modernity, 29–30, 45; as root of butoh, 2–3, 4, 6, 11–13, 19–20, 30; seeks childhood roots, 45; as

shaman, 14–15; spirituality in, 46, 157; *Summer Storm*, 81–90; as surrealist, 6, 22, 30, 66, 71; as terrorist, 94–95; tests boundaries, 174; unique vision of, 33. See also *Ankoku Butoh* (Hijikata's darkness dance), *butoh-fu* (Hijikata's collage notation)

Hijikata Tatsumi and Ohno Kazuo (Fraleigh and Nakamura), 2, 82, 178, 237n1, 238n8, 239n2, 241n7, 242n4

Hijikata Tatsumi DANCE EXPERIENCE no Kai, Hijikata's first recital, 216, 238n16, 238n18

Hiroshima, Peace Park, 4; bombing of, 11, 32, 54, 61, 85, 117

Hitler, Adolf, 109, 117, 119

Hokotai (butoh walk), 27–28, 48, 49, 138

Hokusai, Katsushika, 18

Hosoe, Eikoh, 30, 117

Hoyer, Dore, 98, 110, 139–43

humor, 112, 116, 121, 125, 174

Humphrey, Doris, 21, 76, 244n9

I Can't Help Falling in Love With You (Presley), 223

Ichikawa, Hiroshi, 65–69, 241n8, 241n10

i-ki (Yoshioka and Manger), 158–60

Il Barbiere di Siviglia (Rossini), 120

imagery: elemental, 216; imagination in, 71; morphing of, 14–16, 224; of sand, 15, 66, 193, 203; tangible embodiment of, 82, 84; third eye, 60; transforming through, 45. See also *butoh-fu*

Impressionism, 16–19

India, 6, 57, 104, 123, 170, 172; Bingham in, 228; Fujiwara in, 229; letter from, 179–80; Murobushi in, 231

Inner Material/Material (Hijikata), 32, 66, 75, 85, 157, 241n5, 245n1

Iraq, 104

Ishii, Baku, 21

Ito, Michio, 23–24, 238n19, 238n21

Ito, Morita, 55

Ito (Piñón), 192–93

It's All Moonshine (Yoshioka), 15

JADE Festival (Tokyo), 91, 93, 98, 242n1, 242n6

James, William, 91, 100

Japanese aesthetics, 27, 130

Japanese animism, 235

Japanese nativism, 2, 25, 94

Japonisme, 3, 25, 237n5, 238n9, 238n10, 245n1; global alchemy of, 16–20, 60

jazz, 25, 131, 170, 219, 228, 239n23

jibun (part of nature), 156–58

Jinen Butoh company (Takenouchi), 38–39, 149, 235

Jomon Sho company (Sanki Juku), 130

Jooss, Kurt, 21, 140

Jung, Carl, 3, 64, 237n3, 241n15, 242n16, 242n18; collective unconscious of, 64, 67, 70–71, 73, 114

Junichiro, Koizumi, 104

Kabuki, 3, 18–19, 35, 60, 89, 103; gender transformations of, 98, 194; Gungi as scholar of, 178, 232; Okuni as female founder of, 31, 205–6, 209; *Tohoku Kabuki* of Hijikata, 20, 83, 215

Kamaitachi, Hosoe's photographs of Hijikata, 30

Kasai, Akira, 15, 34, 41, 60, 69, 113; *Butoh America*, 72; at root of butoh, 51–52, 71

Katsura, Kan, 135, 231, 233, 235

Kawamoto, Yuko, in *Shinonome Butoh*, 57, 59, 152

Kaze Daruma (Wind Daruma, Hijikata), 30, 47, 84–85, 240n11, 240n15

Ki (or *Chi*), 129

Kinjiki (Forbidden Colors), 2, 15, 23, 29, 85, 157; in eye of beholder, 214; flashback, 177; origins of butoh, 223; three famous performers of, 213; "What is Kinjiki?" 172–75

Kobayashi, Saga, 81

konpaku, Buddhist concept used by Ohno, 96, 216

Kosaku, Yamada, 21

Kreutzberg, Harald, 5, 21–22, 97, 102

Kugara (Shinto dances), 207

Kuu (Emptiness, Ohno Yoshito), 218–25
Kyoto University, 81

Laage, Joan, 33, 102–8; biography, 230
La Argentina Sho (Admiring La Argentina, Ohno), 49, 75, 96–99, 223, 232
Laban, Rudolph, 5, 21, 43, 51, 102–3, 108, 144
Le Dernier Eden (Ikeda, Murobushi, and Yoshioka), 156
Ledoh, 135–38; biography, 230–31
leprosy, 30, 35, 49–50, 80–82, 87–88
Letter from India, 179–81
Limon, Jose, 195
Linke, Susanne, 140–44, 156, 231, 244n7, 244n8; biography, 236

Ma, the space between, 6–7, 12, 16, 167–71, 187, 195
MA (Endo), 167–71
Mahatma Gandhi, 3, 175, 179–81, 245n2
Mai, internal dance, 124
MAMU Dance Theater (Endo), 170, 228
Manger, Joachim, 154, 156–59, 235–36
Manning, Susan, 109, 243n7
Masumura Katsuko, 22
material, 28, 29, 45; body as, 66–67, 69, 74–76, 128; in butoh, 30, 32, 45, 48, 157, 224–25
materialism, 5, 11, 27–29, 67, 94, 241n7
Matsumoto, Chiyoe, 172, 177–79
meditation, 16, 28, 55, 58, 65; Kasai's use of, 52, 60; *ma* in, 162
Meiji era, 17, 19, 237n4
Message to the Universe, Ohno's poem at age ninety-two, 181
Messy Beauty (Weissbach), 183–86; *ma* in, 183
metamorphosis: in Buddhist groundlessness, 42; in butoh themes of nature, 217; in costumes, music, and stage settings, 43, 56; dancer's consciousness of, 11–13, 42; embodying otherness, 48; in Ephia Gburek's dance, 69; of the fetus, 45; as healing, 1, 64; in Hijikata's

blend of world sources, 30; in the human, 194; in *Kinjiki,* 174; linked with alchemy, 11; metamorphic context of butoh, 33, 64; *Metamorphosis of Okuni* with Kai Takei, 205–6; metaphysical method of butoh, 13; in mysterious movements, 184; in Ohno's "cosmology and studying of the soul," 181; in political shifts and pain of Japan, 35; in Rotie's *Brutality of Fact,* 147; shamanic aspects of, 12–13; spurs global evolution of butoh, 34; surrender in, 55; in "three Fly-Girls," 89; as transitive, 42; unique in butoh, 30; values and means of, 2, 12. *See also* transformation
metaphysics, 73, 213–14, 239n25; in butoh, 51, 74–76, 169
methods, morphological in butoh, 49–62, 86, 115, 129, 156, 218–19, 224; technique of hidden arms, 131
Mezur, Katherine, 33–34
Mikami, Kayo, 45–46, 52, 74, 240n12, 241n11, 242n27
Miya, Misako, 22
modern dance movement, 23–29, 31, 35, 46, 50; embers in Ohno, 98; existential context of, 64–65, 72, 242n24; expressive body of, 75; falling motions in, 76; improvisation in, 76; Ohno escapes, 222; space and time in, 120. *See also* American modern dance, German modern dance, *Neue Tanz*
Modern Forms (Horst), 24
Monet, Claude, 18–19, 224
Montreal Festival of New Dance, 11, 124, 244n8
morph, 6–7, 14, 17, 32, 36, 41; from the Greek *morphos,* 44–45; morphic abilities, 53–55, 72
morphology: alchemical, 41; alternative to social constructivism, 65; *butoh-fu* as records of, 43; choreographic challenge of, 43; in convergence of difference, 187; in costume, 56–59; as explanation of bodily types, 41; globalizing, 12, 31,

76; hidden in stones, 39; in Hijikata, 17, 74; nondualistic, 46–47; in Ohno's dances, 97; osmotic in Ashikawa, 33; of pain, 49–50; philosophical questions concerning, 63; of shedding, 50–52; of small things and slow emergence, 61; somatic solution, 49; of squatting, 52–53; state of becoming, 55, 216; as study of forms and transformation, 44; of technology and nature in Yoshioka, 156; tolerant and inclusive, 2; transformative aesthetic of, 216, 224. *See also* metamorphosis, transformation

Motofuji, Akiko, influential woman in the beginning of butoh, 16, 51, 117, 173, 214

Mourning (Eiko and Koma), 196–200

Mr. O's Book of the Dead (Ohno Kazuo), 51, 232

Murobushi, Ko, 201–4, 229, 231

mythology, 24; mythic archetypes, 71

Nagasaki, bombing of, 11, 54, 85, 117

Nakajima, Natsu, influential woman in the beginning of butoh, 16, 123. See also *Niwa*

Nathan, John, *Japan Unbound*, 4, 237n4

nativism: Japanese, 2, 25, 55, 93

nature: in Barbe, 162; in butoh, 13, 32, 38–39, 41, 54; in Eiko and Koma, 197; in Hijikata, 55, 69, 71; in Ohno Kazuo, 69, 95, 99, 101; in Ohno Yoshito, 59; in SU-EN, 134; in Takenouchi, 149; in Yoshioka, 156–58

Nazis, 103, 109, 119, 243n7

Needleman, Jacob, 45, 240n9

Neoexpressionism, 98, 116, 140

Neue Tanz, 5–6, 16, 21–22, 25, 46, 97

New York Butoh Festival, 12, 55, 72, 149, 201, 216–20

New Zealand, 6, 31

Nicely, Megan, 34

Nietzsche, Friedrich, 31, 68, 143, 241n12, 244n9

Nijinsky, Vaslav, 71, 129, 222

Niwa, (Nakajima), 11, 115, 123–24, 214

Noguchi, Hiroyuki, 242n1

Noguchi, Isamu, 24, 234

Noh theater, 3, 28, 35, 48, 123–28, 209, 243n1

nonattachment, 2, 45, 62, 223

Nothing Lasts but Memory (Laage), 103–6

nuclear testing, 151

Obsessional Art, 29–30, 73, 103–4

Occidentalism, 93, 242n2

Ochanomizu University, 5

Odori, common word for dance, 124

Offering (Eiko and Koma), 197

Ohno, Kazuo: admires Harald Kreutzberg, 102; aging metamorphosis in dance, 44, 217; attitude toward death, 49, 51, 68, 105, 215; attitude toward the West, 29, 34; "be a stone" instruction, 38; biography, 232; butoh founder, 2–3, 11, 29, 213–17; centennial birthday celebration in New York, 218; Christian, 2, 101, 175, 177; dances embryonic life, 13, 59; dances femininity, 194; dance tours of, 2, 96, 222; global empathy of, 15; global genealogy of, 17; homage to, 240n8, 195; hundredth-year visit with, 1, 175–77; illogical imagery of, 15; life spans history of modern dance, 29; my studies with, 2, 5, 11; nonviolent revolutionary, 3; opposite of Hijikata, 29; as Santa Claus, 173; shamanic dances for healing, 14; as soldier, 2, 39, 85, 94, 96, 104–5; spiritual dancing of, 33; studies modern dance, 102; studio in Yokohama, 1, 173; toothless guru, 175–77; on training, 243n7; transforms war trauma, 51, 173, 215; world-friendly alchemy of, 17, 74, 91–101

Ohno Yoshito, 51, 59, 77, 239n2, 241n24, 242n20; biography of, 232; as butoh founder, 2, 15; dance tours of, 2; forwards legacy of his father, 2, 193, 217, 149, 223; on Hijikata's death, 1, 81, 237n1; his "patience of not starting," 217–18, 225; Japanese traditions in dance of, 3; language of the heart in, 32; performs *Kinjiki*, 2, 15, 173–74, 177, 213–14; *Kuu*, dance of emptiness, 2, 218–24; my visit and improvisation with, 1, 172–77; as shaman, 14; *Suiren* performance, 19; workshop words of, 224–25; as world-friendly alchemist, 3, 17, 34, 44

Okina Mai (dances in admiration of elders), 91

Okuni Kabuki and *Onna Kabuki* (Women's Kabuki), 206

Okuni of Izumo, 205–9

Onigawara (Daemon of the Riverbank, Kei Takei), 205–8

Orientalism, 11, 24, 33, 137, 239n28

Orient-Occident, Linke's dance, 142

Our Lady of Flowers (Genet), 22

pain, 32, 38, 68, 70, 73, 76; archeology and transformation of, 45, 222; in Eiko and Koma, 200; Hijikata dances confinement of infants, 83; mysterious *pathos* in butoh, 42–44, 222; Ohno sees in stones, 39; in Ohno's poetry, 172; shifting the pain body, 49–50; in SU-EN, 132–33; truth of, 85; violence in society, 104

Palucca, Gret, 109–10

Pause (Ledoh), 135–38

Perry, Matthew, 17, 19

phenomenology, 42, 152; Japanese, 47, 65–69; Western, 66–67, 69

philosophy: of butoh, 70–71, 73, 76–78; of classical ballet, 64; Eastern, 131; of existentialist modern dance, 64; Hijikata on butoh as philosophy, 63; Needleman on development of the soul, 45; phenomenology of Ichikawa, 66–67, 69; Takenouchi's *Jinen*, 149; of the weak body in butoh, 230

Pink Floyd, 19, 95, 175

Piñón, Diego, 31, 75; biography, 232–33; Butoh Ritual Mexicano, 191–95; *ma* of, 195

Plato, 171

Please Don't Leave Me (Simone), 170

Poison Dance, 5, 16. See also *Neue Tanz*

Ponifasio, Lemi, MAU, New Zealand company, 31

pornography, 4

postmodern dance, 3, 21, 23, 27, 51, 64–65; in America, 56, 75, 76, 214; butoh difference, 135; Duchamp's influence, 115; in EXIT, 151; in Japan, 6, 22; in Rotie, 144

Presley, Elvis, 3, 95, 223

Pre-Western Japan, 19–20, 45

primitivism, 24

Prometheus, Eguchi Takaya's solo, 6, 25–26

Purepecha culture, 195, 191

Quick Silver (Murobushi), 201–4, 231

Raiken, Nanto, priest of Motsuji Temple, 91–92

Ramasike, Tebby W. T., his TeBogO (TBO) Dance Ensemble, 28, 149, 239n27

Ravel, Maurice, 18

Rebellion of the Body (Hijikata), 23, 35, 83

Ridden by Nature (Kathi von Koerber), 38

Rodin, Auguste, 23

Rose, Kathy, 137

Rossini, Gioachino, 120

Rotie, Marie-Gabrielle, 56–58, 77, 233, 140; biography, 233; *Brutality of Fact*, 146–48; *Flying Chair for Da Vinci*, 144–46

Sabbagh, Cristal, 184

samurai, 34–36, 239n31

Sancta Clara, Abraham, 119

San Francisco Butoh Festival, 135–37, 242n21

Sankai Juku, 32, 47, 54–55, 61, 82

Sartre, Jean Paul, 47, 66, 140, 244n5

The Second Sex (Beauvoir), 139–41

Seiryukai (Harada), 72

Sekine, Nourit Masson, photographer at origins of butoh, 10, 95, 240n19
Sexes and Genealogies (Irigaray), 148
Sexual Personae (Paglia), 139
shadow dancing, 70–71
Shah, Parul, 180
shaking, 12, 15, 52–53, 71, 88, 116–17; internal in *Torn*, 190; of Kazuo and Yoshito, 222; of Ledoh, 137
shamanism: Buddhist, 30; definition in butoh, 11–15; healing potentials of, 12, 216; in *Ito* of Piñón, 191–93; in Japanese nativism, 25, 27, 94; of Kei Takei as Okuni, 205–7; in Mary Wigman, 139; of Murobushi Ko, 231. *See also* shamans, shape-shifters
shamans, 13–15, 23, 46, 52, 155; Hijikata as, 55, 71, 84, 94, 214, 216; in Mexico, 192–93; Yoshioka as, 155–56, 158
shape-shifters, 7, 11–12. *See also* shamans
Shaw, George Bernard, 23
Shawn, Ted, 24
shedding, in butoh, 15, 36, 47, 49–52, 56, 60
Shen & Bones company (Weissbach), 186, 235
Shimizu, Shinjin, 73, 103–4
Shintoism, 94, 104, 207, 209
Singapore, 33, 161, 164
somatics of butoh, 11, 31–32, 42, 49, 66, 191; affective, 53–54, 84, 100, 162; elastic, 23; empathic, 50, 94; experiential, 48; inward, 85; process in, 188; sensations and feelings in, 68, 189, 225; transformative, 16, 49
soul: in butoh, yoga, and Qi gong, 13; in *Chicken Project*, 14; in *Suiren* (Water Lilies), 18
squatting, 36, 52–53, 65, 106, 165; in *Goya*, 118–19; of Kei Takei, 206; in *Summer Storm*, 84, 86–88; in ukiyo-e, 18
St. Denis, Ruth, 21, 24, 137, 142
Stone (Takenouchi), 149
SU-EN, 33, 129, 130, 235, 244n4; biography, 233; *Chicken Project*, 14, 133–34; *Headless*, 131–34

Suiren (Water Lilies, Ohno and Ohno), 18–19, 175, 177, 219, 224
Sumida River (Nakajima and Fujiwara), 123–28
Summer Storm (Hijikata), 2, 30, 34, 74, 81–90, 117; Hiroko in *Gibasa*, 234
surrealism, 21–22, 47, 70, 74 103, 113–15; Hijikata affected by, 2, 83, 215; surreal techniques, 75
Suzuki, Daisetz, 167, 171
symbolism, 19, 35, 241n15

Taanteatro Companhia, *Máquina Zaratustra* (Zarathustra Machine), 31
Takei, Kei, 31, 77; biography, 234; *Onigawara* (Daemon of the Riverbank), 205–9
Takenouchi, Atsushi, 28, 31, 38–39, 75, 237n1, 240n3; biography, 234–35; in Broellin, Germany, 149–54; on butoh as ancient dance, 216; *Requiem in the Killing Field*, 150; as shaman, 14
Tamano, Hiroko, *Anc-ient Dance*, 129–31; biography, 234
Tamano, Koichi, 81, 95, 129, 234
Tan, Leng, 196–200
Tanaka, Min, 69, 75, 77, 96
tango, 95, 96, 98, 194, 219
Tatsuro, Ishii, on shamanism in Asia, 12, 55, 237n2, 239n30, 240n21, 241n1
TEN PEN CHii (art collective at Schloss Broellin), 156, 235–36
theater of cruelty, 73, 104
theater of the absurd, 46–47, 103, 113–14, 201, 243n1, 243n3
"the body that becomes": Hijikata's ontology and image of, 3, 17, 49, 55–56, 68, 157; metamorphic method of, 83, 157
The Thief's Journal (Genet), 22
Thiele, Mathilde, 31, 110
third eye, 57–60
Thoreau, Henry David, 11
Three Studies of Figures at the Base of a Crucifixion (Bacon), 146
Toccata and Fugue in D Minor (Bach), 218

Tohoku Kabuki, 20, 238n11

Tokyo, 4, 17, 20; avant-garde, 20, 29; firebombing of, 85, 117; letter from, 177–79

Tokyo Butoh Festival, 30, 84, 240n15

Tokyo Ghetto, (Shimizu), 104

Torn (Weissbach and Bingham), 187–90

Toru, Iwashita, 55

The Touch of a Vanished Hand (Lynch), 17

Toulouse-Lautrec, 18

transformation: act, action or process of, 42–43, 72, 222; amorphous materiality in Hijikata, 45; in butoh endings, 43, 115; *butoh-ka* as vessels of, 57; in butoh metaphysics, 76; in butoh morphology, 35, 41, 61; darkness and integration in, 1; in Ephia and Jeff Gburek, 68; in face of everyone, 171; facial in Fujiwara, 128; in Fleming, 78; as gender reversal in Japan, 98; gender shifts in Piñón, 194, 195; in *Goya*, 120; in Hijikata's "Being Jealous of a Dog's Vein," 75; images of, 37–41; Jung's symbols of, 70, 249; in Ledoh, 138; male to female in Kabuki, 20; male to female in Piñón, 206; as morphology, 44; psychological, 28; in shadow dancing, 70; shamanist art of, 14; of spirit, flesh, and material, 75; in *Verwandlungsamt*, 116; in *Yin Yang Butoh*, 40. *See also* morphology

ukiyo-e, 18–20, 59–60, 83, 89, 238n11, 238n21; in butoh's global cycling, 224

Unearthed (Fujiwara), 55–56

United States, 4, 6, 19; innovative dance of, 18, 23–25; Kasai's butoh for dancers of, 41; military intervention of, 17, 19, 30

ursprung, origins of butoh, 213–17; political, 216

Utah, 37–38, 40, 90

values, 4, 12, 31, 35, 41, 49; performative, 186; spiritual, 67

van Gogh, Vincent, 18

The Varieties of Religious Experience (James), 100

violence, 29, 66, 73, 104

virtue, 20, 98; in Gandhi, 179; in Ohno's dance, 99–101

Voicing Blue (Laage), 106

wabi sabi, 167, 217

wagoto, 103

Waguri, Yukio, 34, 51, 81, 229, 235, 237n1; categorizes and performs Hijikata's *butoh-fu*, 43, 61, 215; as shaman, 14

Waiting for Godot, 114

Waltzin' Mathilde (Grenke), 109–11

war, 29, 35, 74, 76, 94, 95; antiwar messages of butoh, 2, 30, 61, 83–87, 104–6, 215; killing fields of, 14, 39, 151

weak body: images of Hijikata, 55, 62, 64, 66, 75; living in your own body, 176; as philosophy, 230; physical and psychic strength of, 82; as revolutionary, 94

Weidman, Charles, 24

Weissbach, Lani Fand, 187–89, 227; biography, 235; *Waking Woman/Messy Beauty*, 183–86

Wellspring (Fujiwara), 55–56

Westernization, of Japan, 4, 19, 94

Western rationality, 46

the white opus, 53–55

Wigman, Mary, 21–22, 25, 31, 98, 107–8, 110; feminism in, 139–40; foundation of dance Expressionism, 5, 21–22, 46, 142; my studies with, 5, 85, 109; shapes of space in, 102–3, 143, 238n22

Witch Dance (*Hexentanz*, Wigman), 46, 139

women, 139–40, 148; in butoh, 16, 53, 72, 132, 158, 209; "Comfort Women," 104–5

World War II, 86–87, 98, 103–5, 109, 148; butoh born out of, 11, 19; Hijikata's experience of, 29, 85, 129, 214; Japan after, 4, 11, 23, 45, 83, 93, 116; Ohno in, 2, 96, 173

Xenakis, Iannis, 142

YAS-KAS, 82

Yeats, William Butler, 23

Yin Yang Butoh (Takenouchi), 39–40, 240n3

yoga, 13, 24, 52, 57–58, 85, 128

Yokohama, Japan, 1, 172–74, 176, 223, 230, 232

Yoneyama, Kunio, Hijikata's given name, 85

Yoshioka, Yumiko, 31, 48, 231; biography, 235–36; performs *i-ki*, 158–60; in Schloss Broellin, 155–60; as shaman for our times, 155; squatting in classes of, 52; use of sand, 15

Yuasa, Yasuo, 65–66

Zen: connection to art, 167; in Endo's *MA*, 169, 228; *ma* in, 6, 16, 62, 162, 228; Ohno performs in temples, 101; riddle, 66, 114; "Statues of *Rakans*" in *Summer Storm*, 87; in *Sumida River*, 128. *See also* Buddhism

Zen and Japanese Culture (Suzuki), 167, 245n1

Sondra Fraleigh is a professor emeritus of dance at the State University of New York College at Brockport.

The University of Illinois Press
is a founding member of the
Association of American University Presses.

University of Illinois Press
1325 South Oak Street
Champaign, IL 61820-6903
www.press.uillinois.edu